The Big Onion Guide to Brooklyn

THE
Big Onion Guide
TO
Brooklyn

TEN HISTORIC WALKING TOURS

SETH
KAMIL

AND

ERIC
WAKIN

WITH A FOREWORD BY

KEVIN BAKER

NEW YORK UNIVERSITY PRESS

New York and London

NEW YORK UNIVERSITY PRESS
New York and London
www.nyupress.org

© 2005 by New York University

ISBN 0-8147-4785-X (paper)
ISSN 1542-488X

New York University Press books are printed on acid-free paper,
and their binding materials are chosen for strength and durability.

Manufactured in the United States of America
10 9 8 7 6 5 4 3 2 1

CONTENTS

FOREWORD

SOME YEARS AGO, the *New York Times* ran a feature on the many guided tours operating in New York City. It made for hilarious reading. Innocent tourists were being told, among many other whoppers, that trained seals lived in a fountain in the courtyard of the Ansonia and that an orchestra performed on the roof every night. The guides on one bus tour liked to point to a dingy-looking first-story apartment on the Upper East Side with a large stuffed animal in the window . . . and inform their unsuspecting marks that this was the home of Jacquie Onassis.

This sort of business is what has long been affectionately known among New Yorkers as a "racket." Big Onion Walking Tours, by contrast, is the real deal. It was founded in Manhattan in 1991 by Seth Kamil, who was paying his own way through Columbia University as a graduate student in American history and scrambling to make a little cash on the side. Thirteen years later, Kamil is running a full-time business, employing over two dozen equally fervent and well-qualified guides, and Big Onion is widely recognized as the very best at what it does.

In this eagerly awaited volume, the Big Onion rolls through Brooklyn, and the devotion of the authors to their home borough is evident on every page—from their introduction to the city of homes and churches, through their championing of Prospect Park over Central Park as Olmsted and Vaux's greatest creation, to a loving exploration of Sunset Park. Want to find the last great stained-glass window created by Louis Tiffany or the highest point in all of Brooklyn? This is your guide. Want to find the Martyrs' Monument in Fort Greene, the old Brewers' Row in Williamsburg, the finest nineteenth-century mansions, brownstones, row houses, and churches? This is your guide.

But *The Big Onion Guide to Brooklyn* is so much more than a topographical guide to the borough. This is a work of extraordinary depth. With nearly every word from the authors, history becomes palpable. One can trace the course of entire peoples through a great world city. Here are the rise and fall of neighborhoods, faiths, men and machines, customs and folkways. Here one can lament the demise of the Brooklyn Navy Yard and the flight of the Dodgers, rage against the hubris of Robert Moses and admire the philanthropy of Charles Pratt, and gape at the vanished wonders of Coney Island's Dreamland and Luna Park. One can chart the history of the largest Polish community this side of Warsaw in Greenpoint; Little Norway, from its beginnings on Hamilton Avenue; Brooklyn's own Chinatown on "Big 8th Street"; and the African American presence in Bedford-Stuyvesant that dates back at least to the villages of Weeksville and Carrville.

Following the Big Onion around town is like following a guide who is full of savvy, streetwise digressions—and the authors are wonderful digressers, whether they are filling you in on where to get the best Malaysian food or on a chilling ghost story from Park Slope. In the chapter on Sunset Park alone, there are enlightening sidebars on Robert Moses and the Gowanus Expressway, St. Rocco, Jackie Gleason, Pure Land Buddhism, and the terrible

Luckenbach Pier explosion. Better yet—in this terrifically literate work—the authors' sidebars often give us Brooklynites in their own words. You can read the eulogy written for the old city of Brooklyn when it was "consolidated" into Greater New York; Shirley Chisolm, America's first black congresswoman, describing how her mother taught her to love books; Victoria Woodhull charging the Reverend Henry Ward Beecher with adultery in the trial of the (nineteenth) century; a friend of Thomas Wolfe watching him write atop his refrigerator on Montague Terrace; and Walt Whitman on crossing Brooklyn ferry—and growing up on Cranberry Street.

The best way to see Brooklyn is with a live Big Onion guide, on one of their public or private tours. The second best is to grab this book, and a stray apple or a roll, and set off through the streets of this incredible borough. But *The Big Onion Guide* can also be read late at night, in the comfort of one's own bed. Like all the best travel writing, it leads one on a journey through time and the human condition, as well as through physical space. Thomas Wolfe famously wrote that only the dead know Brooklyn; why should they have all the fun?

KEVIN BAKER, 2004
Author of the *City of Fire* trilogy: *Dreamland*,
Paradise Alley, and *Strivers Row*

INTRODUCTION

BROOKLYN. The name means so many different things to people. Millions of people call Brooklyn "home," and, in fact, more Big Onion guides live in Brooklyn than in Manhattan. Many of our neighbors, while living only a few miles from Manhattan, rarely venture into "the city." Those of us living "out here" encounter our share of visitors who regard Brooklyn as immense and overwhelming. But, to us, Brooklyn is a refreshingly vast and mystical place of 2.8 million people living in a network of intimate neighborhoods and enclaves. What is often funniest, are those we know (mostly Manhattanites) for whom "I'm moving to Brooklyn" means nothing positive. We like it that way. Where else is it so easy to stroll the Main Street of your neighborhood, passing the shopkeepers you know by name and greeting neighbors, and then hop a subway to Times Square (now faster than ever with the revived N express running across the Manhattan Bridge)? Keeping that idea of faraway Brooklyn current makes our home that much more livable.

Named in 1625 as the enclave of Breuckelen, this place grew to become the third-largest city in America. Anglicized to "Brooklyn," the city ceased to exist on January 1, 1898, when it was swallowed up into the City of New

York. For more than a century Brooklyn has thus been a part of what many consider the greatest city in the world, of which Manhattan was really the twentieth-century center. But Brooklyn, perhaps the most livable urban environment in America, is the future of our city.

Big Onion Walking Tours has been leading walking adventures since 1991, focusing on the social history of specific neighborhoods by weaving together key events, important people, historic facts, and architectural gems into a well-rounded story. We began in Manhattan, and it took nearly five years before we ventured into Brooklyn with our first tour. This book is a departure for us. Many of the walks within it are not currently offered by Big Onion Walking Tours. Each chapter explores a distinct portion of Brooklyn. Please remember that Brooklyn is a constantly changing place and the walks presented here are up-to-date as of 2004.

The walking tours in this book, if walked at a moderate pace, should take between two and three hours, with Williamsburg and Green-Wood Cemetery taking a bit longer. All of these walks begin and end at or near a subway station. Each of these tours will take you to important historic sites and cultural institutions, as well as past some true neighborhood shops and restaurants. We encourage you to take a break and venture inside.

Our first tour is of downtown Brooklyn and Brooklyn Heights, the oldest urban part of Brooklyn and, with more than 600 antebellum homes, the city's first landmark district. Written by Eric Wakin, this chapter explores the architecture and history of Manhattan's "nearest country retreat," in the words of Hezekiah Pierrepont. Our second walk, written by Leonard Benardo, is through the Fort Greene and Clinton Hill neighborhoods. Slightly east of downtown Brooklyn, these areas are becoming increasingly known for their history and mid-nineteenth-century housing stock. Our Bedford-Stuyvesant chapter was written by Eric Wakin. Bedford-Stuyvesant is the largest African American neighborhood in New York City, an area steeped in architectural and cultural history.

The book then moves north, into Williamsburg. An ever-changing neighborhood, Williamsburg is Italian, Latino, Hasidic, and hipster all at once. Written by Big Onion guide and neighborhood resident Jennifer Fronc, this chapter covers many of the highlights of this vast district. Next we come to the northernmost corner of Brooklyn, Greenpoint. Created by longtime Big Onion colleague Thorin Tritter, Greenpoint is an amazing neighborhood that has moved from being a nineteenth-century industrial center to become a thriving contemporary Polish neighborhood.

The second half of our book covers five districts south of Flatbush Avenue, beginning with Park Slope, known as "Brooklyn's Gold Coast." Park Slope is one of the best-known residential neighborhoods in Brooklyn, and this chapter, written by Annie Polland, describes the reasons this "suburb on the subway" is so desirable. Park Slope is found along the western side of Prospect Park, the emerald jewel of Brooklyn. Written by Seth Kamil, our park walk explores Frederick Law Olmsted and Calvert Vaux's greatest creation.

Keeping with the naturalist theme, we then move to Green-Wood Cemetery for a unique tour focusing on famous Brooklynites buried within this historic garden cemetery. The Green-Wood Cemetery chapter was written by Seth Kamil. The great multiethnic neighborhood of Sunset Park, adjacent to Green-Wood, provides the ninth chapter of our book. Written by Eric Wakin and based on research by Jamie Wilson, this walk moves through a neighborhood known for its diverse cultures, wonderful food, and eponymous park.

Our final chapter explores Brooklyn's playground, Coney Island, the great "Sodom by the Sea." Coney Island is legendary. Written by Leonard Benardo, this walk explores both the past and present of this great area. Coney Island is everything Brooklyn—a tremendous history that continues to undergo a dramatic revitalization and rebirth.

This second Big Onion book would not have been possible without the tremendous support and assistance of a number of important people. We first would like to express our appreciation to everyone at New York University Press. Thanks to all our Big Onion colleagues who contributed to this work and who help lead our walking tours. Thanks to Jessie Kelly, president of the Brooklyn Historical Society (BHS), for offering access to most of the photographs used in the book, and to Sean Ashby, also of the BHS, for guiding us through the photo archives and doing the legwork to get most of the images. We will be forever indebted to Professor Kenneth T. Jackson, who continues to mentor and advise us on all matters historical. Thanks to Stephen Brotmann for his unerring advice and counsel. Thanks to Andrew Alpern for yet again offering some of his encyclopedic knowledge of New York to improve our text. Finally, we are grateful to Kevin Baker for taking time away from his brilliant novels to contribute a foreword to our endeavor.

Thanks to everyone who has ever joined us on a Big Onion Walking Tour for coming out rain or shine, 365 days a year, to join us as we walk the city we love.

We would like to dedicate this book to Traci Farber Kamil, born in Brooklyn and now living seven blocks from her parents' high school alma mater, and Lawrence Wakin, who with his brother, the coauthor, has returned to (part of) the family's roots in Brooklyn.

SETH KAMIL AND ERIC WAKIN

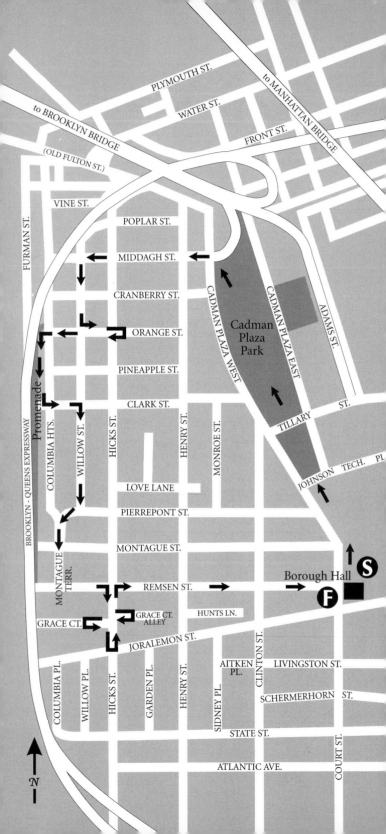

1 DOWNTOWN BROOKLYN AND BROOKLYN HEIGHTS

Manhattan's "Nearest Country Retreat"

> Start: Take the A, C, or F train to the Jay Street Borough Hall stop; or the 2, 3, 4, or 5 to the Borough Hall stop; or the M or R train to Court Street and walk a block to Borough Hall.

OUR TOUR BEGINS at Brooklyn Borough Hall, which sits on a plaza between Court and Adams streets in "downtown Brooklyn," an area sometimes also called the Civic Center. You're actually standing at the back of Borough Hall, if you are on the Joralemon Street side (the south side), because the grand entrance faces north, toward Manhattan. Borough Hall was the city hall of the City of Brooklyn until 1898. Although most New Yorkers don't know it, Brooklyn and New York were separate cities until 1898, when they were consolidated into greater New York City—the current five boroughs—an event that many in Brooklyn viewed with horror (see sidebar). Opposition notwithstanding, with consolidation Brooklyn's 1848 City Hall became merely "Borough Hall." The building was actually originally designed by Calvin Pollard, but the man who supervised its construction was Gamaliel King. In the tradition of Jeffersonian republicanism, King was first a grocer and then a carpenter, who only later became an architect. The restored glint of the 1898 cupola atop Borough Hall is thanks to the recent work of Les Metallers Champenois, which also restored the copper skin of the Statue of Liberty.

Borough Hall sits amid a civic center that has undergone a number of changes in the past 150 years. While many buildings are now gone, there is still ample evidence of the past around you. For example, the 1926 Municipal Building is across Joralemon to the south of Borough Hall and next to the 1994 Brooklyn Law School Annex. Across the street to your west is George L. Morse's 1901 Temple Bar Building, with its three cupolas. Some in Brooklyn consider the Temple Bar Building to be Brooklyn's finest tall structure after the Williamsburgh Bank Building (see our Fort Greene and Clinton Hill chapter for more on the latter).

As you walk north around the eastern side of Borough Hall, note that the greatest changes to this civic center were inspired by city redevelopment projects from the 1930s through today. The blocks to the east are part of downtown Brooklyn designated "Metrotech," in which yet more master-plan redevelopment is currently ongoing. Here office space has been created for Chase Manhattan Bank, the new Fire Department Headquarters, Keyspan, and others. The largest change wrought by Metrotech is visible a few blocks east in the form of the 1999 Marriott Hotel, the first hotel to be built in Brooklyn since 1928's Leverich Towers, which we'll see on this walk.

Probably the most destructive of the urban renewals that affected downtown Brooklyn was the one that razed an elevated train and many buildings to create the Cadman

An early view of what was then Brooklyn's City Hall and is now its Borough Hall, showing a bustling plaza in front. Image courtesy of the Brooklyn Historical Society.

Plaza strip, along which you are walking, which stretches northward from Borough Hall. For New York's greatest builder and destroyer, Robert Moses, Cadman Plaza was "to Brooklyn what the great cathedral and opera plazas are to European cities" and "as much the pride of Brooklyn as the Piazza San Marco is the pride of Venice and the Place de la Concorde the cynosure of Paris." Judge for yourself as you walk northward.

THE CONSOLIDATION OF NEW YORK—THE DEATH OF BROOKLYN

The idea of Brooklyn joining New York was contentious in the nineteenth century, much like the idea of Staten Island seceding from New York City was contentious in the mid-1990s. Indeed, the consolidation referendum passed by only a few hundred Brooklyn votes in 1894. Although Brooklyn actually needed to be connected to New York's copious aqueduct system, many prominent Brooklyn citizens didn't want to merge what they saw as corrupt New York with pristine Brooklyn.

Even after the consolidation referendum passed, a group of businessmen (including A. A. Low and Henry Pierrepont—two of

Brooklyn's wealthiest landowners), along with cultural and religious leaders, formed the League of Loyal Citizens to oppose consolidation. The League's vision of Brooklyn was of a white, prosperous, Protestant borough that wasn't teeming with Manhattan's immigrants.

League spokesperson St. Clair McKelway, editor of the **Brooklyn Eagle,** which sponsored an anti-consolidation song contest— "Up with the Flag of Brooklyn" won the $300 prize—wrote an editorial against consolidation in 1894:

> "Brooklyn is a city of homes and churches. New York is a city of Tammany Hall and crime government. Rents are twice as cheap in Brooklyn as in New York and homes are to be bought for a quarter of the money. . . . Government here is by public opinion and for the public interest. If tied to New York, Brooklyn would be a Tammany suburb, to be kicked, looted and bossed as such. Vote against consolidation now and let the speculators wait till a better time, when New York will offer something like fair terms."

In spite of the League's opposition, of course, Brooklyn and New York were joined, and at the December 31, 1897, observation of the change, Will Carleton's "The Passing of Brooklyn" was read aloud.

> Now while the bells of the steeples turn golden,
> Now as the year has waxed sacred and olden,
> And the new century clearer and clearer
> Flashes its headlights another mile nearer
> And moments are nigh
> When the fierce gongs and strong trumpets braying
> Once more the triumphs of time are displaying,
> When does a feeling of sadness surround us?
> As when the blade of bereavement has found us?
> Not because moments fall dead in their flying;
> Not that we know that a twelvemonth is dying;
> Never with tears is Time's havoc anointed,
> Years at their birth have their death-days appointed

With never a sigh.

No; we are grieved that a maiden of sweetness,

Full of life's vigor and joy and completeness,

With the rich charms of young womanhood laden,

We are aggrieved that this fair, comely maiden,

At midnight must die.

When the Old Year, for his death scene already,

Creeps on the stage with steps slow and unsteady,

Praying the fall of the curtain to linger,

He will lift up his long tremulous finger

To this maiden and cry,

"Death now must enter! But not for me only;

You are to render my passing less lonely;

When Father Time, his white grave-garments bringing,

Sharpens his scythe with twelve strokes loudly ringing,

You with me must die!"

➤ Walk north (toward Manhattan) around the left side of Borough Hall and through Cadman Plaza.

As you walk, notice the 1957 New York State Supreme Court building on your right. Although there has been no uproar like that in Alabama about the Ten Commandments, you can clearly see a bas-relief of Moses and his tablets on the wall of the building immediately to the left of the entrance.

On your left is the restored 1908 Borough Hall subway station kiosk. Cadman Plaza is decorated with statues, as many civic spaces are. At various points you will see representations of Christopher Columbus, done by Emma Stebbins, who designed the Angel of the Waters central statue in Central Park; of Robert F. Kennedy by Anneta Duveen; of former mayor of New York William Gaynor by Adolph Weinman (see his home in our Park Slope chapter); and, most famously, of Brooklyn Heights preacher Henry Ward Beecher by John Quincy Adams Ward. We shall return to Beecher later in the tour.

Continuing northward, you cross Johnson Street and see the mammoth 1891 U.S. Post Office in front of you, to your right. This fantastic 1891 building has several later additions that don't fit in with its Romanesque Revival origins. Beyond the Post Office is a federal courthouse more reminiscent of late-twentieth-century corporate architecture than anything else.

Continue walking north until you come to a set of steps on your left. Walk up these steps and approach the 1951 Brooklyn War Memorial at the north end of Cadman Plaza. Over 300,000 Brooklynites served in the armed services during World War II, and Robert Moses wanted something substantial to honor them. A more elaborate monument and series of buildings was planned, but what resulted was one nearby building and the 100-foot-wide stone wall monument. The wall is bordered by two statues designed by Charles Keck, who also designed those at Columbia University's 116th Street entrance in Manhattan. One is of a male warrior, symbolizing victory, and another is of a woman and child, symbolizing what soldiers fight to preserve. As a memorial, the structure did not receive much praise, with the nastiest criticism perhaps coming from Leslie Katz in the *Nation*, who described it as "a billboard made of stone, with two apathetic stone giants doing a television commercial for grief on either side."

In the distance is the Clock Tower Building, recognizable by the eponymous clock on top of it. Developer David Walentas spent $30 million converting the former 1915 Gair Building into loft apartments that sell for hundreds of thousands of dollars. Those in the clock tower itself were selling for $1.5–2 million. The neighborhood around the Clock Tower Building is called DUMBO, for Down Under the Manhattan Bridge Overpass; the Manhattan Bridge is immediately east of the Brooklyn Bridge, to which Court Street/Cadman Plaza West leads.

➤ **Walk west to Cadman Plaza West (Court Street) and cross at Middagh Street.**

As you cross Cadman Plaza West (the road), you will note the modern buildings that divide the historic district of Brooklyn Heights from the Civic Center/downtown Brooklyn neighborhood. These high-rises and townhouses were built in 1967 and 1968, just a few years after Brooklyn Heights was designated a historic landmark, but also, alas, after the townhouses that once stood here were razed.

The tall apartment buildings immediately north of Middagh are called Cadman Plaza North; the lower-rise townhouses and apartments between Henry Street and Court Street/Cadman Plaza West are called Whitman Close. Believe it or not, they were all designed by Morris Lapidus, who was the architect of the Fontainbleu Hotel in Miami. The tall apartment buildings and townhouses a few blocks south, around the intersection of Clark and Henry, are called Cadman Towers. Just after Lapidus's buildings went up, *Progressive Architecture* magazine dubbed them "monuments in a vacuous space" and noted that the ground around them is "wasted, because it bears no direct relationship to people who lie, not on it, but above it."

It's ironic that the greatest poet the United States has ever known should have his name affixed to the faceless townhouses that are part of this urban renewal. But it was at 98 Cranberry Street, on the southwest corner of Fulton Street (now Cadman Plaza West), at the printing press of Andrew and James Rome, that Walt Whitman set the first edition of *Leaves of Grass* in 1855. The building was demolished in 1964, just a year before the neighborhood was designated a historic district.

Whitman was born on Long Island in 1819 but spent much of his youth and quite a bit of his adult life in Brooklyn. As Whitman remembers it, "From 1824–28 our family lived in Brooklyn in Front, Cranberry, and Johnson Streets. In the latter, my father built a nice house for a home, and afterwards another in Tillary St. We occupied them one after the other, but they were mortgaged, and we lost them." His parents moved to Long Island in 1836, but Whitman stayed to apprentice as a printer. In the 1840s and 1850s he lived between Manhattan and Brooklyn, while editing the *Brooklyn Daily Eagle* and the *Brooklyn Freeman.* It was from the cities of Brooklyn and New York that Whitman got so much of the material for his poetry, including his love for ferries:

> My life . . . was curiously identified with Fulton ferry, already becoming the greatest of its sort in the world for general importance, volume, variety, rapidity, and picturesqueness. Almost daily later. . . . I cross'd on the boats, often up in the pilot houses where I could get a full sweep, absorbing shows, accompaniments, surroundings. . . . The river and bay scenery . . . the hurrying splashing seatides—the changing panorama of steamers, all sizes, often a string of big ones outward bound to distant ports —the myriad white-sail'd schooners, sloops and skiffs, and the marvelously beautiful yachts . . . what refreshment of spirit such sights and experiences gave me.

➤ **Walk west on Middagh to Willow Street.**

At Middagh and Hicks you will pass the new offices of the *Brooklyn Eagle,* which folded in 1955 but has been resurrected recently.

Brooklyn Heights is New York City's first historic district, and you get an entirely different view of the community from the inside—standing on Middagh—than from the outside—standing on Cadman Plaza. The Heights is also New York's first suburb, with more than 600 homes built before the Civil War on an area that had been orchards, gardens, and pasture, with a few mansions scattered about.

Hezekiah Pierpont (he Anglicized the spelling of the family name, which is "Pierrepont") bought 60 acres here in 1804, shrewdly recognizing that its proximity to Manhattan made it a perfect suburb. Pierpont was also a major backer of Robert Fulton's steam ferry project. And as soon as ferries started running from Manhattan to Brooklyn Heights, the land became even more valuable for development. Pierpont advertised his 60 acres of property in 1823 as "the nearest country retreat" for businessmen from Manhattan. Homeowners could be near enough to see ships and businesses in the harbor but far enough from the waterfront sailors' neighborhoods to feel comfortable. As the streets were laid out, Pierpont named them after prosperous Brooklyn families—Livingston, Remsen, Joralemon, Hicks, and, of course, Pierrepont.

But why is there also a Cranberry, an Orange, and a Pineapple Street in Brooklyn Heights? The story is that Mabel Middagh Hicks, a descendant of two wealthy Brooklyn families, was upset at all the family names on the streets, so she put up her own more colorful ones. The board of aldermen eventually let them remain. Is it true? We don't know, but it's too good not to mention.

Another great old Heights story, this one not true, concerns Mabel's relatives, the Hicks brothers—"Milk" and "Spitter" Hicks. The Hicks family did have a farm here, and they likely sold produce in Manhattan. Supposedly, the word "hick" to describe a country bumpkin comes from the phrase "here come the Hicks," uttered by Manhattan residents as they saw the Hicks approaching by boat to sell produce. It's a great story, but "Hick" is a seventeenth-century British abbreviation for "Richard."

HISTORIC PRESERVATION LAW

Before the 1965 historic-district law that preserved Brooklyn Heights's character, property owners and the city could and did destroy homes at will here and elsewhere. In 1953 construction for Robert Moses's Brooklyn-Queens Expressway (BQE) razed parts of Columbia Heights, Middagh Street, and Poplar Street. Other losses over the years included the beautiful Brooklyn Savings Bank at Pierrepont and Clinton; the Church of the Restoration on Monroe; and many private homes on Henry, Monroe, Clinton, and Clark. Cadman Plaza destroyed much of the eastern Heights.

In the face of all the destruction, a group of neighborhood residents got together in 1958 and formed the Community Conservation and Improvement Council (CCIC, pronounced "kick"). CCIC joined with the Brooklyn Heights Association, which helped keep the neighborhood intact in the face of Moses's plans for the BQE, and in 1959 proposed a historic zoning designation for the neighborhood, like that which had been granted to Boston's Beacon Hill.

It took a while, but in January 1965 the U.S. Department of the Interior declared the Heights a historic district, and in April 1965 the New York City Landmarks Preservation Law passed. Brooklyn Heights became the first such neighborhood in New York. Once a neighborhood is designated a historic district under the Landmarks Law, it is very rare that any of its buildings is torn down because the owner must first convince the Landmarks Preservation Commission that it is impossible to earn a reasonable financial return without the demolition. The Heights continues to look like it does because an effective landmarks law was passed and later upheld by the U.S. Supreme Court, and then a band of concerned citizens fought to have the Heights designated a historic district.

Returning to Middagh Street, Middagh was one of the first streets laid out in the Heights and, as such, has the greatest collection of wooden houses in the neighborhood, most from the 1820s. Perhaps the most famous house on Middagh, though, was torn down to make way for the BQE. Number 7 Middagh housed a remarkable collection of writers from 1940 to 1945. George Davis, the literary editor of *Harper's Bazaar* rented the house and invited his friends to come live with him. Carson McCullers and W. H. Auden each took a floor, reportedly paying $25 per month. Paul and Jane Bowles also lived at number 7 as permanent residents. Others came and went, staying for a night or longer. These residents included Gypsy Rose Lee (the ecdysiast, as H. L. Mencken might say), Anaïs Nin, Leonard Bernstein, Salvador Dali, Aaron Copland, and Richard Wright and his family.

Anaïs Nin described the house in her diary: "An amazing house, like some of the houses in Belgium, the north of France, or Austria. [George Davis] filled it with old American furniture, oil lamps, brass beds, little coffee tables, old drapes, copper lamps, old cupboards, heavy dining tables of oak, lace doilies, grandfather clocks. It is like a museum of Americana."

To Carson McCullers, who was inspired by nearby Sands Street to create the character Cousin Lyman in *The Ballad of the Sad Café*, "The street where I now live has a quietness and sense of permanence that seem to belong to the nineteenth century. The street is very short. At one end, there are comfortable old houses, with gracious facades and pleasant back yards in the rear." Paul Bowles described the home as a place in which "each one did his work and minded his business; residents saw one another generally only at mealtimes. Auden sat at the head of the table and conducted the conversations."

When you reach Willow Street, note 24 Middagh, the

1829 Eugene Boisselet House. Several guidebooks call this house the "queen of Brooklyn Heights," and who are we to argue. It is an almost perfectly proportioned and exquisitely detailed, wooden Federal house with a rear cottage.

Turn left on Willow and walk two blocks to Orange. Turn left on Orange and walk one and a half blocks to Plymouth Church of the Pilgrims.

The Italianate 1849 Plymouth Church of the Pilgrims was designed by Joseph Wells. It was the home church of the most famous preacher and one of the most famous abolitionists of the nineteenth century, Henry Ward Beecher. We passed J. Q. A. Ward's Beecher statue in Cadman Plaza, but the Beecher statue in the grass courtyard here and the bas-relief of Lincoln are both by Gutzon Borglum. Borglum is best known for defacing Mount Rushmore with presidential faces, but he also, ironically, began the giant Confederate memorial carving on Stone Mountain in Georgia. This statue shows Beecher "auctioning" a slave to his congregation to save her from being returned to slavery under the Fugitive Slave Act. Although Beecher was the best-known white abolitionist in the North, he was also the subject of his own "trial of the century" in the 1870s.

THE BEECHER TRIAL

There is a "trial of the century" at least once a decade. Think Sacco and Vanzetti, the Lindbergh-baby kidnapping trial, the Rosenbergs, Charles Manson, O. J. Simpson, and so on.

Henry Ward Beecher's 1874 trial for "alienation of affection"—he had an affair with a married parishioner—captured the attention of the city in the post-Civil War decade. Beecher's postwar fame was only exceeded by that of his sister Harriet Beecher

Reverend Henry Ward Beecher, a leading abolitionist, stages a mock slave auction from the pulpit at Plymouth Church. Image courtesy of the Brooklyn Historical Society.

Stowe, author of **Uncle Tom's Cabin,** which outsold all books except the Bible in the 1850s.

Beecher was America's leading abolitionist and spoke widely, using Christianity to condemn slavery. He was so popular that extra ferries, called "Beecher's Boats," were run on Sundays to bring attendees from Manhattan to hear him preach in his 2,800-seat church. By 1859 Beecher was making thousands yearly as a minister. Both Abraham Lincoln and Mark Twain came to hear him speak. It is hard to impress upon the modern reader the national stature of a preacher like Henry Ward Beecher in the nineteenth century—think Billy Graham, Jesse Jackson, and Norman Vincent Peale all rolled into one.

So it was quite a surprise when this man who advocated high moral standards in others was accused of having a moral lapse himself by having sex with a woman other than his wife. Beecher managed to hush up his affair with parishioner Elizabeth Tilton until it was brought into the open by several New Yorkers, including Victoria Woodhull and her sister Tennessee Claflin, both noted equal-rights advocates, spiritualists, investors, and feminists.

Woodhull had the radical idea that a woman's sexual needs are equal to a man's and that love (sex) should not be controlled by anyone but the parties involved. She called it "free love," noting, "I have an inalienable, constitutional and natural right to love whom I may, to love as long or as short a period as I can, to change that love every day if I please"—a fairly radical idea for the mid-nineteenth century, and perhaps for today as well.

Woodhull and Claflin's Weekly declared Beecher a closet free lover and urged him to come out in the open. (The twentieth-century equivalents of Woodhull's public announcement were the 1990s posters pasted up in New York "outing" supposedly straight men and women as being gays and lesbians.) Woodhull cleverly drew the link between her struggle for "social freedom" with Beecher's for freedom from slavery.

> "I propose . . . to ventilate one of the most stupendous scandals which has ever existed in any community. . . . I intend that this article shall burst like a bombshell into the ranks of this moralistic social camp.
>
> I am engaged in officering, and in some sense conducting, a social revolution on the marriage question. This institution . . . has outlived its days of usefulness, and the most intelligent and really virtuous of our citizens have outgrown and are systematically unfaithful to it. It is obvious the human animal demands free love. . . .
>
> The immense physical potency of Henry Ward Beecher is one of the greatest and noble endowments of this great and representative man. His only crime is not to openly admit his having frequently indulged in the practice of free love."

Woodhull, Claflin, and her publisher were almost immediately jailed for obscenity after publishing their charges. Other newspapers reprinted their article, but no one else was arrested. Woodhull's plight became a cause célèbre, and Beecher's subsequent six-month-long civil trial for "alienation of affection," brought by Elizabeth's husband, Theodore Tilton, became a fascinating entrée into sex, infidelity, and free love in Victorian America. The trial ended with a hung jury, and two inquiries by the church exonerated Beecher, although historical evidence has long since shown that he was clearly "guilty." Following the trials, Beecher's stature deteriorated a bit and Theodore Tilton moved to France and died unhappily; Elizabeth moved in with her daughter and is buried in Green-Wood Cemetery in a grave that does not announce her name.

The last word should go to a contemporary paper, which wrote, "The trial was a fine illustration of the power of money and the tricks that can be played with the law." Amen.

➤ **Turn around and retrace your steps on Orange to walk one block past Willow to Columbia Heights.**

The corner of Orange and Columbia Heights has several examples of neighborhood construction undertaken by the Jehovah's Witnesses. The Witnesses were founded near Pittsburgh in the 1870s but moved their world headquarters to Brooklyn in 1909. Today they own at least 36 properties valued at well over $200 million, with that value increasing as the Brooklyn waterfront and DUMBO become more fashionable. While the Witnesses have torn down many Heights buildings, they have also beautifully restored many others. It's important to note that when the Witnesses bought many buildings in the neighborhood, it was not the desirable and unaffordable place to live that it is now.

The 12-story building at 97 Columbia Heights, on the northeast corner of Orange Street, is the Margaret Apartments, formerly the 1889 Hotel Margaret. The Witnesses were renovating it when it burned down in 1980. The Landmarks Law required height restrictions on new construction, but the Witnesses made a successful argument for rebuilding the structure to its former height because that was the height of the building when they began renovations. Betty Smith wrote *A Tree Grows in Brooklyn* here in 1943, and H. G. Wells often stayed here when visiting New York.

The cookie-cutter brick building on the southeast corner (107 Columbia Heights) was finished in 1959, before historic preservation laws went into effect. Note how it overwhelms its neighbors. The building at 124 Columbia Heights, on the river side of the street, sits atop what was 110 Columbia Heights. Washington Roebling, the chief engineer of the Brooklyn Bridge, lived in this house for several months after having a nervous breakdown (or suffering a severe case of the bends, depending on whom you ask) and for weeks at a time watched through a telescope as his bridge went up. (See our *Big Onion Guide to New York City* for more on the Brooklyn Bridge.)

The poet Hart Crane rented what he was convinced was Roebling's room in 110 Columbia Heights from 1924 to 1929. He wrote of the bridge, "And up at the right the Brooklyn Bridge, the most superb piece of construction in the modern world, I'm sure, with strings of light crossing it like glowing worms as the Ls and surface cars pass each other coming and going."

➤ **Walk down the ramp at the end of Orange Street to the Promenade.**

As you stand and look out over the harbor to downtown Manhattan, you have a modern version of the view that merchants living in the Heights but working in Manhattan had when they wanted to look upon their business on South Street in New York City 150 years ago. From here you can also see why the neighborhood is called "the Heights." Many of the streets that today end at the Promenade once sloped down from the heights above to the shoreline. Also from here in 1776 George Washington evacuated Long Island (Brooklyn), fleeing with his troops

A view of the Brooklyn Heights Promenade cantilevered over the Brooklyn-Queens Expressway on opening day in 1950. To the right are the homes of Brooklyn Heights and to the left the warehouses along the waterfront. The Brooklyn Bridge is in the distance. Photo courtesy of the Brooklyn Historical Society.

across to Manhattan under cover of fog and then northward to Harlem and out of New York, living to fight on and win the Revolutionary War.

Listen for the roar of the traffic beneath where you stand. The Promenade (or Esplanade, as some call it) is a cantilevered walkway over the two-level Brooklyn-Queens Expressway, which Robert Moses had built through the community in 1953. The building of the BQE and the destruction it wrought on much of the neighborhood was a primary cause for Heights residents to come together to protect their homes by seeking landmark designation. Indeed, Moses had initially proposed that the BQE cut diagonally through what is today the Heights historic district, which would have destroyed it as Moses had many other neighborhoods. By some miracle, the Brooklyn Heights Association prevailed upon him to change his design so the highway skirted the neighborhood. Moses did so, although he insisted on the public Promenade rather than allowing the homeowners along Columbia Heights to maintain their private backyards all the way to the edge of the bluff.

➤ **Walk two blocks along the Promenade and then turn left on Clark and walk a block back to Willow.**

Along Willow Street, there are examples of most of the architectural styles in the Heights. The home at 101 Willow, at the corner of Clark, is an excellent 1838 Greek Revival home. Note the Greek Ionic portico over the front door and high basement. The current owner of this house actually had bricks from the back of the home moved to the front, where they would make it look appropriately aged. To your left (north) is the 1928 Leverich Towers Hotel, another grand Heights hotel that is now a meticulously restored Jehovah's Witness residence hall.

Look ahead (east) down Clark to the St. George Hotel, which takes up most of the left side of the block between Hicks and Henry. The St. George Hotel defined residence-hotel elegance in the late nineteenth and early twentieth centuries. It began with 30 rooms and was built in stages from 1885 to 1929, until it had over 2,600 rooms, making it the largest hotel in the United States for many years. That honor now goes to one of the mammoth 5,000-room hotels in Las Vegas. In 1931, rooms here were $3.50 with bath, $2.50 without, while a top Manhattan hotel was $8.

Many New Yorkers had coming-out parties, weddings, and anniversaries in the hotel's 11,000-square-foot ballroom. The St. George was also a favored hangout of the Brooklyn Dodgers. Today the St. George has been divided into several separate residential buildings. Its salt-water

EL ST. GEORGE SWIMMING POOL
Clark Street, Brooklyn, N. Y.

The Hotel St. George saltwater swimming pool ca. 1950 ("cleaner than the ocean ever has a chance to be"), with its mirrored ceiling, from a contemporary postcard. Image courtesy of the Brooklyn Historical Society.

swimming pool (billed as "cleaner than the ocean ever has a chance to be") with mirrored ceiling is gone. The St. George was also the site of the largest fire ever in Brooklyn. Early Sunday morning, August 27, 1995, a man using a blowtorch to remove copper pipes to sell for scrap started a fire in the 51 Clark Street part of the hotel. The fire spread to several attached buildings and grew to 18 alarms, bringing 500 fire fighters to the neighborhood to extinguish the blaze.

➤ **Cross Willow and walk south as you note the different styles along the block.**

On the Promenade side of the street is 108–112 Willow, three Queen Anne–style buildings built in the 1880s and that mix elements from across architectural history—terra cotta, shingles, bay windows, gables, and a small tower. It is a bizarre style that somehow works and makes it difficult to see where one house ends and another begins.

Continuing along, note the Gothic Revival town-houses, on your right, built in the late 1820s and 1830s. The giveaway architectural signs are the large blocks that make up the outer walls and the Tudor arched windows. Further along on your left is 109 Willow, a Colonial Revival building with exposed outside shutters.

The three Federal-style townhouses set back from the street at 155, 157, and 159 Willow, to your left, are some of the earliest in the Heights, having been built in the 1820s. Note the arched dormered windows on top of two of the houses. At some point the owner of the other house extended the third floor upward and did away with the dormers. A plaque on the middle house says that it hid an underground storage space that was used to hide runaway slaves as they escaped northward to Canada from the South. You can see the glass brick that is the roof of this space if you look down at the sidewalk. Playwright Arthur Miller owned No. 155 in the early 1950s and wrote *The Crucible* here.

The carriage house at 151 Willow is an 1880 addition to the block, although it looks older. The stars on the front of the building actually cover iron tie rods that go through the building and support the walls. Note the name posted on the tree inside the wrought-iron fence.

THE BARDS OF BROOKLYN

Crowds of men and women attired in the usual costumes, how
   curious you are to me!
On the ferry-boats the hundreds and hundreds that cross,
      returning home, are more curious to me than you suppose,
And you that shall cross from shore to shore years hence are
      more to me, and more in my meditations, than you might
      suppose.

—WALT WHITMAN, "Crossing Brooklyn Ferry"

At three o'clock in the morning when the rest of the city is silent and dark, you can come suddenly on a little area as vivacious as a country fair. It is Sands Street, the place where sailors spend their evenings when they come here to port. At any hour of the night some excitement is going on in Sands Street. The sunburned sailors swagger up and down sidewalks with their girls. The bars are crowded and there are dancing music, and straight liquor at cheap prices.

—CARSON McCULLERS, "Brooklyn Is My Neighborhood"

I live in Brooklyn. By choice. Those ignorant of its allures are entitled to wonder why.

—TRUMAN CAPOTE, "A House on the Heights"

Under thy shadow by the piers I waited;
Only in darkness is thy shadow clear.
The City's fiery parcels all undone,
Already snow submerges an iron year . . .

O Sleepless as the river under thee,
Vaulting the sea, the prairies' dreaming sod,
Unto us lowliest sometime sweep, descend
And of the curveship lend a myth to God.

—HART CRANE, "To Brooklyn Bridge"

➤ Turn right on Pierrepont Street and walk one block.

To your right (north) the ugly brown townhouse at 222 Columbia Heights was built to fit in with the others under the strictures of the Landmark Law. It gets an A for effort and a D for design. Next-door at 218 and 220 Columbia Heights are two examples of the Renaissance Revival style, an opulent, Italianate design. The three townhouses at 21, 23, and 25 Pierrepont Street, which you just passed on the right, are also in this style. Note the continuous balcony-like balustrade that ties them together.

➤ **Turn left and walk south a bit, passing Pierrepont Street, to Pierrepont Place, which becomes Montague Terrace.**

Notice, on the Promenade side, two of the three original mansions designed by Richard Upjohn in 1857. At 3 Pierrepont Place is the former home of Abiel Abbott Low, a merchant who became rich through trading with China and moved to the Heights in the mid-nineteenth century. His son Seth Low was the only person to be both mayor of Brooklyn, in 1884, and of New York City, in 1901. In between, he was president of Columbia University and presided over the campus's move from midtown Manhattan to Morningside Heights. Low also donated $1 million of his personal fortune to fund the construction of Columbia's Low Library.

The mansion at No. 2 was the home of Alfred Tredway White, a wealthy merchant and philanthropist whose charitable motto was "philanthropy plus five percent." White funded model tenements for the poor in Brooklyn.

The playground bordering No. 2 and the walkway to the Promenade are all that remain of the third of Upjohn's mansions. Demolished in 1946, it had been the home of Henry Pierrepont.

Walk south on Montague Terrace, passing No. 5, where Thomas Wolfe lived in the early 1930s while finishing *Of Time and the River*. A friend described his place:

The chief piece of furniture was an old table, work worn and ancient but still sturdy. It was marked by many cigarette burns and its surface was dented like a shelf after a hard battle. . . . At the right, as one entered, and opposite the windows, was one alcove containing a gas range and another with an electric refrigerator which bumped and hummed as refrigerators did then. Tom claimed that this sound stimulated him by its rhythm. On the old table and on this refrigerator he did most of his writing.

➤ **Turn left on Remsen and walk one block. Turn right on Hicks.**

Look left on Hicks to the corner of Montague Street at the 1913 Hotel Bossert, now a Jehovah's Witness dormitory. Another grand Heights hotel, the Bossert was known as the Waldorf-Astoria of Brooklyn and boasted a two-story, rooftop restaurant with a nautical theme, called the Marine Roof.

Walk a few steps along Hicks and enter Grace Court Alley on your left. Walk down the alley and look at the former carriage houses that served Joralemon and Remsen mansions.

➤ **Return to Hicks Street and turn left. Walk a few steps more and cross the street to enter Grace Court.**

On the corner of Grace Court and Hicks is Grace Church, Richard Upjohn's 1849 Gothic Revival work. Walk down Grace Court and enjoy the stunningly deep gardens that stretch back from the Remsen Street houses. The end of Grace Court has its own mini-Promenade. Arthur Miller lived in 31 Grace Court and wrote *Death of a Salesman* here, before moving to Willow Street. In 1955 Miller sold his Grace Court place to W. E. B. Du Bois, who said at the time, "We couldn't have rented there. We had to buy. When we first came, the FBI swarmed around the neighborhood asking questions." Du Bois stayed until 1961.

➤ **Return to Hicks. Turn left and walk back to Remsen Street. Turn right and walk a block to Henry Street.**

At the corner of Remsen and Henry is Our Lady of Lebanon Maronite Church. Yet another Richard Upjohn structure, this one was completed in 1846 as Church of the Pilgrims, just before Upjohn went on to do Grace Church. The congregation moved to Plymouth Church (of Beecher fame) in the 1930s, rechristening that congregation Plymouth Church of the Pilgrims. You may have noticed the doors on this church. They were salvaged from the ocean liner *Normandie*, which sank in the Hudson River in 1942. In a bit of historical irony, before the Lebanese Christians moved into this church, it was home to the decidedly anti-immigrant and anti-consolidation Reverend Storrs, who argued that Brooklyn should remain "a New England and American city" and not merge with New York. Needless to say, Storrs's vision didn't come to pass, and so we end at this example of polyethnic downtown Brooklyn as a fitting coda to our chapter, standing at an immigrant church in a much changed and still changing neighborhood.

➤ Continue on Remsen three blocks to return to Brooklyn Borough Hall where we began.

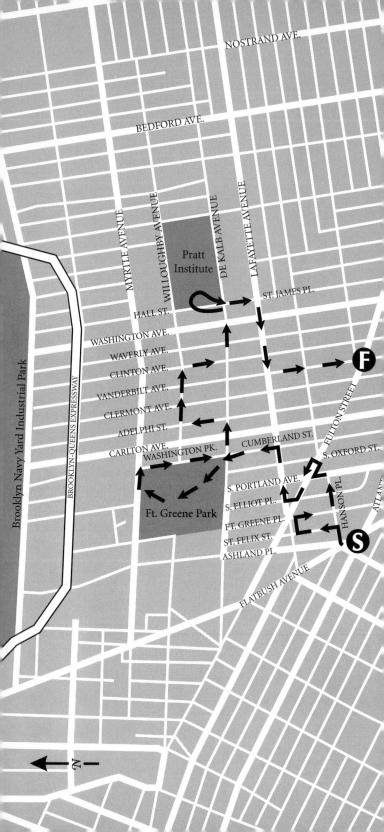

2 FORT GREENE AND CLINTON HILL

From Revolutionary War to Cultural Center

➤ Start: The Hanson Place entrance of the Atlantic Avenue subway stop (2, 3, 4, 5, B, and Long Island Rail Road), steps from the Pacific Street stop (D, M, N, R).

FORT GREENE AND CLINTON HILL are two of Brooklyn's loveliest neighborhoods with some of the finest brownstone streets and row houses anywhere in New York City. We will walk through them sequentially in this tour, beginning with Fort Greene and following with Clinton Hill.

The neighborhood of Fort Greene, bounded by Atlantic Avenue to the south, Flatbush and Clinton avenues to the west and east, and Myrtle Avenue to the north, is named for Revolutionary War hero Nathaniel Greene (1742–1786). Major General Greene, from Rhode Island, was, among America's officers of that period, second in importance only to his close comrade George Washington. Greene's efforts as commander of the Southern Department from 1780 to 1783 are considered his greatest contribution to the colonists' struggle against the British Crown.

Like most of Brooklyn, Fort Greene was largely farm-land until the early to mid-nineteenth century. By the 1840s, skilled black workers, mainly shipbuilders, settled in large numbers in Fort Greene, establishing at the time the foundation for a middle-class black community. Together with Clinton Hill, the neighborhood was a suburb of Brooklyn Heights and a stable middle- and working-class area, though it did not reach the apotheosis of luxury of its western neighbor. By the 1870s, over half of Brooklyn's black population lived in Fort Greene. The 1930s saw the neighborhood's first real decline as the Depression devastated homeowners, and residences that had turned to rooming houses (for Navy Yard workers) skyrocketed in number. The Navy Yard's closing in 1966 was a blow to Fort Greene residents, but middle-income families, many of them black and Latino, returned soon after, attracted by affordable brownstones that could be had for less than $25,000. The neighborhood's turning point was its graduation to landmark status in 1978. It was subsequent to this recognition that revitalization—or, in today's parlance, gentrification—began to advance in earnest.

The past two decades have seen the ascension of fashionable restaurants, galleries, coffeehouses and (the inevitable) real-estate agencies in this artist-populated area ("Brooklyn's SoHo," as it is sometimes called). What this change means is the partial reconfiguration of the population, as longstanding community members are edged out and new urban professionals take their place. But unlike gentrification patterns in other city neighborhoods, where the price paid for revitalization is often the displacement of lower-income minority residents by middle-class whites, Fort Greene's transformation has happened largely across racial lines. This change is testament to the neighborhood's longstanding history of racial and social-class diversity and the prevailing sense, despite gentrification, of racial amity.

On the institutional side, the expanding arts complex of the historic Brooklyn Academy of Music (BAM) is one of several examples of Fort Greene's renaissance. In fact, Fort Greene rightly lays claim to being the cultural epicenter of Brooklyn, and the neighborhood's revitalization certainly is partially attributed to (and a function of) BAM's development. Artistically, while Fort Greene's most celebrated resident, Spike Lee, has decamped for the Upper East Side, other notables like jazz legend Cecil Taylor and TV and film personalities Chris Rock, Rosie Perez, and Wesley Snipes remain.

Look up at the Williamsburgh Bank Building (now HSBC Bank), at 1 Hanson Place. Notice the antiquated "h" at the end of Williamsburgh here. Only until incorporation and consolidation with Brooklyn in 1852 did the neighborhood of Williamsburg to the north carry that additional "h." But "h" or no "h," the Williamsburgh Bank is the largest building in Brooklyn, at 512 feet (by comparison, there are well over a hundred buildings in Manhattan taller than it). Built between 1927 and 1929, this nicely massed Spanish Revival, Art Deco setback structure is well known for its four clocks (one on each face of the building's tower) as well as its plethora of dentist offices. The clocks themselves were the largest in the world until surpassed by one in Milwaukee in the early 1960s. It should be mentioned that while the Williamsburgh Bank holds Brooklyn's tallest-building award, the tallest actual structure goes to the radio/TV tower atop Brooklyn Technical High School (later on this walk).

Notice that both the Ashland and Hanson street signs are brown in color. This color signifies a street's landmarked status and indicates that buildings cannot be changed without the consent of the Landmarks Preservation Commission. You will encounter a large number of Fort Greene's landmarked streets over the course of this tour.

A 1946 view of the Williamsburgh Savings Bank, which dwarfs everything around it. Photo courtesy of the Brooklyn Historical Society.

Next-door to the Williamsburgh Bank Building is the gothicized Hanson Place Central United Methodist Church, built coterminously with the Williamsburgh Bank and by the same architects (Halsey, McCormack & Helmer).

➤ **Walk along Hanson Place to St. Felix Street and take a left. Keep walking until you reach Lafayette Avenue.**

On the left side of the street is the Brooklyn Music School and Playhouse (126 St. Felix Street). Established in 1912, this is Brooklyn's community school of the performing arts. Inside are classrooms, dance halls, and a 266-seat theater. The school's credo is "to provide training in music and dance of the highest quality without regard to income, age, previous experience, or professional aspirations." Speaking of high-quality music, the late great Betty Carter, jazz vocalist extraordinaire and champion of local community arts, lived across the way at 117 St. Felix Street.

Notice all the cast-iron bishop's-crook streetlamps as you walk down St. Felix Street. A supremely handsome turn-of-the-twentieth-century light source, with its massive size yet intricate detail, this lamppost style is considered by many to be the benchmark of ornamental lighting. It was under the reign of Mayor Rudy Giuliani that the city began putting these handsome posts back into circulation. For contrast, on the corner of Lafayette and St. Felix Street have a look at a typical banal 1970s lamppost, standing, ironically, only several feet away from a bishop's crook. Progress?

On Lafayette, you stand before the legendary Brooklyn Academy of Music.

BROOKLYN ACADEMY OF MUSIC

The Lincoln Center of Brooklyn? The flowering cultural mecca of New York's largest borough? The nation's oldest performing arts center? Well, it's all of the above, and more. You stand before one of Brooklyn's great institutional achievements: America's oldest continuously operating performing arts center and an exploding complex of music, theater, dance, and film. As an institution, BAM (pronounced "bam") actually dates way back, from 1861, when it housed the Philharmonic Society of Brooklyn as well as other musical and theatrical productions in a building on Montague Street in Brooklyn Heights.

In its early years, BAM was also an important lecture site, showcasing among others Booker T. Washington, Mark Twain, and Henry Stanley, with his account of the discovery of Dr. Livingston. Following its death by fire in the Heights, a new structure designed by Herts & Tallant, leading theater architects of the day, went up on the present site on Lafayette Avenue in 1906. In BAM's new theater, the Metropolitan Opera presented some of its performances. In the Met's final season at BAM, during a performance of **L'Elisir d'Amore**, the great tenor Enrico Caruso suffered

An early-twentieth-century view of the Brooklyn Academy of Music, where practically everyone from Enrico Caruso to Twyla Tharp has performed. Photo courtesy of the Brooklyn Historical Society.

a throat hemorrhage; his own final Met performance was two weeks later.

After World War II, BAM fell on hard times, and its performance spaces were often employed by such things as martial-arts studios and language classes. BAM's renaissance occurred under the vital and thoughtful stewardship of Harvey Lichtenstein, who from 1967 until he stepped down in 1999 helped mastermind the transformations here. Lichtenstein now heads the BAM Local Development Corporation (LDC) in its efforts to further expand the cultural district. In its most recent venture, 80 Hanson Place, around the corner, will soon be home to around 30 arts and services groups. BAM LDC has received a remarkable $80 million in pledged city and state funding, with which it hopes to attract an additional $600 million of private investment. This will include, beginning in 2005, construction of a visual and performing arts library as part of the Brooklyn Public Library system.

Today BAM houses the Howard Gilman Opera House (2,109 seats) and the Harvey Lichtenstein Theater (874 seats). Across the street on Lafayette are the new studios for the Mark Morris Dance Group and Twyla Tharp. According to the management at BAM, its mission is twofold: to present internationally significant artists with an avant-garde orientation and to serve Brooklyn's ethnically diverse population. Its success in all this is best seen in its wide-ranging support and ongoing expansion.

➤ **Turn right on Lafayette and walk one block to Fort Greene Place. Turn right and walk one block back to Hanson Place.**

Hanson is a lovely landmarked street with a number of especially attractive row houses, including No. 92 from 1858; No. 104 with its Deco front, wide lintels, and handsome brick; No. 115 with its broad girth; and No. 133 with its charming pinwheel designs.

At the end of the block, observe firsthand the ongoing development of Atlantic Center, a 26-acre retail and housing complex. The IRT, BMT, and Long Island Rail Road have long converged under the center, creating what Governor George E. Pataki called "the busiest transportation hub in Brooklyn." At press time, a second shopping mall is being built above the terminal as part of the overall $200 million project to transform the complex. Once upon a time, Brooklyn Dodgers fans petitioned owner Walter O'Malley and Brooklyn borough president John Cashmore to place Ebbets Field here (the southern part of it, to be exact) rather than schlepping it out to Los Angeles. Brooklyn residents still rue the day. Sports fans may get their wish, though, as the New Jersey Nets, under Bruce Ratner's developmental supervision, use eminent domain to take over land around and on the neighboring rail yards to build a new Frank Gehry–designed stadium (at press time, debate over its establishment still rages).

➤ **Turn left on Hanson Place and walk two blocks to South Portland Avenue.**

Stop at the Seventh-Day Adventist Church (88 Hanson Place, corner of South Portland Avenue). Like the Lafayette Avenue Presbyterian Church later on this tour, this church functioned as a way station for the underground railroad. An 1860 George Penchard–designed Baptist church building, it has been operated since 1958 by a Seventh-Day Adventist congregation founded by Caribbean immigrants. Looking at the lovely pastel Neoclassical row of four fluted Corinthian columns with capitals holed with rosettes, one could be in southern Alabama with this church design.

➤ **Take a left on South Portland and walk one block to Fulton. Turn right and walk two blocks to Cuyler Gore Park.**

The "Cuyler" is for Dr. Theodore Ledyard Cuyler (1826–1909), first minister at the Lafayette Avenue Presbyterian Church (see below for church details). The "Gore," derived from a term for a small triangular piece of material, denotes a small triangular park (Brooklyn has four other "Gore" parks: Cooper, Grant, Memorial, and Underhill).

A short detour for the horticulturally minded: traverse several blocks further east to Fulton Street between Cumberland and Carlton. Marty Markowitz, Brooklyn's borough president, announced this block the 2002 winner of the Greenest Block in Brooklyn contest.

➤ **Return along Fulton a few blocks to South Elliott Place. Turn right on South Elliott.**

Fulton has become the main commercial drag of Fort Greene, populated by a wealth of restaurants, boutiques, architectural firms, galleries, and, yes, real-estate agencies. You will find on or around Fulton five—count 'em, five—

French restaurants (which corresponds perfectly with the French influx into Fort Greene); New York's first South African restaurant; a Senegalese restaurant (where for $7.95, at press time, you can have tiebou dieun, the national dish of Senegal); and the sumptuous Southeast Asian restaurant, Cambodian Cuisine.

Cambodian Cuisine, at 87 South Elliot Place between Lafayette Avenue and Fulton, is, at press time, multiethnic Brooklyn's sole Cambodian restaurant. With 140 or so dishes, it is an encyclopedic sampling of home-grown Khmer cuisine. In front of the restaurant stands a statue of little-known Civil War general Edward Fowler (his anonymity is ensured by the unfortunate absence of any biographical information accompanying his statue). Cast in 1902, it shows the forgotten Union general in full proud pose. Born in 1827, Fowler was the colonel of the 14th Regiment during the Civil War. Although seriously wounded at the second battle of Bull Run and at Gettysburg, he kept command of his regiment, a group known as the "red-legged devils." Fowler is buried in Brooklyn's Green-Wood Cemetery. The sculptor, German-born Henry Baerer, is perhaps best known in New York City for his bust of Beethoven in Central Park.

Standing at the statue, look back west toward the Williamsburgh Bank Building. Its lovely mass comes now into full view.

➤ **Take a right on Lafayette and walk two blocks to South Oxford Street.**

The Lafayette Avenue Presbyterian Church (85 South Oxford Street) is one of Brooklyn's great churches and at one time was the largest Presbyterian church in America. It is a growing, multiracial, multicultural, midsize (350 members) body. According to the current pastor, David

Dyson, the church today is "two-thirds black and one-third everything else."

The church, built immediately before the Civil War and founded by abolitionists, was a critical site on the underground railroad. In fact, downtown Brooklyn itself was sometimes known as the Grand Central Terminal of the underground railroad. The church preserves letters written by the aforementioned Theodore Cuyler, who remained thirty years as the church's first preacher and was an outspoken opponent of slavery. These letters discuss fugitive slaves hiding in the basement heating tunnels when other regular hiding places were compromised or under surveillance.

Within the church, a must-see experience is one of Louis Comfort Tiffany's great Brooklyn-church achievements in stained glass, and also his very last. Regrettably, the once 200-foot steeple, one of Brooklyn's highest points in the nineteenth century, was dismantled during the early-twentieth-century construction of the independent subway line. The church also has an exceptional gospel choir—the Inspirational Ensemble—that has performed for two presidents, the Pope, and various royals and dignitaries. The Ensemble worked as the original singers on jazz-great Donald Byrd's *Nutcracker in Harlem* and is included on some of John Cale's recent work. On a related note, in Boerum Hill you can find the former Cuyler Presbyterian Church, which began as an extension of the Lafayette Avenue Church to support its growing programs. In 1907 Cuyler Chapel established itself as an independent organization. As times change, so do (sometimes) churches, and Cuyler Presbyterian was converted into residential use in the early 1980s.

Before leaving, have a look across the street at two fine-looking apartment buildings. On the opposite corner of

Lafayette and South Oxford is 101 Lafayette, also known as the Griffin, and across from the Griffin, at 65 South Oxford, is the Roanoke. The Griffin was a lovely Art Deco hotel when finished in 1932, and after an early 1990s conversion, it is now a cooperative apartment building. The Roanoke was one of Brooklyn's first luxury apartment buildings when finished in 1893.

➤ **Walk a block further on Lafayette to Cumberland and take a left, walking toward DeKalb Avenue and Fort Greene Park.**

The building at 260 Cumberland was the home, from 1929 to 1965, of the great twentieth-century modernist poet, author, and Pulitzer Prize winner Marianne Moore (1887–1972). In 1935, T. S. Eliot wrote that her poems are "part of the body of durable poetry written in our time, in which an original sensibility and an alert intelligence and deep feeling have been engaged in maintaining the life of the English language." Moore was also a devoted sports fan, supporting the Brooklyn Dodgers and writing the liner notes to Muhammad Ali's record *I Am the Greatest*. Moore attended Sunday services at the Lafayette Avenue Presbyterian Church, fitting for one who grew up with a grandfather who was a Presbyterian minister.

Once you reach DeKalb Avenue have a look back west, where you can see Brooklyn's tallest structure: the 597-foot radio/TV tower atop Brooklyn Technical High School. DeKalb, by the way, is named for Johann DeKalb, a German baron who came to America with the Marquis de Lafayette in 1777 and became a Revolutionary War hero after the Continental Congress appointed him a major general. He was mortally wounded in South Carolina in 1780.

➤ **Enter Fort Greene Park at the corner of Dekalb Avenue and Washington Park (the street).**

Brooklyn's first park, 30-acre Fort Greene Park was founded in 1847 on the urging of Walt Whitman, who expressively voiced Brooklyn's need of a "lung." It was redesigned in 1864 by Frederick Law Olmsted and Calvert Vaux, before they turned to their masterful work outfitting Prospect Park.

A fort did originally exist here—Fort Putnam it was called—built in 1776. Nathaniel Greene actually contributed to the fort's construction. And it was from here that General Greene guaranteed Washington's retreat and safe passage across the East River during the Battle of Brooklyn, helping to hold off British troops as Washington escaped via the Brooklyn Heights waterfront. Later, Fort Putnam, like all of New York City, would be occupied by the British until the war's end in 1783. The fort was renamed in 1812 for General Greene, and a garrison was stationed on the site. In 1847, Washington Park became the official name (now curiously the name of the street with a gorgeous row of Italianate brownstones, once Fort Greene's grandest address, at the eastern end of the park, off DeKalb, where we entered). The park officially became Fort Greene Park in the early twentieth century.

Standing within the park is Stanford White's brilliantly designed Prison Ship Martyr's Monument, a large-scale reminder of the devastating conditions to which American revolutionary prisoners were subjected at the hands of the British. Between 1776 and 1782, 11,500 Continental soldiers died from disease and starvation while held captive by the British on ships anchored offshore in Wallabout Bay (now called the Channel), the present site of the Brooklyn Navy Yard. The number of dead prisoners was almost

Stanford White's Prison Ship Martyr's Monument in Fort Greene Park commemorates the 11,500 Continental army soldiers who died during the Revolutionary War aboard British prison ships anchored off what is today the Brooklyn Navy Yard. The monument was completed in 1908, two years after Stanford White was murdered by Harry Thaw. Image courtesy of the Brooklyn Historical Society.

three times the number of soldiers who died in all the battles of the American Revolution. Many of their remains are entombed in the Martyr's Monument.

Unveiled in 1908, this structure is actually the third incarnation of the Martyr's Monument. The first, set up by New York's Tammany Society in 1844, stood near the Brooklyn Navy Yard waterfront; the second was a large stone crypt in Fort Greene Park itself. This third design is an impressive and imposing 145-foot fluted Doric column topped by a huge bronze urn (its height makes it a visual landmark throughout the neighborhood). The column is often cited as the tallest free-standing Doric column on earth, if you enjoy superlatives.

Despite the painful history memorialized in the park, it has functioned as a wonderful respite from the hustle and bustle of urban life. Hazel Rowley, author of the biography *Richard Wright: The Life and Times*, describes the great American writer's employment of the park: "Wright got up early . . . around 6 AM—sometimes earlier at the height of summer. Clutching his lined, yellow legal pad, a fountain pen, and a bottle of ink, he walked to nearby Fort Greene Park. He climbed to the hill, where he sat on a bench, looking down on the brownstones and, in the distance, the ragged tenement houses by the Brooklyn Navy Yard, and filled page after page with his scrawling handwriting." This happened in 1938–39.

➤ **Return out of the park at the Myrtle Avenue entrance and walk back along Washington Park (the street) in the direction you came two blocks. Make a left on DeKalb and walk one block to Carlton.**

As you look at the lovely homes on Carlton (like so many Fort Greene blocks, a landmarked street), check out 267 Carlton, on the corner. This was the 1873 house of shirt maker and merchant C. P. Piper. Located there today is the Yvon Morisset Gallery, a leading exhibitor of Haitian art. In the other direction, at 175 Carlton, you'll find the home where Richard Wright began working on his classic *Native Son*.

Across the street is the fine Edmonds Playground. Have a sit-down here and take in the active street life around you. Ronald Edmonds, by the way, was a major African American educator (1935–1983). Born in Michigan, he was director of Harvard's Center for Urban Studies and worked for a time at New York City's board of education.

➤ **Continue on Dekalb one block to Adelphi. Turn left and walk one block to Willoughby.**

On the left side of the street, with its lovely tower, witness the sadly condemned Church of St. Michael and St. Mark (in New York the signal of an X on the façade denotes a building's structural unsoundness; though in some instances, especially in Brooklyn, it might signify stickball). The future here is uncertain.

Across the street from the church is the 1951 Clinton Hill School/PS 20. Another fine playground adjoins the school; this one is named for Albert Lysander Parham (1914–1990), a beloved local philanthropist who contributed $250,000 to renovate the former Clinton Hill Playground in the year he died.

> **Turn right on Willoughby and walk one block east to Clermont.**

On the southeast corner is the attractive and quite literally named French Speaking Baptist Church (Eglise Baptiste d'Expression Francaise, 209 Clermont). This church was once the Jewish Center of Fort Greene (and before that it was the Simpson Methodist Church), and you can still see a Star of David above the portals. It is fitting for a French-speaking church to be on Clermont Street, which derives its name from the French for "clear mountain." In the New York context, Clermont was the Hudson River seat of the politically and socially prominent Livingston family of New York for more than 230 years. Interestingly, while the actual street name is derived from Robert Fulton's first steamboat, the *Clermont*, it was Robert Livingston who pushed Robert Fulton to leave Paris (where he was seeking a painterly career) and return to the United States to pursue steamboat design. See nearby Fulton Street to close the circle.

Just a few doors down, at 171 Clermont, are the Armory Towers, a textbook example of adaptive reuse. Turned into rental units in 2000, this structure once housed the Clermont Armory: the Third Battery National Guard of New York (see the lobby for photographic evidence). The Clermont Armory, constructed in 1873, was the oldest standing armory in New York City. The Armory was built for the New York State 23rd Regiment, which saw action in the Civil War, in World War I, and at Normandy in World War II. Stand across the street and admire the creatively executed I-beams supporting the massive center arch of the façade.

➤ **Continue on Willoughby two blocks to Clinton Avenue, the dividing point between Fort Greene and Clinton Hill.**

Clinton Hill is named not for William Jefferson but rather for DeWitt Clinton, New York mayor, governor, and senator in the first quarter of the nineteenth century. "Clinton" is the name realtors have pinned on Manhattan's West Midtown neighborhood as well (though it remains "Hell's Kitchen" to most natives). Clinton Hill is on the eastern border of Fort Greene (up the hill from it, literally) and is roughly bounded by Myrtle Avenue on the north, Atlantic Avenue on the south, Clinton Avenue on the west, and Classon Avenue on the east. The slightly smaller Clinton Hill historic district, designated as such in November 1981, is bounded by Myrtle, Vanderbilt, Putnam, and Classon avenues.

The English purchased Clinton Hill, one of the highest areas in Brooklyn, from the Dutch in the seventeenth century. As farmland, the area was parceled and sold for development in the mid-nineteenth century to prosperous merchants who had been forced out of Brooklyn Heights. Quite rapidly, Clinton Hill—or "The Hill," as it was known—became second only to Brooklyn Heights in terms of elegance. By the third quarter of the century, Charles Pratt helped spearhead a millionaire's row on the ultrafashionable Clinton Avenue, where he built for himself a spectacular mansion, then, as wedding presents, a mansion each for four of his sons. Quite justly, Clinton Avenue at the time was considered the 5th Avenue of Brooklyn. Overall, Clinton Hill has one of the city's largest concentrations of row houses from the post–Civil War period.

During the 1950s, so-called urban renewal under Robert Moses transformed the area with the erection of many of the high-rises now situated around Pratt Institute. In recent years, though, many of the same indicators of the gentrification process in Fort Greene hold true for Clinton Hill. Contributing in this regard has been the superb quality of the housing stock and the extensive public investment targeted at maintaining the historic status of the neighborhood. Evidence of such gentrification are the numerous homes now transcending the $1 million threshold.

➤ **Turn right on Clinton Avenue.**

Walking down Clinton Avenue between Willoughby and DeKalb is one of the finest urban aesthetic experiences in New York. And this is certainly what was intended by Charles Pratt when he had built for his sons four of the great mansions of latter-day Brooklyn. All except one are still standing here. His fifth son opted for Park Avenue. Pratt's own mansion, No. 232, is on one of the highest points of elevation in Brooklyn. The remaining wedding presents for his sons—numbers 229, 241, and 245—are all curiously located across the street from the father's. Just enough room to keep lingering Oedipal resentment in check.

Charles Pratt's mansion, on the west side of the street, is today part of St. Joseph's College. Founded in 1916, St. Joseph's motto is *esse non videri*: "to be, not to seem." Pratt, in his penchant for the material, would have heartily agreed. Next-door on the corner is the modernist 1964 McEntegart Hall. Across the street are the remaining sons' homes: today No. 229 is the home of the Pratt Institute president; the lovely Romanesque Revival No. 241 is the residence of Brooklyn's Roman Catholic bishop emeritus, Thomas V. Daily (a former top deputy to Boston's former Cardinal Law, who has been accused of covering up sexual abuse of children in the Church); and No. 245 belongs, like Pratt senior's home, to St. Joseph's. Take your time and savor the comeliness of the homes and the block.

Charles Pratt, who moved to Clinton Hill in 1870, was born in 1830, one of eleven children of a Massachusetts carpenter. After working for a Boston firm specializing in paints and whale oil, he moved to New York, where his interest in petroleum expanded the already established Astral Oil, whose slogan modestly averred that "the holy lamps of Tibet are primed with Astral Oil." Pratt eventually took over Astral, creating Pratt Oil Works in Greenpoint and thereby spearheading the largest and most successful company in Brooklyn. In 1874, it merged with Standard Oil, for which Pratt became a lead partner, paving the way for Rockefeller's Standard Oil and today's Exxon-Mobil.

Pratt was a member of the Washington Avenue Baptist Church, but offended by the pastor (see below for details) he left and founded the Emmanuel Baptist Church on Lafayette Avenue. In his obituary, the *New York Times* descriptively noted that "personally Mr. Pratt was short and stout with a very broad pair of shoulders and a sharp pointed face. He was of a happy jovial disposition and had a very happy family circle. He leaves a wife and eight

Mansions along Clinton Avenue built by New Yorker and oil millionaire Charles Pratt for his sons and himself. Photo courtesy of the Brooklyn Historical Society.

children." By the time of his death in 1891, Pratt was best known for his enormous philanthropy, a goodly portion of which went to his beloved Pratt Institute. In fact, the day before his death was spent at Pratt discussing the addition of two new buildings.

For Pratt's Brooklyn legacy outside the terrain of Fort Greene and Clinton Hill, check out the 1886 Astral Apartments in Greenpoint, commissioned by Pratt to house his refinery workers (on Franklin Street between Java and India). Its model was the Peabody Apartments in Southwark, London. As noted by the *American Architect*, Pratt intended his Astral Apartments of 1886 to house "the widow who has lived in affluence but has been reduced in circumstances," "the shop-girl," "the clerk, or tradesman," and "the great body of first-class mechanics who have families."

➤ **Turn left on DeKalb and walk three blocks to the corner of Hall Street and the main entrance to Pratt Institute. Enter Pratt Institute at the Hall Street gates. Pratt covers the blocks between Willoughby and DeKalb avenues and between Hall Street and Classon Avenue.**

Named for Charles Pratt, its 1887 founder and donor, Pratt Institute is one of the world's leading universities of art, design, and architecture. The school has grown over the past century from 5 to 25 acres, populated today by some 4,000 students. The campus is a wonderful agglomeration of architectural styles, sculptural elements, and industrial motifs. We suggest you spend some time walking around the campus grounds, as its richness can only be alluded to in the context of this tour.

In front of you as you walk in stands the library, originally founded as Brooklyn's first free public library and only in 1940 made part of Pratt Institute's system (though it was Pratt himself that set it up originally). The library celebrated its centenary in 2002.

Around Ryerson Walk is the 1887 East Building (formerly the Machine Shop Building), one of two original campus buildings, which contains the engine room and boiler designed specifically so that Pratt, if his educational adventure failed, could readily transform its efforts into a shoe factory. In its look, it has the decayed gracefulness of a Dickensian London industrial structure. Go inside and check out the nineteenth-century Ames Iron Works steam engines still supplying through its generators a goodly amount of the campus's energy. Appreciate the various cats camped out in the boiler room, à la Rome (you are requested not to feed them).

Pratt's main (and other original) building, dressed in neo-Romanesque, boasts a most handsome porch (added in 1895) and clock tower. Today it includes the offices of the president, the provost, and the dean of the School of Art and Design.

Across the river, Pratt purchased the upper six floors of a West 14th Street building in 1999 at a cool $11.5 million, for a permanent home for its Manhattan operations. But Brooklyn remains the school's headquarters, and to underscore the point, in the same year Pratt installed 26 large, compelling (often industrial) sculptures on the grounds of the campus. By a range of well-known and near-well-known sculptors, they provide the campus with a lovely open-air museum-like feel. Enjoy as you stroll the campus grounds.

Some prominent alumni of Pratt over the years include actor and director Robert Redford, painter and sculptor Eva Hesse, photographer Robert Mapplethorpe, and painter Ellsworth Kelly.

➤ **Return from the Pratt campus and turn left on St. James Place (Hall turns into St. James as you walk south) until you get to Lafayette.**

The lovely and landmarked 1869 Higgins Hall structure is the home of the Pratt Institute's School of Architecture. It was originally Adelphi Academy, a private school. Henry Ward Beecher, the prominent, progressive nineteenth-century minister, laid the building's cornerstone. The building was tragically gutted by fire in 1996, requiring a complete rehabilitation. See its 1887 partner, the South Building, next-door.

Look diagonally across Lafayette to see Emmanuel Baptist Church (279 Lafayette Avenue). Finished in 1887, this imposing edifice, with one of New York's most extraordinary church interiors, was recently the beneficiary of a terrific $2.3 million restoration (finished in 2001). Designed by well-known architect Francis Kimball (see his Montauk Club on the Park Slope tour) and financed by (who else?) Charles Pratt, it is an attempt at medieval French Gothic accompanied by lovely yellow Ohio sandstone.

The church itself was an offshoot of the Washington Avenue Baptist Church. Apparently Emory Haynes, the pastor of the Washington Avenue Church, offended the church's wealthiest parishioner, Charles Pratt, by a satire of monopoly men in one of his books. Like J. P. Morgan, who around the same time left the Union Club in anger to form the Metropolitan Club, Pratt bade farewell to the capitalist-needling Pastor Haynes and became the principal donor of this new church on Lafayette Avenue. In fact, Charles Pratt became so closely identified with the Emmanuel Church that it was often known as the Astral or Standard Oil Church.

Whatever happened to Emory Haynes? Haynes, who had previously converted to Baptism from the Methodist faith, returned to Methodism and, according to the *New York Times* in 1891, moved to Boston and became "addicted to driving fast horses, and to writing novels." Charles Pratt died the same year.

➤ **Turn right on Lafayette and walk two blocks to Waverly Avenue and Underwood Park (Lafayette between Washington and Waverly avenues).**

This charming park was the site of the great mansion of John Thomas Underwood (1857–1937), the noted typewriter manufacturer. Underwood's typewriter revolutionized the industry, and his Hartford, Connecticut, factory was by 1915 the largest in the world. To represent the "World of Tomorrow," the 1939 World's Fair chose to

The yellow-clapboard Skinner House at the corner of Lafayette and Vanderbilt, built in the mid-nineteenth century and still standing strong. Photo courtesy of the Brooklyn Historical Society.

feature a state-of-the-art Underwood typewriter. Underwood generously donated his plot to the city, thus allowing for the park you see today.

➤ **Continue along Lafayette until you get to Vanderbilt, stopping at Steele Skinner House (southeast corner of Lafayette and Vanderbilt).**

Savor this yellow-clapboard house for being an exemplary holdout from the mid-nineteenth century. Facing diagonally across Lafayette, you will see Our Lady Queen of All Saints Church (northwest corner of Lafayette and Vanderbilt). The awkwardness of the church's name belies the grandeur of this cast-stone pile. Built in 1913, it was the pastoral home of the future cardinal of Chicago (and the first cardinal west of the Allegheny Mountains), George Mundelein. Mundelein, who also commissioned the church, created the modern archdiocese in Chicago, where he ventured in 1915, just a few years after the present church's completion. Try to figure out who the 36 saints are that adorn Our Lady Queen.

➤ **Look next-door at Clermont and Lafayette.**

Here is the stately polychromatic terra-cotta 1906 Brooklyn Masonic Temple, reminiscent, it is said, of fifth-century Greek temples. Like most aspects of the Masonic movement, its history is steeped in mystery. It's enough to appreciate the façade.

➤ **Take a left on Clermont to see Bishop Loughlin Memorial High School (357 Clermont Ave).**

This school is one of New York City's oldest Catholic high schools, originating in 1851 on Jay Street. The school moved here in 1933, when the diocese changed its name to honor John Loughlin, Brooklyn's first Roman Catholic bishop (1853–1891). Loughlin was 35 years old at the time and was immediately faced with the rise in Brooklyn of the fiercely anti-Catholic Know-Nothings, a political party with brief but potent support. In fact, former New Yorker Millard Fillmore, the thirteenth president (he succeeded Zachary Taylor when the latter died in 1850) ran on the Know-Nothing ticket in 1856, garnering a tidy 22 percent of the vote. A century later, Bishop Loughlin's graduating class of 1961 included Rudy Giuliani.

From here, walk south down Clermont a few blocks to Fulton Street. To your right is the Lafayette Avenue stop of the C train, and to your left is the Clinton–Washington Avenue stop. If you are seeking some respite after hoofing it around the lovely Fort Greene and Clinton Hill neighborhoods, now is your time to continue south, straight down Clermont, cross Atlantic Avenue, turn left for half a block, and then continue south on Vanderbilt Avenue until you hit Prospect Park. From the vantage point of Brooklyn's most magnificent green space, one can relax and reflect until it's time to begin the charming brownstone neighborhood walk of Park Slope (see chapter 6).

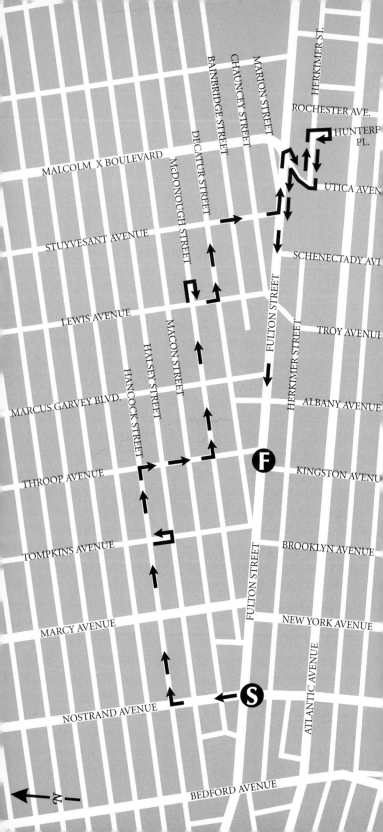

3 BEDFORD-STUYVESANT

"In Those High Rooms Life Soared and Ebbed"

➢ **Start: The Nostrand Avenue stop on the A or C train at the intersection of Nostrand and Fulton Street.**

THIS WALK TAKES you through a small but historic part of Bedford-Stuyvesant, New York's largest African American neighborhood, which contains some of the most beautiful row houses in the city, spectacular churches, and one of New York's oldest free black communities. It has also been home to, among others, composer Eubie Blake, congresswoman Shirley Chisolm, musician Richie Havens, actress Lena Horne, poet June Jordan, drummer Max Roach, and boxer Floyd Paterson. In the 1960s and '70s, Bed-Stuy was one of the most impoverished neighborhoods in America, but today it is being revived by longtime residents and some newcomers who have renovated homes, created new businesses, and helped rebuild the community.

Like most Brooklyn neighborhoods, there are no formal lines denoting where Bedford-Stuyvesant begins and ends, but its rough area is as follows: From where you stand when exiting the subway, the neighborhood stretches

A fanciful, nineteenth-century sketch of what the artist imagined Bedford Corners, the forerunner of Bedford-Stuyvesant, might have looked like in the eighteenth century. Image courtesy of the Brooklyn Historical Society.

almost 30 blocks northward to Flushing Avenue, across which lies Williamsburg. Some would argue that Bed-Stuy ends only two blocks south at Atlantic Avenue, while others, present authors included, say it stretches 10 blocks further to Eastern Parkway, where Crown Heights begins. Broadway cuts the neighborhood into a pie-piece-shaped wedge to the east, separating it from Bushwick, while Classon Avenue makes its western boundary, with the neighborhoods of Fort Greene, Brooklyn Heights, and Park Slope lying beyond.

The two streets that give the neighborhood its name both run north-south through it—Bedford Avenue to your west and Stuyvesant Avenue to your east. Bedford Corners was the town that grew up to the west, where in 1668 Thomas Lambertse opened an inn "for the accommodation of strangers . . . with diet and lodging and horse meals." The area was ideally situated for an inn, thanks to the crossroads that took travelers south to the town of Flatbush or north to Bushwick, east to Jamaica (in today's Queens), and west to the ferry that took commuters from Brooklyn Heights to Manhattan. Both the first Dutch settlers and the subsequent English ones "bought" the land from the Canarsee Indian tribe by bartering goods for what the Indians considered land use but the colonists saw as land ownership.

In the late 1700s, the area had only 200 residents, a third of whom were slaves, marking a continuous black presence in Bedford-Stuyvesant extending back likely to its earliest settlement. Given that Brooklyn's total population at the time was less than 2,000, the Bedford Corners area was one of the most populous. The most prominent family, the Lefferts, owned almost half the land in the area and were the largest slaveholders.

The changes that created a modern Brooklyn in the nineteenth century began with its transformation from a collection of towns like Bedford into a single incorporated city. The nineteenth century brought a railroad, the right-angle-grid street system, and horse-pulled omnibuses to the neighborhood of Bedford Corners. With transportation came development, and the farmers sold their land to builders, who bought lots and built row houses. An 1854 advertisement in the *New York Times* touted land and homes as "first class improvements . . . elegant and costly dwellings . . . convenient and easy of access of New York . . . a remarkably healthy and pleasant part of the city of Brooklyn."

As the population of farmers gave way to one of the middle class, a continued housing boom in the late nineteenth and early twentieth centuries brought most of the row houses you see today, along with some of the more luxurious apartment buildings like the Alhambra and Renaissance on Nostrand Avenue. In the late nineteenth century, Abraham Abraham, a founder of A&S, and Frank Woolworth both lived in the neighborhood still called Bedford to the west and Stuyvesant to the east, but which eventually merged to become "Bedford-Stuyvesant."

In the late nineteenth and early twentieth centuries, as immigration to New York grew, more immigrants moved to the neighborhood, including Italians, Irish, and Eastern European Jews. Between the world wars, blacks from the southern United States moved north and settled in Bedford-Stuyvesant for the economic opportunity the city offered, with perhaps more black migrants settling here than in Harlem after about 1920, attracted by the easier possibility of owning a home. The Duke Ellington–Billy Strayhorn composition "Take the A Train" sings the praises of the IND subway, which beginning in the 1930s took people to and from Bed-Stuy and Harlem. Bed-Stuy thus became a thriving black middle- and working-class black community.

Keeping in mind that Bedford-Stuyvesant had always had a black community, especially in Weeksville and Carrville (see sidebar), this community was augmented by immigrants from the West Indies and migrants from the South, who became a majority in spite of white racism. Indeed, in 1929, white William Blackshear, the rector of St. Matthew's Protestant Episcopal Church, announced that he did not want blacks worshiping in his church. Bedford-Stuyvesant was certainly a majority-black community by the 1950s, and by the 1960s it emerged as the largest black neighborhood in the United States. Bed-Stuy elected the first black congresswoman in history, Shirley Chisolm, in 1968.

Bedford-Stuyvesant was ravaged by poverty, unemployment, and drugs in the 1960s and 1970s. But, as we noted, residents have long been committed to working with the police and each other to stabilize the neighborhood. As homes have been renovated and new ones built by the New York City Department of Housing Preservation and Development, Bed-Stuy has returned as the preeminent place in the city for African American home ownership. Of course, with development come rent rises, and the neighborhood becomes less an exclusively black neighborhood and one in which other New Yorkers see opportunity.

Before walking north on Nostrand Avenue, note Carver Bancorp at the intersection with Fulton Street, recently rededicated here. Carver is a community institution founded more than half a century ago by clergy and business people in Harlem. Its logo of interlocking, open C's is derived from the African symbol for unity and reflects Carver's commitment to urban New York—"building wealth block by block"—and reflects their extensive mortgage lending in Bedford-Stuyvesant.

➤ **Walk north on Nostrand Avenue.**

The six-story terra-cotta and brick apartment house on the west side of Nostrand between Macon and Halsey streets is the 1890 Alhambra Apartments. In spite of its name, there is nothing really Moorish about the building. Architect Montrose Morris (more on him below) designed both this building and the 1886 Renaissance apartment house, with its cylindrical turrets, a block further north, on the southwest corner of Hancock Street. The Alhambra is more impressive above street level, where stores were added in the 1920s, detracting from the power of the building. Looking up, you can enjoy the chimneys, dormered windows, arched colonnades, and peaked roofs.

Walking north, you've passed Halsey Street, one of a number of Bed-Stuy streets named after naval heroes. William F. Halsey was born in 1882 in New Jersey and graduated from the U.S. Naval Academy (Annapolis) in 1904. As Admiral "Bull" Halsey, he qualified as a pilot when he was 52 and commanded the U.S. Pacific Fleet's air force. Halsey's Third Fleet played a major role in the battles in the Pacific during World War II, including the crucial 1944 Battle of Leyte Gulf.

James Naughton's 1886 Girls' High School, one of the oldest public high school buildings in New York City. Its alumnae include singer Lena Horne, writer Paule Marshall, and Shirley Chisolm, the first black woman to be elected to Congress. Photo courtesy of the Brooklyn Historical Society.

Between Halsey and Macon streets, across the street from the Alhambra, stands James Naughton's 1886 Girls' High School, the oldest public high school building in New York City, although it is now used as an adult education center. Girls' High School and its brother school, Boys' High School, both evolved from the girls' and boys' divisions of Central Grammar School, built in downtown Brooklyn in 1878. The former 1891 Boys' High School, also by Naughton, is on Marcy Avenue between Putnam and Madison streets (we'll point it out later on the walk). Boys' and Girls' High School now exists as a single entity at 1700 Fulton Street, which you'll see at the end of the tour.

The list of famous alumni of Boys' includes writers Norman Mailer and Isaac Asimov; critic Clifton Fadiman; composer Aaron Copland; all-star basketballer Connie Hawkins; and William Levitt, whose Levittown development on Long Island redefined suburban sprawl in the post—World War II era. Girls' alumnae include singer Lena Horne; writer Paule Marshall; and congresswoman Shirley Chisolm.

SHIRLEY CHISOLM

Shirley Chisolm was born in Brooklyn in 1924 but moved to her parents' home in Barbados shortly afterward, only to return to Bedford-Stuyvesant when she was 10. She earned her B.A. from Brooklyn College and an M.A. from Columbia University. Chisolm went into politics and strongly supported education and employment issues. She was elected to the state assembly and wanted to run for Congress, but Bed-Stuy was made up of five different electoral districts, none of which had a black majority, thus making it extremely difficult for a black candidate to be elected to national office. A lawsuit finally forced New York to redraw the electoral districts to create a congressional district whose voters were a black majority. In 1967 the community of Bed-Stuy elected Shirley Chisolm to Congress, making her the first African American woman ever to serve.

Chisolm wrote in her autobiography, **Unbought,** about the importance of education while growing up: "We had to read, too, even if we did not want to. We all had library cards and every other Saturday Mother took us to the library to check out the limit, three books each. Each of us had a dictionary and our Christmas presents were books, often one of those endless 'adventure' series such as Nancy Drew or Bobbsey Twins stories."

➢ Walk to the corner of Hancock Street and turn right. Walk two blocks to Tompkins Avenue. As you pass Marcy Avenue, look to your left for the former Boys' High School, the Romanesque building with circular towers two blocks to the north.

Although not within the nearby Stuyvesant Heights historic district, the three blocks of Hancock between Nostrand and Throop have some of the most magnificent housing in the neighborhood. Montrose W. Morris (1861–1916), of Alhambra and Renaissance fame, was the architect responsible for many of the houses along these blocks of Hancock Street. Morris had his own architectural firm by the time he was 22 and cleverly built his own house at 236 Hancock between Marcy and Tompkins as an example of what he could do. Indeed, the story is that developer Louis Seitz, who paid for the Alhambra, saw Morris's work here and hired him because of it.

Morris did a beautiful job of designing individual row houses that, when taken together in groups, seem to be larger and more magnificent structures than any of their individual parts. This style is evident in the 1886 row from Nos. 236 to 244. Notice how Morris uses flat roofs on the end houses in this row (including his own at No. 236) and mansards and gables in the middle ones to create what is almost an optical illusion of a single large structure.

Other beautiful houses along Hancock are No. 232, at the southeast corner of Marcy, an 1888 Queen Anne beauty with projecting bays; Nos. 255–259, with the seemingly incongruous third-floor loggias that work well here; the 1880 strip at Nos. 246–252, which combine terra cotta and columns; and the "queen" of Hancock Street, No. 247, a gigantic 80-foot-wide almost-palazzo home with central stairway, built for water-meter manufacturer and millionaire John C. Kelly.

Author Paule Marshall, who grew up in Bedford-Stuyvesant, in her 1972 book *Brown Girl, Brownstones* described the homes she saw:

Looking close, you saw that under the thick ivy each house had something distinctively its own. Some touch that was Gothic,

The "queen" of Hancock Street, No. 247, is a huge Romanesque pile with a double entry stoop. It was built more than 50 feet wide on an 81-foot-wide lot for millionaire water-meter manufacturer John C. Kelly. Photo courtesy of the Brooklyn Historical Society.

Romanesque, Baroque or Greek triumphed amid the Victorian clutter. Here, Ionic columns framed the windows while next door gargoyles scowled up at the sun. There, the cornices were hung with carved foliage while Gorgon heads decorated others. Many houses had bay windows or Gothic stonework, a few boasted turrets raised high above the other roofs . . . in those high rooms, life soared and ebbed.

Bedford-Stuyvesant's housing stock was what attracted people who wanted to own their own homes from the nineteenth century through the twentieth. It was one of the few neighborhoods in which African Americans in New York could buy homes in the early nineteenth century and again in the twentieth century. Currently, Bed-Stuy's beautiful homes are attracting newer, wealthier buyers, both black and white, leading to rising property values and gentrification. Following the destruction of many homes in the 1960s and 1970s, the New York City Department of Housing Preservation and Development started funding the rehabilitation of many brownstones, while building other new housing. Today many houses sell for $500,000, with others of particular architectural merit going for much more.

➤ **Turn right on Tompkins Avenue and walk to No. 404.**

The building at No. 404 is the former site of a cigar and candy store owned by Russian immigrants Morris and Rose Michtom. In 1903 the Michtoms put a small, stuffed toy bear in their window with a sign reading "Teddy's Bear," and that's why every child in America today has a teddy bear. What's the story behind this stuffed animal?

In November 1902, President Teddy Roosevelt was bear hunting in Mississippi. Roosevelt's game catcher, Hold Collier, lassoed a small bear, knocked it unconscious, and tied it to a tree for the president to shoot. Roosevelt refused (although—and this part of the story is usually forgotten—he did ask someone to "put it out of its misery," and a hunter did so with a knife).

When reporters got wind of the story, they wrote about Roosevelt's "sportsmanlike" conduct. Cartoonist Clifford Berryman of the *Washington Post* drew a cartoon of a black bear roped by a white catcher—"Drawing the Line in Mississippi"—with Roosevelt turning away in disgust. The message of the cartoon was that Roosevelt was disgusted by Southern racists. Berryman's bear evolved into a cub, as he drew further cartoons and Americans took to them, with the race message forgotten.

Back in Brooklyn, Morris Michtom supposedly wrote to Roosevelt requesting the right to use his name on the bear, and the president wrote back, "I don't think my name is likely to be worth much in the toy bear business but you are welcome to use it." Boy, was he wrong.

➤ **Return to Hancock and walk east one block to Throop. Turn right on Throop and walk three blocks to MacDonough.**

As you walk south, you'll pass the Newman Memorial Methodist Church at Macon Street, a curiously named street for today's Bedford-Stuyvesant because Nathaniel Macon was a North Carolina representative and senator who was a strong supporter of slavery.

On the corner of Throop and MacDonough are two spectacular churches. The 140-foot-high campanile (reminding you of St. Mark's in Venice) identifies the 1889 First AME Zion Church, on the southwest corner. The building got its start as the Tompkins Avenue Congregational Church, with an auditorium that could hold over 2,000 worshipers. Across the street, on the northwest corner, is the 1880s Stuyvesant Heights Christian Church, with its beautiful stained-glass windows.

➤ **Turn left on MacDonough.**

As you continue eastward on MacDonough, you'll walk past an interesting structure: the free-standing and lonely house at 97 MacDonough is the 1888–1889 Eastern District Grand Tent #3, Grand United Order of Tents of Brooklyn. You may be more familiar with Kiwanis, Elks, and Odd Fellows, but the Tents is one of the earliest and most important African American women's fraternal lodges in the United States. Founded in Norfolk, Virginia, by two former slaves—Annetta Lane and Harriet Taylor—with two abolitionists—Joshua Giddings and Joliffe Union. The Tents' name is derived from one of its purposes: "to care for their sick, bury their dead, shelter the stranger and the outcast, and spread their tents over fallen humanity."

On the corner of MacDonough and Throop is the 1895 pinnacled, Gothic Revival Our Lady of Victory Roman Catholic Church, built with Manhattan schist—the bedrock on which most of New York's skyscrapers stand.

Continue on MacDonough, past Marcus Garvey Avenue (Sumner Avenue) to the corner of Lewis Avenue. As you cross Marcus Garvey, look to your left several blocks north at the enormous 1894 castle that is the 13th Regiment Armory of the New York National Guard, where Billie Holiday sang in the 1940s and Bobby Kennedy spoke in the 1960s.

➤ **Continue on MacDonough to Akwaaba Mansion at No. 347. You are now in the Stuyvesant Heights historic district.**

Akwaaba is a bed-and-breakfast in the heart of Bedford Stuyvesant. Monique Greenwood, the former editor in chief of *Essence,* and her husband, Glenn Pogue, bought the Italianate 1860 home in 1995 from the Lilly family for $225,000. The Lillys were only the fourth family, and the first black family, to own it and only managed to buy it by pooling family money in 1940. Akwaaba, which means "welcome" in the Akan language of Ghana, has 18 rooms, many with fireplaces. Greenwood took her own advice— she is the author of a book subtitled *The Black Woman's*

Grand homes along Bainbridge Street in the Bedford-Stuyvesant landmark district, circa 1941. Photo courtesy of the Brooklyn Historical Society.

Guide to Creating the Life You Really Want—and decided that building a business of her own with her family was what she really wanted. Around the corner on Lewis Avenue, Greenwood and Pogue have opened Akwaaba Café and other shops as well.

➤ **Walk back to Lewis and turn left. Walk one block to Decatur.**

On the southeast corner of Decatur and Lewis is the 1894 Mount Lebanon Baptist Church, with its shingled, terra-cotta tower stretching up into the sky.

➤ **Turn left on Decatur, then right on Stuyvesant, and walk to Fulton Street.**

As you pass Bainbridge Street, look to your left at the land-marked houses, especially Nos. 113–137. Across Fulton Street and a bit to your left is the new Boys' and Girls' High School, which boasts a new athletic field built by

Take the Field, a nonprofit group co-founded by New York Giants co-owner Robert Tisch.

You are standing next to Fulton Park, named for Robert Fulton, who designed the first steam ferryboat from Manhattan to Brooklyn. Inside the park is a statue of Fulton holding a small model of that boat, the *Nassau*. There is currently an effort to rename Fulton Street after abolitionist Harriet Tubman, who helped more than 300 slaves escape to freedom on the underground railroad. Fulton Street was used to move slaves from Brooklyn churches into the historic black community of Weeksville and to Canada. But since Fulton Street passes through many community districts, each board would have to approve the renaming, and we've yet to see that kind of cooperation in New York.

> ➤ Turn left on Fulton and walk one block. Turn right on Malcolm X Boulevard / Utica Avenue and walk one block to Herkimer. Turn left on Herkimer and walk one block to Hunterfly Road.

The few wooden houses on Hunterfly Road are all that is left of Weeksville and Carrville, two of the oldest free black communities in New York City. The original towns were about a mile apart on many acres of farmland south of Atlantic Avenue. Weeksville was named after early settler James Weeks, but Carrville's etymology is unclear. It may be a linguistic twisting of "Crow Hill," another name for the area.

Black slaves were a large part of the population of the town of Bedford, living and working on farms owned by wealthy white families like the Lefferts. After New York State abolished slavery in the 1820s, emancipated slaves began to buy land here. The first black landowner was William Thomas, a New York City chimney sweep who bought land and moved here from Manhattan in 1832.

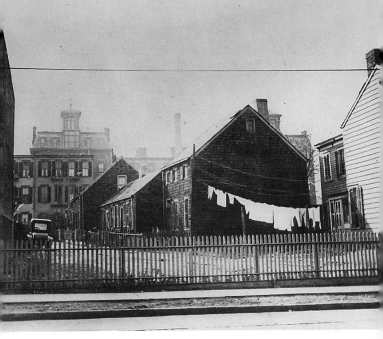

The Hunterfly Road houses of Weeksville as they looked in 1920. Weeksville was one of the oldest free black villages in New York and included a school, several churches, an orphanage, an old-age home, and a cemetery. The Weeksville homes are now being restored by the Society for the Preservation of Weeksville and Bedford-Stuyvesant History. Photo courtesy of the Brooklyn Historical Society.

Henry Thompson, president of the African Woolman Benevolent Society, bought land in 1835, and James Weeks bought plots from Thompson. Somehow Weeks's name stayed with the land and not Thompson's.

By 1850 Weeksville and Carrville had more than a hundred black families. Colored School No. 2 had opened in Carrville in 1841, moving to Weeksville in 1853. The community was served by Bethel Tabernacle AME Church in Weeksville from 1847 and by Berean Baptist Church in Carrville in the early 1850s. It also had an orphanage, a burial society, an old-age home, and a cemetery.

What did people do for money? The 1850 U.S. census listed occupations including laborer (this would be mostly farm labor), seaman, sailmaker, horse dealer, grocer, cigar maker, shoemaker, carpenter, cook, speculator, preacher, and teacher. The 1875 census listed 675 black residents.

Weeksville was a stop for slaves escaping to Canada on the underground railroad, and it also became a place of defense for blacks during the 1863 Draft Riots in New York, during which angry whites attacked and killed blacks across the city. The *Christian Recorder* newspaper reported, "In Weeksville and Flatbush, the Colored men who had manhood in them armed themselves and threw out their pickets every day and night, determined to die defending their homes. Hundreds fled there from New York. . . . And so in every place where they were prepared, they escaped being mobbed."

African Americans built their own community here since they were excluded from the white community around them. Black abolitionist Henry Highland Garnet founded the African Civilization Society here to aid Southern freedmen on land donated by a son-in-law of former slave-owner Leffert Lefferts. The community built the Howard Colored Orphan Asylum (named after General O. O. Howard, commissioner of the U.S. Freedmen's Bureau after the Civil War). Dr. Susan Smith McKinney-Steward, the first African American woman to become a physician in New York State, was born and raised in Weeksville, as was Moses Cobb, one of the city's first African American police officers.

What happened to the community? It was pushed out by development; people moved away to other parts of the city and houses were torn down. All that is left of the original settlement are these four houses. New Yorkers James Hurley, Delores McCollough, and Patricia Johnson reached out to preserve the houses in the 1960s. They created the Weeksville Society, which later spawned the Society for the Preservation of Weeksville and Bedford-Stuyvesant History. They collected tax documents, census records, and histories, and the Landmarks Preservation Commission designated the houses landmarks in 1970.

After literally decades of struggling, Weeksville and Carrville will be receiving preservation monies. Recently, Senator Hillary Clinton, Brooklyn borough president Marty Markowitz, and others appeared at a groundbreaking for a multimillion-dollar restoration of the four houses and construction of an education and cultural center. To date, $3 million has come from the borough of Brooklyn and $400,000 from Washington's Save America's Treasures program, established by Bill Clinton.

> Retrace your steps to Fulton and turn left.

As you walk west, you will pass 1397-B Fulton, site of the Brooklyn chapter of the NAACP. The NAACP was formed in 1909 when W. E. B. Du Bois's Niagara Movement joined with a group of prominent white liberals on February 12, 1909, the centennial of Abraham Lincoln's birthday. The organization has fought tirelessly for equality, education, and enforcement of the Fourteenth and Fifteenth Amendments. In 1954 the NAACP Legal Defense and Educational Fund brought the *Brown v. Board of Education* lawsuit, overturning the "separate but equal" idea of schooling for blacks and whites.

In New York in 1917, the NAACP forced the city to abolish laws that segregated municipal housing and has continued to fight for equality.

> Continue to the Kingston-Throop C train stop at the intersection of Throop and Fulton streets.

On your left, across the street, is Restoration Plaza, a complex of offices, stores, and the Billie Holiday Theater, built by the Bedford-Stuyvesant Restoration Corporation (BSRC), formed in 1967 as the first nonprofit community-development corporation in the United States. BSRC was established at the urging of the Central Brooklyn Coordinating Council, an umbrella organization of community groups, with the help of then-senators Robert F. Kennedy and Jacob K. Javits. It works with residents to improve neighborhoods, build housing, provide health care, and encourage economic development.

You've now come essentially in a circle from where you began, through residential Bedford-Stuyvesant to its commercial center along Fulton Street.

4 WILLIAMSBURG

A "Polyglot Population"

➤ Start: The Bedford Avenue L train stop at Bedford Avenue and North 7th Street. Please note: This walk is substantially longer than others in the book.

WILLIAMSBURGH (which was spelled with the final "h" until 1855) started as a small farming community. In 1797 the first ferries in Williamsburgh left for Manhattan from Thomas Morrell's farm on Grand Street at the East River. Because farmers could now easily send their goods to market, the area began to boom. Richard Woodhull, who operated a rival ferry from Metropolitan Avenue, hired the army's chief engineer, Lt. Col. Jonathan Williams, to survey the area in 1802. Although Williams never lived in Williamsburgh, his name was somehow given to the area. By 1827, Williamsburgh had over 1,000 residents and was incorporated as a village. And in the 1830s, the village began building wharves and docks along the waterfront.

It wasn't until the mid-nineteenth century, though, that Williamsburg began to develop into an industrial center. There were two main reasons for this transformation. First, Brooklyn was becoming a tax haven for Manhattan business owners, and Brooklyn boosters began to publicize it as a refuge from Manhattan's high taxes. Second, after

Hecla Architectural Iron Works, long gone from Williamsburg, but whose decorative ironwork adorns Brooklyn Borough Hall, Manhattan's St. Regis Hotel, the Dakota apartment house, and the interior of Grand Central Terminal. Image courtesy of the Brooklyn Historical Society.

the village of Williamsburgh merged with the city of Brooklyn in 1855, Brooklyn began to fund the development of roads in the Williamsburg section. As a result, industry flourished. The Pfizer drug company started its Williamsburgh plant in 1849, providing jobs for many German immigrants. The Astral Oil Works, New York's largest oil refinery, was located at North 12th Street and the river. Astral was established by Charles Pratt, and in 1874 Astral merged with Rockefeller's Standard Oil (see our Fort Greene and Clinton Hill chapter for more on Pratt and his Pratt Institute). Bayside Fuel now occupies this site. Williamsburg was also home to the Hecla Architectural Iron Works, which was a foundry on North 12th Street. Its decorative ironwork festoons Brooklyn Borough Hall, the St. Regis Hotel, the Dakota apartment house, and the interior of Grand Central Terminal.

With all this industrial growth and a concomitant population boom, the neighborhood required a different kind of housing stock. The townhouses and mansions that had been built decades earlier no longer served the needs of the community, so speculators began converting these older buildings into rooming houses, as well as building rows of tenement apartment buildings to house the industrial work force. As a result, in the last quarter of the nineteenth century, Williamsburg became an immigrant enclave. With the opening of the Williamsburg Bridge in 1903, even more immigrants (mainly Jews, Italians, and Slavs) began moving from Manhattan, making Williamsburg a veritable extension of the Lower East Side.

In 1939, the *WPA Guide to New York City* described "Williamsburg, the area extending fanwise from the Williamsburg Bridge to Flushing and Bushwick Avenues" as having "a large polyglot population." Indeed, this is still the case. However, many people are only familiar with Williamsburg's Northside neighborhood, with its art galleries, bars, and boutiques. But Williamsburg contains multitudes, and this walking tour will take you through not only the recently gentrified Northside but also the Latino, Hasidic, and Italian sections of Williamsburg.

➤ **Begin by walking east on North 7th Street, away from Bedford Avenue. Turn left on Driggs Avenue and head up to North 11th Street. Notice the warehouses and factories, interspersed with tenement apartment buildings. Turn left on North 11th Street and head over three blocks to 79 North 11th Street, at the northeast corner of Wythe Avenue.**

As you walk through the Northside section of Williamsburg, the large number of bars and taverns is striking. Neighborhood residents, both old-timers and newcomers alike, complain about the noise and foot traffic that come along with every new bar and nightclub. Williamsburg's economy, though, has a close relationship, historically and currently, with alcohol. The first distillery was established in Williamsburg in 1819, and the area has been a brewing center since the 1850s. In the late nineteenth and early twentieth centuries Williamsburg was home to dozens of breweries. Brewers' Row was a 10-square-block area that alone contained 11 breweries.

The F&M Schaefer Brewing Company and the Williamsburg Bridge. Schaefer started making beer in Williamsburg beginning in 1916 and closed in 1976, leaving the borough without homegrown beer until the Brooklyn Brewery opened in 1996. Photo courtesy of the Brooklyn Historical Society.

In 1916, Schaefer opened its Williamsburg brewery between South 9th and South 10th streets and between Kent Avenue and the river. During Prohibition, Schaefer was able to stay afloat by brewing "near beer" in its Williamsburg facility. The Williamsburg plant closed in 1976, and for 20 years Williamsburg was without a brewery. But in 1996, the Brooklyn Brewery opened its headquarters in Williamsburg, in a nineteenth-century steel foundry. This building contains a 70,000-square-foot brewery and warehouse, as well as a 300-seat facility. Call the brewery at 718-486-7422 for a schedule of events and tastings.

➤ **Walk back on North 11th Street one block to Berry and turn right. Walk three blocks south to the People's Firehouse at 113 Berry Street.**

During the New York City fiscal crisis of the 1970s, it was determined that eight firehouses could be closed with no impact on fire fighting. Engine Company Number 212, located at 136 Wythe Avenue, was one such house. The fire truck was to be taken out on Thanksgiving night, 1975. The neighborhood decided to rally and prevent the city from shutting down their firehouse. Protesters took over the firehouse and lived there for a year and a half until the city finally gave up and allowed Engine Company 212 to stay open. The People's Firehouse, here at 113 Berry Street, is a community organization that continues to fight for the interests of neighbors and the community and is a legacy of this struggle. In an odd twist of fate, the current New York City budget crisis has caused the municipal government to reconsider some of the tricks they used in the 1970s, namely, shutting down firehouses. Sadly, Engine Company 212 was closed in May 2003 in spite of strong neighborhood protest, and one of its engines was removed to Governors Island in New York harbor, which is largely uninhabited—an ignominious end to the People's Firehouse.

➤ **Continue south one block to North 7th Street and turn left. Walk one block to Bedford Avenue and turn right.**

Many of Williamsburg's industrial buildings, factories, and warehouses were abandoned in the 1970s; by the 1980s, artists from Manhattan started reclaiming these large, affordable, and well-lit spaces as studios. The New York City Board of Estimate approved the use of these former industrial spaces as residences in 1985. This, and the abundance of cheap, large spaces, created a surge of

Manhattan artists into the neighborhood in the 1980s. Many observers note that Williamsburg staged a remarkable comeback in the 1990s. They point to all the commercial activity on Bedford and to the decrease in crime as causing people to actually want to live and recreate in Williamsburg. However, the boom on Bedford Avenue does not translate into prosperity for every resident of the Williamsburg district, and the Northside hardly represents the bulk of the neighborhood's population. Longtime residents of Williamsburg have mixed feelings about this transformation. They recognize that the neighborhood is safer and cleaner and that the streets are once again bustling. But as unscrupulous landlords try to squeeze out the "old-timers" in favor of the "new people" (whom they can charge $1,400 for a one-bedroom apartment off the Bedford Avenue subway stop) and as more and more bars open on quiet, residential side streets, this blessing can only be considered mixed.

The Real Form Girdle Factory Building, at 218 Bedford Avenue, is an interesting example of the reuse of industrial space in this neighborhood. This building had actually been a girdle factory through the early twentieth century. About four years ago, when entrepreneurs started to realize the residential real-estate value of these old buildings, the upper floors of this particular building were converted into loft-style apartments. At street level is Williamsburg's first "mall," which contains a café, a yoga studio, an art-book store, a fantastic record store, and boutiques. It's probably just a matter of time before Starbucks and the Gap take over this formerly underground, subversive little corner of Brooklyn.

As you continue down Bedford Avenue on your way to Grand Street, you will pass the site of Williamsburg's first public school. The school was built in 1826 on the south side of North 1st Street between Berry and Bedford Avenues. In 1843 Williamsburg was divided into three school districts, and in 1850 a school was built in each district. When the City of Brooklyn subsumed Williamsburg in 1855, it also took over the administration of education and the building of schools throughout the district, one of which is featured later in this walk.

➤ **Continue south on Bedford Avenue to Grand Street and turn right.**

As you walk, notice the mix of industrial and residential buildings. It is hard to imagine that this was once where Williamsburg's wealthy businessmen and manufacturing magnates lived and worked. Notice the building at 33–35 Grand, between Kent and Wythe, on the north side of the street. This was home to the North Side Bank, designed by Theobald Engelhardt and built in 1889. This building serves as the only reminder of a particular aspect of the neighborhood's history; its close proximity to where the ferry from Manhattan used to land probably meant that it was a bustling establishment during business hours. Notice that along the top one can barely discern where it once read "North Side Bank." In another transition, this building then became home to the J. Nikolas Guaranteed Lacquers Company, and it is now a residential building. Neighborhood activists and the building's owner have recently expressed interest in having this building designated a historical landmark.

Continue down Grand to the Grand Ferry Park at the East River. This is where Morrell's farm was located and where the first ferry ran between Williamsburg and New York. This is the neighborhood's only waterfront park, and the views of Manhattan are stunning.

From the park, you get a fantastic view of the Williamsburg Bridge. In 1884, state senator Patrick McCarren, who controlled the Brooklyn Democratic organization through the early twentieth century, began lobbying for a bridge to Manhattan. Legislation for this bridge was finally passed in 1895. Construction began on November 7, 1896, and the bridge opened to the public on December 19, 1903. Civic leaders hoped that the bridge would attract members of the city's upper classes to Williamsburg; ironically, though, the population movement worked in reverse. The elite fled, and recent immigrants who had been living on the Lower East Side poured into the neighborhood. Leffert L. Buck and Henry Hornbostel, inspired by French architect Alexandre Gustave Eiffel, designed this bridge. Upon completion, it became the longest suspension bridge in the world, with a main span—between the towers—of 1,600 feet, beating out the Brooklyn Bridge's 1,595 feet. The Williamsburg Bridge in total is 7,308 feet long; each of the four cables is 2,985 feet long, and the steel towers reach to 35 stories. The total construction cost was $30 million. The first elevated train over the bridge crossed in 1905.

Turn around and walk a block back to Kent Avenue and turn right. To the right is the mammoth American Sugar Refining Company, manufacturers of Domino Sugar (292–350 Kent Avenue between South 2nd and South 5th streets). Until recently, this was the last sugar refinery left in Williamsburg. In the 1880s, there were seven such plants on the Brooklyn waterfront, and by 1887, more than half the sugar consumed in the United States was being produced in Williamsburg. Domino started in Manhattan as the William and F. C. Havemeyer Company on January 1, 1807. The company moved to Brooklyn in the 1850s, and some of these buildings date to the 1860s, although the processes were eventually all automated.

The buildings and towers added in the twentieth century provide striking and beautiful contrast to the original nineteenth-century structure. Note the size of the garages

An 1890s view of the American Sugar Refining Company, which made Domino Sugar until closing in 2004. By 1887, over half the sugar consumed in the United States was being made in Williamsburg; now, none is. Image courtesy of the Brooklyn Historical Society.

at street level of this building; probably too small by today's standards, these garage doors remind us of the size of the wagons and carriages that were being used in the nineteenth century. Notice, too, on the east side of Kent Avenue, between South 4th and South 5th streets, the brick warehouses. Presumably these buildings housed industries affiliated with the large sugar refinery across the street. Notice in particular the faded painted sign that reads "cotton BAGS burlap." Presumably this business provided the sacks in which the refined table sugar from across the street was distributed.

This plant was recently the site of a bitter, protracted labor dispute. On June 15, 1999, 300 workers, members of the International Longshoremen's Association Local 1814, went out on strike. The workers wanted Tate & Lyle, the British company that owns Domino, to preserve the 40-hour week and their seniority rights. The union was also concerned about the company's plan to cut 110 jobs. Most of the strikers had been with the company for 20 years and so had been involved in early strikes and job actions against the company. The Teamsters', Laborers', and Boilermakers' locals all walked the line in solidarity. After a year on the picket line, the strikers' unemployment benefits ran out, and the company was not caving to the union's demands. Many workers ended up having to get new jobs, walking the picket line before and after work and on days off. In April 2000, the union accepted a new contract, the details of which were still largely not known to workers at the time they voted to return to accept the contract. The strikers returned to work, defeated. Many blamed the ILA for selling out their workers and making concessions to the capitalists. It was a Pyrrhic victory; the plant stopped making sugar altogether in 2004.

➤ **Continue down Kent to Broadway and turn left.**

Here are two cast-iron buildings reminiscent of the cast-iron district of SoHo. At 97 Broadway is an 1870 building that was home to the Kings County Fire Insurance Company. Notice the segmental arches on Corinthian colonnettes. At 103 Broadway is another 1870s factory. It is now a residential building. Considered beautiful and unique by modern standards, cast-iron buildings were merely seen as economical and practical in the late nineteenth century. As cast iron was strong, durable, and fire resistant, it became the practical choice for factories and warehouses. The façades could be selected out of catalogs; they often reproduced classical and Italianate architectural elements, most notably arched window bays and columns. Once considered utilitarian eyesores, cast-iron buildings are now often described as "beauties" and "marvels." Perhaps low-slung, cinder-block structures will be prized by late-twenty-first-century architecture buffs.

➤ **Continue east on Broadway to the gravel parking lot where Bedford Avenue, South 6th Street, and Broadway intersect.**

Broadway and South 6th Street in 1925. The elevated trains provide the fastest connection between the neighborhood and Manhattan. The Kings County Savings Institution is on the near left, and Williamsburgh Savings Bank is in the distance. Photo courtesy of the Brooklyn Historical Society.

Notice the yellowish building at 109 South 6th Street, which was built in 1891 by W. W. Cole. This was the Bedford Avenue Theatre. The actress Fanny Brice opened the theater with her production of *A Jolly Surprise*, which was a comic farce. In 1897, the theater was renamed the Empire Theatre, and the Little Egypt Burlesque Company was featured here. Little Egypt herself was known for performing an indecent "hoochy koochy"—a bellydance—in a revealing costume. Although Little Egypt received notoriety and bad press for her lascivious dancing, her audience would have been just as disreputable and poorly behaved. In the late nineteenth century, burlesque houses were wildly popular among working-class men and slumming gentlemen, not only for the performances but also for the prostitutes who often worked in such theaters. The building was sold in 1908 for $850,000, and part of the structure was demolished during construction of the Williamsburg Bridge.

Ahead, at the northeast corner of Broadway and Bedford (135 Broadway), is the Williamsburg Art and Historical Center, housed in this stunning 1868 Second Empire–style building. This building was erected to house the Kings County Savings Institution, which was chartered on April 10, 1860. For the first seven years of its existence, the Kings County Savings Institution operated out of Washington Hall, which was a civic building located at Bedford Avenue and South 7th Street. In 1867, this lot was purchased and the architectural firm of King & Wilcox was hired. In 1921, the Kings County Savings Institution officially changed its name to the Kings County Savings Bank. In 1969, a merger between the Kings County Savings Bank and the American Savings Bank created the United Mutual Savings Bank, which was in existence through the 1980s.

In 1996, artist Yuko Nii founded the Williamsburg Art and Historical Center in this building, which is now a New York City landmark and on the Department of the Interior's National Register of Historic Places. Fundraising is still underway for the building's restoration. Yuko Nii is a painter with an M.F.A. from Pratt. The Williamsburg Art and Historical Center is based on her "bridge" concept. Her goal was to start a "multifaceted, multicultural art center whose mission is to coalesce this diverse artistic community, and create a bridge between local, national and international artists." Nii was named a Brooklyn "Woman of the Year" in 1998 for her service to the community and a "Woman of Excellence, Vision and Courage" by Governor Pataki in 2001. The Williamsburg Art and Historical Center hosts art exhibitions, dance performances, theater, music, poetry readings, film screenings, and annual festivals.

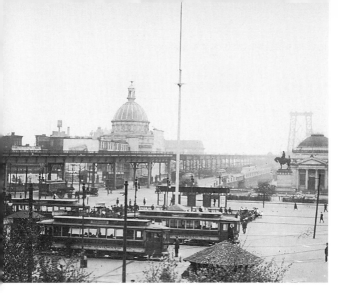

An amazing 1920s view looking west toward the Williamsburg Bridge, with its plaza streetcars and the Williamsburg Savings Bank in the foreground. Photo courtesy of the Brooklyn Historical Society.

➤ **Continue one block east on Broadway to Driggs Avenue and the Williamsburg Savings Bank at 175 Broadway.**

Architect George B. Post designed this bank in 1875. Post is better known for the New York Stock Exchange, but his credits also include City College and the Brooklyn Historical Society. The Williamsburg Savings Bank exemplifies "City Beautiful Classicism," with its use of limestone and marble and the classical-inspired dome. Go inside to admire the interior of the bank, designed by Peter B. Wright. The rotunda of the dome is 100 feet high and features glass panels etched with the letters "WSB." Six-pointed stars also adorn the dome. Note that there is no figurative imagery in the interior design. The building was restored in the 1990s, most noticeably the newly gilded dome, by Platt Byard Dovell and is now home to HSBC Bank.

Look across Driggs to the northeast corner of Broadway and Driggs, where there is another cast-iron beauty, the former Sparrow Shoe Factory Warehouse. Notice how this façade features fluted Corinthian pilasters. This building was designed by architect William B. Ditmars and built in 1882. It seems doubtful that this particular building launched Ditmars's career, but 20 years later he was designing churches on Central Park West. The building is now used as a warehouse. But notice along this stretch of Broadway the newly refurbished cast-iron factory buildings that have been turned into luxury condominiums. It is perhaps just a matter of time before this one is also turned into housing.

At 178 Broadway, across from the Williamsburg Savings Bank, is the world-renowned Peter Luger steakhouse. Peter Luger was started by German immigrants in 1876 as "Charles Luger's Café, Billiards, and Bowling Alley." By 1847, two-thirds of Williamsburg's population was German. The area was attractive to German immigrants because of the regular ferry service to Grand Street in Manhattan, which was the commercial center of Kleindeutschland.

Peter Luger himself was reputed to be an ornery steak tyrant. Until his death, the only thing on the menu was porterhouse steak. No chicken, no fish, no vegetables. Porterhouse. It is rumored that if a customer complained about the steak, Luger would come to the table, taste it himself, and then inform the customer that the steak was fine and that he didn't know what he was talking about. And yet scores of people put up with this odd behavior because the food was just that good. Luger died in 1947, and his children sold the restaurant to Sol Forman, himself a longtime patron of the restaurant.

Forman is a classic New York success story: born to Russian-immigrant parents in 1903 on the Lower East Side of Manhattan, as a teenager, he and his siblings started a metalware factory, which was located across the street from the restaurant. Forman had been bringing his clients and customers to the steakhouse for years. He took over in 1950, making very few changes to the winning Peter Luger formula. Forman died in 1999; his daughters are now running the restaurant. Peter Luger may have rolled over in his grave when the Formans added an air conditioner to the dining room, a shrimp cocktail to the menu, and a Peter Luger credit card for 80,000 valued customers, but his spirit still presides over the place. While they now take reservations, they don't take anyone else's credit cards, they won't cook your steak well-done even if you insist, and they don't treat Manhattanites in suits any better than the Brooklyn guys in work pants.

> **Walk one more block east on Broadway to Roebling and turn right.**

As you head down Roebling, it is hard not to notice the way the Brooklyn-Queens Expressway slices through what was once downtown Williamsburg. Bob Moses, the evil architect of modern New York, plowed this highway through the neighborhood in 1957. Other, wealthier Brooklyn neighborhoods, like Brooklyn Heights, were able to convince Moses and his minions to reroute the highway around their areas. But Williamsburg was not as lucky, and the BQE dealt a deathblow to an already struggling neighborhood. More than 2,200 units of low-income housing were destroyed. This was bad timing, since in the decades following World War II, the neighborhood was receiving floods of new immigrants, particularly from the Dominican Republic, Latin America, Poland, and other Eastern European nations. By the 1980s, manufacturing and other industrial concerns were fleeing the neighborhood. Housing stock was crowded and insufficient for the large immigrant families, on both the Latino and Hasidic sides of the neighborhood. Williamsburg continued to experience a population boom in the 1990s, both from the influx of white, middle-class hipsters and from the rapid population growth in the Hasidic Jewish community. The City of New York has responded by rezoning land and buildings that had previously been approved for manufacturing only, particularly south of Grand Avenue.

> ➤ **Continue down Roebling two blocks to South 9th Street and turn right. At 179 South 9th Street, between Roebling and Driggs, is the 1853 New England Congregational Church.**

This building exemplifies the changes Williamsburg has gone—and continues to go—through. Williamsburg was an elite enclave through most of the nineteenth century, and this Italianate-style church is evidence of this heritage. This building was one of the first Congregationalist churches to be built in Brooklyn. Thomas Kinnicut Beecher, the younger brother of Henry Ward Beecher, was its minister. The congregation—made up of wealthy Brooklynites of Anglo-Saxon stock—met in nearby lecture halls until they established a permanent home for their congregation. The lot was purchased for $38,000, and construction began in 1853. Thomas Little (who, a few years later, went on to work on the controversial Tweed Courthouse) was the architect. Henry Ward Beecher spoke at the cornerstone-laying ceremony. Next-door, at 177 South 9th Street, is the church rectory, which was built in 1868. The Congregational Church was destroyed by fire in 1893 and restored in 1894. In 1955, La Luz del Mundo Church moved into this historic building, which it restored in 2001. The building was designated a landmark on November 24, 1981, by the Landmarks Preservation Commission.

➤ **Continue west on South 9th Street for two blocks to Bedford Avenue and turn left, heading down to Clymer Street.**

As is evidenced by the presence of both La Luz del Mundo Church and the signs in Hebrew and Yiddish in front of apartment houses, both Satmar and Latino families populate this section of Williamsburg. Relations between the two groups have not always been amicable, but in recent years their respective community organizations have teamed up, most notably to defeat a garbage incinerator proposed for the waterfront.

As you continue down Bedford Avenue, the area becomes more uniformly Jewish. This area has been an Orthodox Jewish neighborhood since the early twentieth century, when legions of Russian and other Eastern European Jewish immigrants moved to the area from Manhattan's Lower East Side. The Satmar community in Williamsburg, however, dates only to 1946. The founder of the Satmar Hasidim, Grand Rabbi Joel Teitelbaum, escaped the Nazis and went first to Switzerland on December 5, 1946. Teitelbaum and some of his followers then left Europe for Williamsburg, which was already a heavily Orthodox community. After World War II ended, Polish and Hungarian Jewish survivors began migrating to the community and reestablishing their lives here. December 5 remains the most important secular date for Williamsburg's Satmar Hasidim; every year they celebrate the Grand Rabbi's escape from the Nazis. Currently, about 25,000 Satmar Hasidim live in Williamsburg. The community manages a network of yeshivas and social services. It is responsible for feeding and caring for the impoverished and elderly, as well as educating 8,500 students. They also run a matzo factory, a kosher meat market, and a loan company. The community also owns real estate estimated to be worth tens of millions of dollars, according to the *New York Times.*

At 500 Bedford Avenue at Clymer Street is the International Jewish Rescue Organization. This was Grand Rabbi Joel Teitelbaum's house. Teitelbaum died in 1979 without a son. According to Hasidic custom, the oldest son of the Grand Rabbi assumes leadership upon the father's death. The Satmar community's rabbis got together and selected Moses Teitelbaum, the only nephew, to assume leadership of the neighborhood. There is currently a family feud, though, that is threatening to permanently fracture the Satmar community. In 1999, Moses Teitelbaum appointed his third son, Zalmen, to take over Congregation Yetev Lev D'Satmar. This caused many in the neighborhood to assume that Zalmen, not Aaron, the oldest son, would become the Grand Rabbi upon Moses Teitelbaum's death. Aaron is the rabbi at the Satmar suburban enclave in Kiryas Joel, in Orange County, New York. Factions have formed supporting each brother. Perhaps most interesting, this dispute has had an impact on matchmaking. Parents in each faction refuse to allow their children to marry children from the other side.

As you continue down Bedford Avenue to the northeast corner of Taylor Street, notice the stunning nineteenth-century mansions, which once housed Williamsburg's aristocrats. At 505 Bedford Avenue there is a great example of the reuse of space in Williamsburg. Built in 1896 by the architectural firm Lauritzen & Voss, this was Frederick Mollenhauer's house. Frederick was the son of John Mollenhauer, who founded the Mollenhauer Sugar Refinery in 1867, originally located on Rush Street at Kent Avenue. This building is now the Yeshiva Yesoda Hatora of K'hal Adas Yereim.

➤ **Walk three more blocks south on Bedford Avenue.**

At 559 Bedford, on the northeast corner of Rodney Street, is an 1890 mansion. It is now home to Congregation Arugath Habosem. At 561 Bedford, on the southeast corner of Rodney, is the Hawley Mansion, which dates to around 1875 and was converted in 1891 by Lauritzen & Voss. This building now houses the Young Israel of Brooklyn congregation. Young Israel is an international Orthodox movement, founded on the Lower East Side of Manhattan in 1912. It was a reaction to the damage the Jewish community believed was being done by the growing popularity of the Reform movement (which allowed men and women to sit together during services, which were often conducted in English on Saturday mornings), socialism, and the "Americanization" of younger generations of Jews.

> Continue down Bedford Avenue, crossing over the BQE. Four blocks past the BQE you'll reach Heyward Street. Turn left to 119 Heyward Street, between Bedford and Lee avenues.

This is the former home of Public School 71K, which was built in 1888–89 by James W. Naughton. Naughton was born in Ireland, and his family moved to Brooklyn when he was eight. He was educated at both the University of Wisconsin, Madison, and Cooper Union. Naughton served as the superintendent of buildings for the City of Brooklyn from 1874 to 1876. He then became the superintendent of buildings for the Board of Education of the City of Brooklyn from 1879 until his death in 1898. During this period, Naughton designed all the school buildings built in Brooklyn (see our Bedford-Stuyvesant chapter for some examples). After the consolidation of Greater New York in 1898, New York City took over the administration and building of schools. This building was designated a New York City landmark by the Landmarks Preservation

Commission on February 3, 1981. It is now home to the Beth Jacob School, which is part of United Talmudical Academy Torah V'yirah.

➤ **Continue on Heyward Street two blocks to Marcy Avenue.**

The commercial district of the Hasidic community is on Lee Avenue above Heyward and on Rutledge Street between Lee and Marcy avenues. Notice the kosher bakeries, wig shops, and hat stores catering to the community. If it is Saturday, nothing will be open, as this is, after all, a traditional Jewish community in which the Sabbath is observed from Friday at sundown to Saturday at sundown.

➤ **Turn left on Marcy Avenue and walk five blocks to Keap Street. Turn right on Keap Street to No. 274.**

In Judaism, because one does not have to worship in a consecrated space (as one does in Catholicism, for instance), many congregations are older than the buildings they call home. In fact, many Jewish congregations in New York City started in basements, storefronts, or people's homes, until the congregation had the resources necessary to purchase or erect its own building. Such was the case with Temple Beth Elohim, the first Reform Jewish congregation in Brooklyn, dating to 1851. The building at No. 274 was erected in 1876. In the early twentieth century, American Jewry was becoming more secular as the Reform movement was gaining popularity. But in Williamsburg, things proceeded in the opposite direction: the Jewish population became more Orthodox. This was mostly because the German Jews began moving out of the neighborhood as more Orthodox Eastern European Jews began moving in, mostly after the opening of the Williamsburg Bridge.

In 1921, this building was sold to the Hasidic Bnos Yakov of Pupa Congregation.

➤ **Continue on Keap Street one block to Division Avenue. Turn left on Division to Rodney Street and the Brooklyn Public Library's Williamsburgh Branch.**

In 1901 Andrew Carnegie donated $5.2 million to the City of New York for the construction of library buildings. Of that grant, $1.6 million was designated for the construction of 20 libraries in Brooklyn. Williamsburg was selected for one of the earliest buildings because of the booming population in the district, and this branch was the second to be completed with Carnegie money. Construction began in 1903, and Mayor Seth Low spoke at the cornerstone-laying ceremony. Richard A. Walker, Beaux-Arts-trained architect, designed this branch, which was considered the most beautiful of any of the branches. It opened in 1905. This building was designated a New York City landmark on June 15, 1999, by the Landmarks Preservation Commission. The library now services the predominantly Spanish-speaking community living in the immediate area.

➤ **From here, there are two options: One is to turn right on Marcy, and in about two blocks you'll reach the Marcy Avenue stop on the J, M, and Z lines, which will take you back to Manhattan. The other is to walk east on Broadway to the corner of Union Avenue (about four blocks) to the Broadway stop on the G train, which you can take one stop to Metropolitan Avenue. At this point, you can either switch to the L train to head back to the city or get off and head to the "Little Italy of Brooklyn." If you choose the latter, exit the G train, and you will be at the corner of Union and Metropolitan.**

In 1855, census records reflect that there were no native Italians living in Brooklyn; there were just about 10,000 by 1890. But after the opening of the Williamsburg Bridge in 1903, many Italians found their way to the neighborhood. The large number of both manufacturing and waterfront jobs was an enticement. Many of these new residents hailed from the region around Naples and from southern Italy, bringing with them religious festivals and regional differences that persist to this day.

Looking north, you will notice the BQE. Where you stand was the heart of Italian Williamsburg until the BQE disrupted the community, destroying housing and businesses. On the other side of the overpass is where the Feast of Our Lady of Mount Carmel and Saint Paulinus has taken place every summer since 1903. (The church is at North 8th and Havemeyer.) This feast commemorates the release of St. Paulinus, the bishop of Nola, Italy, from captivity by the Vandals in the fifth century. It is said that Paulinus had volunteered to be a captive in place of a child who had been captured. He did this so that the child's mother, who was a widow, could have her only son back. Legend has it that an Ottoman sultan, who was impressed with Paulinus's courage and bravery, secured his release from prison.

Elements of the story of Paulinus have been re-created in this lively Brooklyn festival. For instance, dozens of local Italian men hoist a boat on their shoulders and carry it through the streets. In the boat is a statue of St. Paulinus and a local man dressed as the "Turk"; this procession is led by a brass band. Also central to this festival is the dancing of the giglio, which is a 3-ton, 85-foot tower that is carried through the street by 120 lifters. The giglio is said to symbolize the lilies that the people of Nola waved as Paulinus returned to town. Both the giglio and the boat were constructed by men in the neighborhood, and it is a great

Since 1903, the centerpiece of the Feast of Our Lady of Mount Carmel and Saint Paulinus is the dancing of the giglio, a 3-ton, 85-foot tower that is carried through the street by 120 men. The giglio, pictured here in 1956, symbolizes the lilies that the people of Nola, Italy, waved in the fifth century to welcome Paulinus back to his home after he willingly offered himself as a hostage in exchange for a kidnapped local girl. Photo courtesy of the Brooklyn Historical Society.

honor to be selected to participate in either of these traditions. This reflects the fact that despite the movement of "new people" into the neighborhood, Italian Williamsburg has been able to maintain its traditions, religious institutions, and community.

➤ Head east on Metropolitan Avenue about four blocks to Graham Avenue, also known as "Via Vespucci."

Along Graham Avenue, pictures of saints and local luminaries decorate the street signs; a beautiful grotto is dedicated to the Virgin Mary; and the fire hydrants are painted red, white, and green, like the Italian flag.

➤ Turn right on Graham Avenue and head south for two blocks to Ainslie Street; on the southwest corner is Cono and Sons O'Pescatore, and on the northwest corner is S. Cono Pizzeria.

Cono is not a universally common Italian name, but it is estimated that a couple of hundred men in Williamsburg bear this unusual name. These men are Teggianese Italians, named after St. Cono, who was born in Teggiano in southern Italy in the twelfth century. This first Cono was said to have been born to an elderly couple, who believed they would never have children. They named him Cono (which means "cone" in English) to represent the Holy Trinity, perfection. As the story goes, the parents merely wanted their son to marry and carry on the family name. But once they found him praying in a burning oven unscathed, they had to rethink their plans for this young man. Cono went on to become a Benedictine monk and perform numerous miracles before he died at 18. However, he was believed to continue to protect his followers after his death and is credited with protecting Teggiano from Allied bombing during World War II. The name Cono was brought to Brooklyn in the late nineteenth century by the thousands of Italians who were fleeing the poverty of southern Italy. To this day, young Brooklyn Italian men and women continue to honor this tradition by naming their sons Cono. The St. Cono American Society was founded in 1935, and the reestablished Society was founded in 1988. It is located at 23 Richardson Street, which was re-named San Cono Strada in 1989.

While you're here, the pizza at S. Cono Pizzeria is the best in the neighborhood. And the calamari at Cono and Sons O'Pescatore is amazing—as is the opportunity to ob-serve neighborhood families coming in for dinner, middle-aged men embracing each other in greeting, and longtime friends speaking to at each other in southern Italian dialect. After a satisfying, filling meal, you need dessert.

➤ So head out, turn west on Ainslie Street, and go one block to Manhattan Avenue. Turn right and head north one block to Devoe Street and Fortunato Brothers, at 289 Manhattan Avenue.

Fortunato Brothers is rumored to be a local Mafioso hang-out; whether or not this is the case, the cannoli and es-presso here are the best available in all five boroughs. Sit down, savor the aromas, the conversations, the atmos-phere.

➤ When you are finished, walk north on Manhattan Avenue to Metropolitan and turn right. Walk one block east to Graham Avenue and the L train.

5 GREENPOINT
American Warsaw

➤ Start: The Greenpoint Avenue G train stop at Greenpoint and Manhattan avenues.

GREENPOINT, on the edge of Queens and adjacent to Williamsburg, is an often overlooked jewel of Brooklyn. Famous for being Mae West's birthplace and the cradle of "Brooklynese," Greenpoint's true appeal is the combination of its long industrial history and flourishing Polish community.

Although originally named for the lush vegetation that covered this spit of land jutting out into the East River, Greenpoint has not been the garden spot of Brooklyn for many years. Instead, beginning in the 1830s, Greenpoint became the site of a wave of development that made it a hub of industrial activity. Its shores became home to shipyards, quickly followed by factories and heavy industry. In particular, Greenpoint became a flourishing home to the five black arts: printing, ceramics, oil refining, glassmaking, and ironworking.

Today, while you can still see the remains of some of the factories and plants that once dominated the local landscape, it is hard to imagine why Greenpoint attracted such development. If anything, Greenpoint seems remote. It is served by only a single subway line, one that has no direct link into Manhattan, and the neighborhood is essentially bypassed by the BQE. Two hundred years ago, at the dawn of the nineteenth century, the area was even more isolated. Most important, Greenpoint was separated from Manhattan by water. While the distance was not far, the cost of traveling across the river was enough to deter development. However, by the 1830s changes in steam power made waterborne transportation the cheapest and most effective means of moving goods and people. New York's waterways became virtual superhighways, and Greenpoint became far more attractive. Its empty shoreline and open space suddenly were only a five-minute ferry ride from Manhattan's swarming streets.

An unlikely pair was responsible for this early development of Greenpoint: Eliphalet Nott, the president of Union College, and Neziah Bliss, a successful steamship builder. Perhaps the friendship between these two was not as strange as it sounds. Nott was an inventor in his own right and a great advocate of improving the education of science. But what brought the men together was more than just a common interest in science; it was money. Bliss saw the vacant shoreline across the river from the crowded piers of Manhattan as the perfect place in which to expand his shipbuilding business, while Nott, who had access to college funds, saw that such a development might result in a lucrative financial return that could help his university and gain himself some recognition. In 1832 the two joined forces and purchased 30 acres along the East River. One year later they added to their holdings, and soon other developers followed. By 1850 two of the city's leading politicians, Mayor Ambrose Kingsland and future governor Samuel Tilden, were amassing property in the area. What followed was an impressive boom that filled the area with heavy industry. To some, Greenpoint became a foul-

smelling, smoke-belching eyesore, but to others Greenpoint's factories were part of a new American industrial
economy and an important source for jobs.

Greenpoint's growth coincided with rising immigration. In the 1830s, Irish immigrants made the neighborhood their home as they found work in the new shipyards
and iron foundries. By the 1870s and 1880s, the Irish had
moved up and out, but new Italian and Eastern European
immigrants took their place on the lowest rung of the economic ladder. Greenpoint became home to these immigrants, much like in Manhattan's Lower East Side. But
while Mulberry Street developed a particular appeal to
Italians, and Orchard Street became associated with Jews,
Greenpoint became a haven for Poles.

In fact, for the past hundred years, Greenpoint has
boasted the largest concentration of Poles outside Warsaw.
This is largely due to successive waves of Polish immigration that have made this neighborhood their home. In the
1880s and 1890s, poor Poles who had been pushed off their
land by industrialization came to New York and settled
in Greenpoint because of the factory jobs. There had, of
course, been earlier Poles in New York dating back to the
1600s; perhaps the most famous is Tadeusz Kosciuszko,
who designed West Point and was crucial to the American
Revolutionary victory at Saratoga (and whose name was
given to a bridge on the BQE not far from here). However, it was the Polish immigrants of the 1890s who began to settle in Greenpoint in the first sizable way. Forty
years later, during the 1930s, a new group of Poles came to
America, escaping the Nazis. Greenpoint appealed to some
because of its existing Polish community. After World War
II, the neighborhood gained more newcomers as Poles
fled communism. More recently, as Poland fought for and
gained independence from Russia, yet another wave of immigrants has helped rejuvenate this community. Perhaps

nothing demonstrates this continued growth more than the fact that some 7,200 new Polish immigrants, equivalent to 19 percent of the existing Greenpoint population, settled here between 1991 and 1994.

Today, even as Asians and Hispanics have moved into the area, walking down Manhattan Avenue is like walking down a street in Warsaw. Fueled by this constant flow of new Polish immigration, the neighborhood has become home to bakeries, butchers, bookstores, and a whole range of other stores that cater to this community. In some ways it is much like Chinatown or Flushing, but the foreign language on the signs is not Chinese or Korean; it's Polish.

Manhattan Avenue, as you can probably tell, is the spine of Greenpoint. As you look to the south, you can see a thriving commercial street, lined with all sorts of business catering to the Polish community. As in many immigrant neighborhoods, the Poles who moved into Greenpoint helped create their own financial lending institutions to get these businesses established, rather than relying on national banks. The largest of these is the Polish and Slavic Credit Union, which is just a few doors west on Greenpoint Avenue. It has branches all over Brooklyn and has assets that rank it among the largest 100 credit unions out of the more than 14,000 in the nation. In addition to providing loans, it funds a variety of performing arts series for this neighborhood.

We are going to walk down several blocks of Manhattan Avenue later, but first let's head north and go down some of the side streets.

➢ **Walk north along Manhattan Avenue one block to Kent Street.**

As you head up Manhattan Avenue, you might notice that the Burger King building looks rather strange. It was originally built as the Chopin Theater, well before fast food took hold of the American diet.

More important to the neighborhood are the Polish and Slavic Cultural Center, located just east of Manhattan on Kent, and the Pol-Am Ksiegarnia (bookstore), on Manhattan and Java. Both seek to maintain a link back to Poland. The bookstore is a fascinating place to explore the world of recent Polish émigrés. Opened in 1985 by Darius and Krystna Kruk, it caters to young Poles who want to Americanize but not lose a connection to their homeland.

> **Turn left (west) on Kent Street and walk one block to Franklin Street.**

As you turn west on Kent, the Polish signs fade away, and instead you find yourself on a street taken right out of the nineteenth century. Its tree-lined sidewalks and graceful homes should suggest to you that this was a street for Greenpoint's middle class. Many of the buildings date to the 1840s, when industrial plants were opening along the shoreline, and this street was where many of the heads of those factories, or at least the foremen, lived. For example, John Englis, owner of the Continental Iron Works, lived at No. 108, while Henry Steers, who built the largest wooden ship ever constructed, lived at No. 128.

A short way down on your left, at No. 130, is a house with pillars that was built by Neziah Bliss, one of the founders of modern Greenpoint. Bliss, a friend of Robert Fulton, was a successful steamship builder in Philadelphia and Cincinnati in the early years of the nineteenth century. In 1827 he moved to New York to compete in the rapidly developing city and began building new steam engines at his Novelty Iron Works at the foot of East 12th Street in Manhattan. He soon sought more room and began eyeing

Greenpoint's shoreline, acquiring his first property there with Eliphalet Nott when they bought 30 acres from John Meserole. Bliss quickly embraced his role not only as shipbuilder but also as real-estate developer, marrying into the Meserole family, which owned much of the area, and later acquiring property north of Newtown Creek to create Blissville. By 1834, Bliss paid for the surveying of Greenpoint and the laying out of streets, establishing the shape of the area that remains today.

There are also two churches on this block that further suggest its middle-class character. The first is the St. Elias Greek Rite Catholic Church, which was originally built in 1870 as the Reformed Dutch Church of Greenpoint. (The Dutch church moved in 1943 to Milton Street.) The second is the Church of the Ascension, which was organized in 1845 and built in 1865, making it Greenpoint's oldest church. In the nineteenth century, both churches served the older, more established Americans in the area, with Dutch and English ancestry, as distinct from the new Irish, German, or Polish immigrants who were just arriving on American shores. They were the churches of factory managers and were thus built in this middle-class section of Greenpoint.

➤ **Turn right on Franklin Street and walk one block to Java Street.**

On Franklin Street, you are close to the piers which were once the industrial heart of the neighborhood. The waterfront, which is obscured because of the buildings but stands just to your west, was once busy with international trade. Raw materials were unloaded onto these shores to feed the factories that then produced finished goods to ship out. Access to the water, cheap land, and the close proximity to New York all helped Greenpoint thrive. But it was

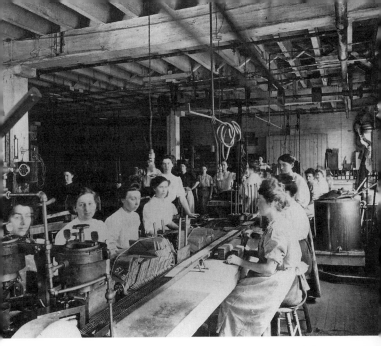

About 1920, inside the Eberhard Faber Pencil Factory, a Williamsburg mainstay from 1872 until 1956, and one of many businesses to leave Brooklyn in the twentieth century. Like many other famous Brooklynites, Faber is buried in Green-Wood Cemetery. Photo courtesy of the Brooklyn Historical Society.

heavy industry that made its home here. From 1840 until 1880, almost half of Greenpoint's population worked in shipbuilding. In addition, by 1883 almost all of the 20 glass factories in Brooklyn were located here, as were a majority of its brass and iron foundries and several large oil refineries and porcelain factories. Today, the flow of international trade has long faded from these shores, but street names like Java and India remain to remind us of what this area was once like.

Another, less exotic industry that made its home in Greenpoint is visible across the street: the Eberhard Pencil Factory, with the notable symbol of a yellow star within a diamond along its roofline and the pencil-based design on its façade. The company was started by Eberhard Faber, the great-grandson of Casper Faber, who opened the first commercial pencil factory in Germany in 1765 after developing a process for binding graphite powder and encasing it in wood. Eberhard Faber emigrated to America in 1848 to establish an import business for his family's pencils. In 1861 he opened America's first pencil factory on the East River, near where the United Nations now stands, but moved to Greenpoint when his Manhattan building burned in a fire in 1872. The company remained a mainstay of Greenpoint, eventually occupying the entire space from Greenpoint Avenue to Kent Street and from Franklin Street to West Street, until 1956, when it moved to Wilkes-Barre, Pennsylvania. The building had various uses after that and was converted into artists' studios in the late 1990s. Now, other than looking at the outside of the old factory, the closest thing to a pencil plant in Greenpoint is the Pencil Factory bar across the street.

➤ **Stop at the corner of Franklin and Java streets.**

Standing on the right side of the street is the dramatic Astral Apartments, covering the block between Java and India. Built in 1886 using a Romanesque Revival architecture that exudes strength, this building was commissioned by Charles Pratt, one of Greenpoint's most famous industrialists and the man responsible for Brooklyn's Pratt Institute. Pratt, a self-made man, established the Astral Oil Company in the 1860s along the waterfront in Greenpoint. His company produced kerosene, a replacement for whale oil, as a source for light. By 1870 his Greenpoint refinery processed 1,500 barrels of oil per day, converting it into 1,100 barrels of kerosene, which was shipped all over the world. Astral's advertisements claimed, "The holy lamps in Tibet are primed with Astral Oil." Even after Pratt merged his company with John D. Rockefeller's Standard Oil in 1874, the Greenpoint refinery continued to thrive. Unlike his partner, however, Pratt became concerned with his responsibility to his workers. He built this apart-

A 1900 advertisement for Charles Pratt's Brooklyn-based Astral Oil Company, which eventually became part of Rockefeller's Standard Oil, devolving into today's Exxon-Mobil. Image courtesy of the Brooklyn Historical Society.

ment building as laborers' housing, seeking to improve on the cheap, dark tenements they might otherwise live in. One year later, he opened the Pratt Institute in Bedford-Stuyvesant as a trade school. (See our Fort Greene and Clinton Hill chapter for more on Pratt.)

If we continued walking north, we would find an increasingly Latino portion of Greenpoint. First, however, we are going to turn back to the south and explore the heart of the Polish community.

➤ Turn around and walk back along Franklin Street two blocks to Greenpoint Avenue.

The two roads that cross here were initially built by the early developers of Greenpoint as a way to attract people and commerce to the area. Franklin Street, named for Benjamin Franklin, is the older road and was opened in 1839 as the Ravenswood, Green Point, and Hallett's Cove turnpike, providing the first complete roadway from Williamsburg to Astoria. This road, Bliss believed, would add a secondary channel of transit to Greenpoint, in addition to the ferry service from Manhattan, and increase demand for his land holdings. Greenpoint Avenue was laid out more than 10 years later, in 1852, and was an opportunistic response to the creation of Calvary Cemetery by Manhattan's St. Patrick's Cathedral in 1848. With the construction of Greenpoint Avenue, ferries would unload their passengers here for visits to the cemetery and thus fuel the local economy.

Greenpoint Avenue, however, was not the original name of this important street. You may have noticed as you walked south from India Street that all the streets, except this one, are in alphabetical order (Hudson, India, Java, Kent, Greenpoint, Milton, Noble, Oak). In fact, Greenpoint Avenue did initially fit within this scheme, as it was called "L" and, later, Lincoln Street. As time passed, however, the name was changed to reflect its centrality to this neighborhood.

Regardless of the name of the street, the sizable Neoclassical building standing on the corner is a sign of the intersection's significance. Opened around 1895 as the Mechanic and Traders Bank, this building attests to the commercial activity in the area. Today, while the commerce has faded, the building remains an important part of the neighborhood, as it houses offices for *Nowy Dziennik* (New Day), a daily Polish-language newspaper that caters to the local community.

➤ **Continue along Franklin for one more block, turn left on Milton Street, and then walk one block to Manhattan Avenue.**

Named for Daniel Milton, who made sailing-ship materials and served the shipyards that moved here in the 1840s and 1850s, this street is lined with houses built in the middle of the nineteenth century. One of the more elaborate ones is the Queen Anne brownstone at 122–124 Milton Street, which was built in 1889 and incorporates a range of materials and styles.

More noteworthy is No. 136, which now serves as home to the Greenpoint [Dutch] Reformed Church that had been on Kent Street from 1848 until 1891 but was originally built as the Thomas Smith residence. Although small compared to later homes, this was a grand house for one of the most successful industrial captains of Brooklyn. Smith's field was porcelain, an industry that America was not known for in the early nineteenth century. However, Smith traveled to France in 1866 and returned with new ideas. He purchased property here in Greenpoint and opened the first successful hard-porcelain factory in America. For decades, Greenpoint was home to Union Porcelain Works, the premier china company in the country, which supplied some of the country's wealthiest families and even the White House.

Further up the street is St. John's Lutheran Church, a remnant of the German population that used to live here in large numbers. Note the German Gothic Revival style and the original name, Evangelish-Lutherische St. Johannes Kirche, on the steeple. If you can get inside, there is beautiful Bavarian woodwork adorning some of the walls, but the church is often closed since the Lutheran population has dwindled.

Continuing along Milton Street, you come to the most visible church in Greenpoint, the Roman Catholic Church of St. Anthony of Padua/St. Alphonsus, which was built in 1874 and includes a spire that rises some 240 feet above the pavement. The split name is because this congregation represents a merger of two churches. St. Alphonsus, which was originally in its own building, initially served a German-speaking population but saw its membership shrink by the 1970s to the point that its independent existence was threatened. Meanwhile, the Church of St. Anthony of Padua, which had been founded in 1856, originally served an Irish community that also saw its numbers decline. The resulting merger, which now also serves the Polish and Latino communities, is a thriving church that marks the symbolic town center of Greenpoint.

➤ **Turn right on Manhattan and then right on Noble after one block.**

Another church, around the corner on Noble Street—named for James Noble, who was a trustee of the Village of Williamsburgh in 1842—emphasizes why Brooklyn was known as the City of Churches. In the space of four blocks, we have already passed six churches. This one, the Union Baptist Church, was originally incorporated in 1847 and moved into this building in 1863. It, like the Anglican Church of the Ascension, served the early residents of Greenpoint. By the 1870s, however, the Baptist community was being replaced by Catholic and Lutheran immigrants, as the neighborhood underwent a transition. Today, the church is empty, but it is known for at least one famous parishioner. From 1874 to 1884, the pastor of this church was Rev. David Hughes, whose son was Charles Evans Hughes, governor of New York, presidential candidate, and chief justice of the Supreme Court.

Overall, the large number of religious institutions in this neighborhood reflects not only the faith of Brooklynites but also the multiple waves of immigrants that flooded into the area, each of which established its own houses of worship. To some degree, these buildings stand as a testament to the success of Neziah Bliss and Eliphalet Nott in establishing Greenpoint as an attractive working and residential community.

The most recent group to embrace Greenpoint, as you already know, are the Poles, and next-door, at No. 155, stands a building that caters to this community. The Polish National Alliance has been called by some the glue that holds this community together. It provides social services and information for older Polish Americans and younger immigrants.

➤ **Walk one block on Noble, turn left on Lorimer, and then walk one block to Calyer.**

As you look left on Calyer, you can see one of the more well-known institutions from this neighborhood, the Green Point Savings Bank, established in 1869 by leading Greenpoint businessmen. The bank is itself a sign of the commercial success of this community and shows the need for credit in this industrial center of the nineteenth century. This site, however, is not the bank's original building, which stood on Franklin Street. This building was erected in 1908, when the bank could claim more than $5 million in deposits. Take a stroll inside to see a gorgeous marble interior. Ironically, while the bank continues to thrive and retains its Greenpoint name, its headquarters is now in Manhattan.

Of course, well before the savings bank drew attention to Greenpoint, the neighborhood was known for the Continental Iron Works, which stood down the other direction

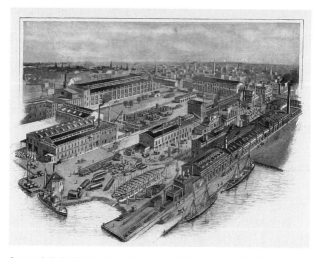

Greenpoint's Continental Iron Works, about 1865, where the Civil War ironclad **Monitor** was built. Image courtesy of the Brooklyn Historical Society.

on Calyer Street, because it was there that the ironclad *Monitor* was built to fight during the Civil War.

THE IRONCLAD *MONITOR*

The "Yankee Cheesebox," as it was called by some detractors, was designed by Swedish engineer John Ericsson, built in Thomas F. Rowland's Continental Iron Works, and included a moving turret assembled by Neziah Bliss's Novelty Iron Works. It was launched on January 30, 1862, and gained fame for its clash with the **Merrimac** at Hampton Roads, Virginia, on March 9, 1862. Even though the battle was a draw and the **Monitor** sank later that year off Cape Hatteras, killing its crew of 16, it served as the prototype for a whole new style of metal-hulled ships, which we continue to rely on today. In addition to its revolutionary iron hull, the **Monitor** was the first ship in the world to include a revolving gun turret, and it included inventions covered by some 280 separate patents. The success of the **Monitor** also served to justify the development of Greenpoint, which had only emerged as a shipbuilding center 30 years before. While the Brooklyn Navy Yard would take over as the dominant home for shipbuilding on the East Coast, Greenpoint's residents were quick to point out that it had laid the foundation for such development.

➤ **Walk one block further on Lorimer to Meserole and turn left. Walk one block and turn right on Manhattan Avenue.**

After passing one of the local elementary schools and the police station, we have now reemerged on the main shopping street. As you walk down the street, look in some of the stores and note how they cater to the Polish community.

For example, step inside Zakopane at No. 714 to see classic Polish folk art, from cut glass to wood carvings. If you are in the mood for something sweet, walk into Stodycze Wedel at No. 772, the Polish equivalent of Hershey's. You might not recognize the names of the chocolates, but the flavor is the same in any language. And for a look at a store that really shows the recycling of space, step inside the Genovese Drug Store at 722 Manhattan Avenue. The exterior hints at the origins of the building, but inside walk down the sloping foyer into the heart of the store. Long before this was a drug store, the building was originally erected as a theater and then later converted to a roller rink. Note what is left of the early decorations: the disco ball that's still hanging from the ceiling and the circular ramps that now make this one of the more wheelchair-friendly buildings in Greenpoint.

➤ **Turn left on Norman and right on Leonard, and then walk to Nassau.**

Norman is one of several streets in the area that harks back to the early settlers of this land. It is named for Dirk Volckersten, known as Dirk "The Norman," a ship's carpenter who settled in New Amsterdam in the 1640s and moved to Greenpoint as its first European resident in 1645. Eight years later, Dirk sold some of his property to Jacobus Hey, who passed it down to his son-in-law Pieter Praa. Praa, in turn, became the largest landholder in the area, acquiring over the course of his lifetime all of Greenpoint, most of Hunter's Point, and 40,000 acres in New Jersey. Although Praa didn't make it onto a street name, one of his four daughters married John Meserole and a granddaughter married Jacobus Calyer, which explains those street names.

As you pass the newsstand at 91 Norman, take a look at the variety of Polish magazines and newspapers offered for sale. You might also see Spanish and Arabic papers alongside the English and Polish ones, a hint at the diversity that still exists in Greenpoint.

A stroll down Leonard Street takes you off the main shopping street but gives you a sense of this neighborhood. You might notice, for example, the well-maintained houses, many of which have new siding. This is a neighborhood where residents are investing in their property and where they consider settling for the long-term. More noticeable is Grace's Day Spa, which opened a few years ago down the street, reflecting the flow of wealthier families into the area. Some people believe Greenpoint is on much the same track as Williamsburg but a decade or so behind. Its comparatively low rents, they emphasize, are attracting new residents who will fuel an economic rise. Also noteworthy is the Greenpoint Islamic Center, which shows some of the diversity that exists in this largely Polish community. Founded in the 1970s, the Center moved here in 1997 and draws from Indians, Pakistanis, and African Americans who have made this neighborhood their home.

➤ **Turn left on Nassau and walk to McGuinness Boulevard.**

Standing on the corner of Leonard and Nassau is the Murawski Apteka, an old family pharmacy that still thrives here, where chains like CVS and Duane Reade have not yet emerged. Like many other local businesses, this pharmacy caters to the Polish community. Inside, for example, you can find traditional Polish home remedies made from various herbs. Some similar items are also available across the street at Ziolko, at 93½ Nassau, although the focus is on Polish cosmetics rather than herbal remedies. But a look inside the Murawski Apteka shows that it is much more than just a pharmacy. For one thing, inside stands a Western Union office, which provides a way for residents to wire money to relatives back home. There is also a bulletin board loaded with private notices about services or items for sale in the community. The pharmacy has become much like the barber shop of small towns across America, the place to learn about what is going on in the community and to get the latest gossip.

MEAT MARKETS AND BANQUET HALLS

As you stroll along Nassau, you will pass several meat markets. Poles are not shy about their carnivorous diets, as a lunch or dinner at any of the local restaurants will prove, and the community supports butchers like few other neighborhoods in New York. These meat markets can be seen in much the same light as the fish markets of Chinatown, where demand for fresh seafood has resulted in a blossoming of competitive establishments. Here, however, the demand is not for fish but for meat. Step inside to see the huge array of beef, pork, and lamb, not to mention the elaborate selection of sausages. You may be familiar with kielbasa, a finely ground pork sausage that has made it to most supermarkets. Less well known are the long kabanosy, which are like Slim Jims; mysliwska, which resemble hot dogs; jalowcowa, one of the few sausages that doesn't include garlic; and kiszka, which is made from a combination of blood, buckwheat, pork skins, and liver. In addition to these products, many of these meat markets offer a variety of Polish foodstuffs, including dried soups, fruit syrups, and traditional condiments.

Another noteworthy aspect of the food in Greenpoint is the establishment of several large banquet palaces. You may have noticed some of these while walking, including the Polonaise Terrace at 150 Greenpoint, the Imperial Palace on Manhattan Avenue, and the Princess Manor at 88–92 Nassau Avenue. These large restaurants, complete with dance floors, cater to the European-style gatherings that continue to be regular occurrences here in this family-based community.

As you continue walking, you'll pass Eckford Street, now solidly Polish but originally named for Eckford Webb, one of the first shipbuilding firms to follow Neziah Bliss and move its yard to Greenpoint.

➤ Turn right on McGuinness Boulevard and walk to Driggs Avenue.

This major thoroughfare feeds into the Pulaski Bridge to Queens. Originally called Oakdale Street, the name was changed in the 1960s to honor Peter McGuinness, longtime Democratic party boss of Greenpoint. Notice the square at Driggs Avenue named for Father Studzinski, a priest for 22 years at the largest local Polish church. As in many immigrant communities, many of the religious leaders in Greenpoint were immigrants themselves. Father Studzinski grew up in Silesia and was ordained in Poland before coming to the United States in 1912 at the age of 25. You

The 1896 St. Stanislaus Church now has the largest Polish Catholic congregation in Brooklyn and has been visited by Pope John Paul II and Lech Walesa. Photo courtesy of Ed James and the Brooklyn Historical Society.

might note that the plaque honoring Father Studzinski was erected by Mayor Koch, an effort to appeal to the Polish community's voting block.

➤ **Turn left on Driggs and walk to Humboldt Street.**

Down Driggs to your left is the Church of St. Stanislaus Kostka, the spiritual heart of the neighborhood. Although a few blocks to the east, it is worth a detour. "St. Stans," as it is often called, was established in 1896 and now has the largest Polish Catholic congregation in Brooklyn. Several thousand congregants gather here each Sunday to attend one of 10 masses, including several in Polish. The church has been visited by Polish dignitaries and leaders, including Pope John Paul II and Lech Walesa, whose names now mark the surrounding intersection. Interestingly, the name of Humboldt Street, in honor of the German naturalist, is a link back to an earlier wave of immigrants that made this neighborhood their home before the Polish community emerged here.

➤ **Turn around and head back along Driggs past McGuinness Boulevard to Leonard.**

As you can tell, Greenpoint still includes some industrial sections. Driggs Avenue is notably different from the commercial shopping street of Manhattan Avenue. However, even here, signs of the Polish community abound. There is, for example, the Polish American Legion building at 519 Leonard Street. Or notice the Jehovah's Witnesses building on Driggs between Eckford and Leonard, which has its sign in Spanish and Polish. More noteworthy is the Polish National Home at 261 Driggs. A look at the sign tells you it was founded in 1914, emphasizing how long Greenpoint has had an established Polish community. The recent newcomers are just the latest of several waves of Polish immigration. The date of 1914 is also an interesting one to consider. Why was this organization established then? The answer has to do with the emergence in Greenpoint of a new generation without firsthand knowledge of Poland. By 1914, the first Poles who had come to the area in the 1890s were watching their children grow up without any memory of the mother country. They established this and other organizations to create a link to Poland for their children and for their children's children. It was a way to ensure the continuation of their culture, and it still serves that purpose today. As the sign says, the Polish National Home "stands as a tribute to our grandparent's dreams, the goals of our parents, and the needs of future generations."

➤ **Continue on Driggs to Lorimer and McCarren Park.**

Beyond the small corner park to your left is a decrepit, seemingly rubble-strewn lot that represents all that is left of one of the great WPA building projects in Brooklyn. Behind the fence and overgrown plants are the remnants of the largest public pool built in the borough. The complex, which included changing pavilions and an elaborate entranceway, was one of 11 pools built by the city under the direction of Robert Moses. Later called by architect Robert Stern "a minor masterpiece," the pool opened in 1936 and was able to hold 6,800 bathers. More than 75,000 people attended the opening celebration, and the pool remained a vibrant part of Greenpoint into the 1970s. As the city's finances worsened, however, upkeep was postponed. In 1983, after funds for much-needed repairs went unallocated, the pool was forced to close and has never reopened. In 2001, the city finally agreed on a plan to renovate the facility, but in the wake of the sudden fiscal crisis, the $30 million price tag means it will probably remain closed for some time yet.

➤ **Step across Lorimer into McCarren Park.**

McCarren Park, encompassing more than 35 acres, is named for a native son, Patrick McCarren, who made good. Born to an Irish-immigrant family in Massachusetts, Pat McCarren moved to Williamsburg, where he attended school and learned the cooper's trade. His success, however, came not in commerce but in politics, winning election as a Democrat to the state assembly in 1881 and the state senate in 1889. When he died in 1909, the board of aldermen named this park in his memory.

More recently, in 1996, the park gained fame, or infamy, as the place where the first Asian longhorned beetle was discovered in America, sparking a frantic effort to stop any further infestation. With no known predators in the United States, the beetle is a serious threat to hardwood trees and has the potential to cause more damage than Dutch elm disease, chestnut blight, and gypsy moths combined. USDA officials believe the beetle entered America inside packing material from China. As to why Greenpoint became an early home, one can only assume the beetles found it as appealing as other immigrants have.

Other, more welcome immigrants have left their mark on the surrounding buildings. On the far side of the park, for example, is the onion-domed Russian Orthodox Cathedral of the Transfiguration. With a design based on the Tsar's Winter Palace in St. Petersburg, the church was built in 1921 and suggests the number of Eastern European immigrants flowing into Greenpoint in the late nineteenth and early twentieth centuries. Its elaborate ornamentation makes it one of the more visible landmarks in the area. If you can get inside, the beautiful interior includes a hand-carved wooden screen on which icons were painted by monks in the Orthodox Monastery of the Caves of Kiev.

➤ **Turn right on Lorimer and walk to Bedford Avenue.**

If St. Stans is the spiritual heart for the Polish community of Greenpoint, the small, fenced-in garden ahead of you is the emotional heart. Walk through the gate and look to your right at Father Jerzy Popieluszko, one of Poland's most recent martyrs. A priest in Poland in the 1970s and 1980s who was an outspoken critic of Communism, Father

Popieluszko continued to speak out even after martial law was imposed in 1981. Although his calls were finally answered with the rise of Solidarity and eventual Polish independence, he did not live to see that success. In 1984, he was arrested by Poland's Communist secret police. Eleven days later his body was found; he had been beaten to death. Local residents here raised money for a statue that was erected in 1990. After vandalism damaged that monument, this statue was rededicated in 1992 in front of a crowd of more than 11,000 people. A decade later, residents continue to light candles and put flowers at the base of the statue.

➤ **Turn right on Bedford to the intersection with Nassau. Walk one block further east on Nassau to Manhattan Avenue to catch the G train at the Nassau Avenue stop.**

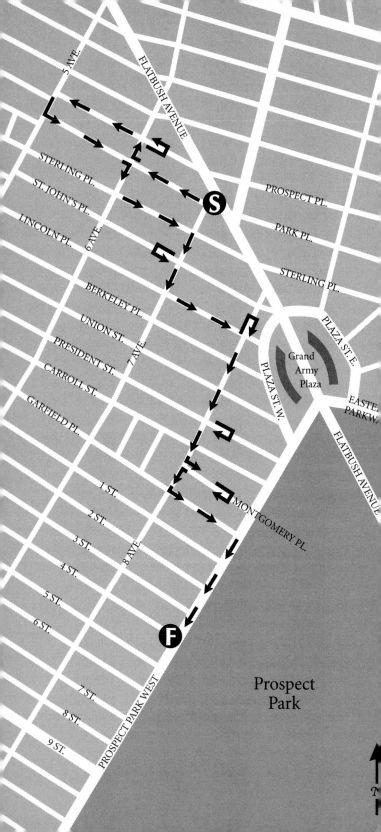

6 PARK SLOPE
"A Land of Terra Cotta and Red Brick"

➤ Start: The corner of 7th Avenue and Flatbush Avenue. To get there, take the B or Q train to the 7th Avenue stop.

IF WE ACCEPT Brooklyn's nineteenth-century moniker, the "City of Homes and Churches," then a case can easily be made that Park Slope was and is the quintessential Brooklyn neighborhood. Rows of brownstones glide down the slope, to be interrupted at points only by Victorian Gothic, Neoclassical, and Romanesque Revival houses of prayer. Even the commercial arteries of 7th and 5th avenues are studded with religious buildings; nineteenth-century structures grace 7th Avenue in the Upper Slope, while more modest storefront churches line 5th Avenue toward the bottom of the slope.

But perhaps more important than the religious buildings are the homes. After all, it was the prospect of owning one's home that lured nineteenth-century middle-class Manhattanites over the Brooklyn Bridge and into the developing area of Park Slope. The 1893 *Guide to Brooklyn and Long Island* is revealing, as it describes Park Slope as "a land of terra cotta and red brick, of gable roofs and dormer windows. It is a charming place of charming homes, of quaint designs, little invaded by flats and apartments." Thus, just as important as the architectural features was the fact that nineteenth-century Park Slope offered the middle class the opportunity to own their own homes; they would not have to settle for the as yet unfashionable "flats and apartments" that were increasingly becoming the lot of their counterparts who remained in Manhattan. Though today many of Park Slope's original single-family homes have been divided into multifamily homes and apartment buildings, over the twentieth century the middle class has become accustomed to apartment home living and has gradually found its way back to Park Slope.

Park Slope is named for its proximity to Frederick Law Olmsted and Calvert Vaux's Prospect Park, as well as for its more basic geography. From the park, the land slopes down to the Gowanus Canal. From the seventeenth century until well into the nineteenth, several families of Dutch and Huguenot descent owned the farmland that would form Park Slope. In the 1850s, a lawyer and railroad investor named Edwin Clark Litchfield saw the potential of the area as a smart residential district and promptly purchased significant tracts of the land and began laying out the streets. The opening of the park in 1873 spurred development in the northern section of the Slope, but this drew not the multitude of Manhattanites that Litchfield dreamed of but, rather, downtown Brooklynites, crowded out of their own bustling residential areas.

The 1883 opening of the Brooklyn Bridge a mile and a half away served as the direct catalyst for the major wave of development in Park Slope. With the opening of the bridge and its cable railway, commuters could forgo the long ferry lines and traverse the East River in short time, which allowed them more time to travel farther into Brooklyn. The wave of development that ensued lasted for several decades, until the extension of the subway by World War I funneled most development into the yet untouched neighborhoods south of Park Slope.

This tour will take us up and down the slope and back and forth in time from the 1860s to the present, tracing the waves of people who came to Park Slope, whether from Brooklyn or Manhattan, Germany or Ireland, Italy or Eastern Europe, and, more recently, Puerto Rico and the Caribbean. We will visit the brownstones and mansions they have lived in and the churches and synagogues they have prayed in. By tracing the various styles of architecture, we are able to appreciate what lends to Park Slope the strong aura of the past that made it, in 1973, the largest landmark district in Brooklyn. But this tour will also venture off the beaten track of the landmark district in order to capture the diversity and spirit that goes hand in hand with the architectural beauty to make Park Slope a premier residential district into the twenty-first century.

➤ **Turn the corner so that you are on 7th Avenue and look to the west at the row of five red-brick townhouses, Nos. 8-16 7th Avenue.**

When this row of Italianate homes was built in 1860, they were the first townhouses to sprout in the territory that would become known as Park Slope. Lone mansions such as Edwin Litchfield's Tuscan villa, within what is now Prospect Park near Prospect Park West, and Charles Higgins's house, at about present-day 9th Street, appeared on the farmland of the area as early as the 1850s, but this row inaugurates the spread of row houses that would lend to Park Slope its trademark characteristic. The style of these homes—brick Italianate with double doors—was similar to many of the homes built in this time in Carroll Gardens and Fort Greene. And like those who settled in Carroll

Gardens and Fort Greene, the people who bought these homes came from the downtown Brooklyn area.

These Brooklynites were able to take advantage of the lines of transportation—horse-drawn carriages—available on Flatbush Avenue, which could bring them to their jobs every morning. Thus, these merchants, lawyers, and editors were pushed out of downtown Brooklyn's increasing crowdedness and lured to the quiet of Park Slope. They were also lured by real-estate ads that promised such luxuries as full bathrooms with tubs and basins, coal- or wood-burning stoves that gave heat, and running water. This brief wave of development was abruptly curtailed with the depression of 1873. Though to the south of this row is another row of houses (you can see the change by noting the shift in the height of the rooflines between numbers 16 and 18), the second row was not built until 1879. This pause in construction due to the unfavorable economic condition also changed the overall character of 7th Avenue. When the first houses were built in the 1860s, 7th Avenue was viewed as a residential sector. However, by the early 1880s, the noteworthy residences were built farther up the slope and to the south, and commercial construction appeared on 7th Avenue.

➤ **Walk across 7th Avenue and amble down the south side of Park Place; we will be making several stops on this block.**

Originally called Baltic Street, Park Place was given its new name in 1873 in honor of the opening of Prospect Park. An early-twentieth-century photo of Park Place that shows the street is now virtually in keeping with its original appearance; the only difference is the small steps on the curbs that nineteenth-century residents used to gracefully exit and enter their carriages.

The age of the brownstones on this street spans from 1868, at the southeast corner of the street, to 1881, at its northwestern end. Most of the row houses in Park Slope were built through speculative development, whereby a builder would buy several lots at a time and construct a row of houses on short-term financing. When the houses were almost completed, prospective buyers could specify finishing details to their liking. Not only does this style allow for striking uniformity, the "mass production" also kept prices down, making the homes affordable to the middle class. An interesting note: in redecorating, many current residents have uncovered bricked-over entryways along the side walls of their first-floor common area. These were the entrances that builders kept in order to easily walk through the row of homes during construction.

Good examples of Italianate homes are Nos. 132–142. These six homes were built in 1868 by real-estate developer Daniel Wells and builder William V. Williamson, who had built on Flatbush Avenue. As you can see, by the late 1860s, the Italianate style seen previously on 7th Avenue now has the brick surface covered with layers of brownstone. Another feature of the Italianate design evident here is the three-story, flush-fronted brownstone over high basements. Note the molding surrounding the arched doorways.

A bit further on are examples of Neo-Grec architecture, at Nos. 112–116. The Italianate style seen previously was increasingly replaced in the late 1870s by the Neo-Grec style. Though still in brownstone, the Neo-Grec style found favor with speculative builders because its architectural details—stylized incised ornaments—were much more easily and cheaply reproduced than the rich foliate forms of the Italianate design. The ornamentation characteristic of the Italianate design was rounded and sculpted, while the Neo-Grec's design was squared off and incised. Furthermore, while the Italianate had a flat, or flush, front, the Neo-Grec incorporated angular bay windows. Here, the bays are two-sided; in later years, when builders focused on the Upper Slope, they introduced three-sided bays. What is notable to the ordinary observer is the way the bay windows achieve a stunning effect on the roofline. The Neo-Grec style was pioneered in France at the École des Beaux-Arts in the 1840s and popularized in America in the 1870s. As the Landmarks Commission notes, the style became so popular that it was used to greater effect in New York than in Paris. This row of four houses was designed by John Magilligan, who eight years earlier had built the Italianate houses to the west of this row. Among these four is one built by Magilligan as a gift to his wife, Mary.

Look at Nos. 100–110. Trick question: Is this row of Neo-Grec homes, designed by the architectural firm of Parfitt Brothers and constructed out of Nova Scotia stone, a "brownstone"? Yes and no. Though the homes are a whitish-gray as opposed to brown, many would describe them as brownstones. Upon their introduction to Manhattan in the 1840s, the close-grained sandstone known as brownstone became so popular that the term "brownstone" in popular parlance began to encompass any row house or townhouse, regardless of color or material.

The original nineteenth-century occupants of No. 90 would probably be surprised to discover that the twentieth century would see real-estate agents and their clients scrambling for this type of housing. In the past twenty years, as the brownstone revival has grown, former carriage houses and stables have become artist studios and homes. This Italianate carriage house served the residents of the corner home, which opens onto 6th Avenue. According to the Landmarks Commission, though the original carriage doors were replaced by an overhead door, the paneled hay-loft door you see is original.

➤ **Walk across Park Place so that you are on the east side of 6th Avenue. Walk one block north, turn right on Prospect Place, and stop midway up the block.**

The row of homes you see at Nos. 77–85 are neither Neo-Grec nor Italianate. They are called "Neocolonial." Though their foundations date to the nineteenth century, the homes were built in the late 1960s. In the mid-twentieth century, Park Slope underwent a decline, especially around the peripheries of the neighborhood, as longtime residents and potential residents took their automobiles, hit the newly constructed highways, and headed out for the suburbs. By the late 1960s, these foundations supported dilapidated, abandoned storefronts. Attempting to encourage neighborhood improvement, Brooklyn Union Gas Company (now known as Keyspan) teamed up with Asen Brothers and Brook to restore the foundations and erect these "Cinderella Project" homes.

➤ **Walk back along Prospect Place. Cross 6th Avenue and stop in front of Nos. 54-64 Prospect Place, on the left side of the street.**

This row of ivy-covered homes is not included in the historic landmark district, and they serve as sufficient justification for wandering out of the confines of the district. Here we have five great examples of the Queen Anne style that hit America in 1876 at the Philadelphia Exposition and came to shape urban row house architecture in the 1880s. Porches, turrets, bay windows, stained glass, and L-shaped stoops (rare in Park Slope) are combined to achieve Queen Anne's characteristic asymmetrical and romantic style.

➤ **Continue walking along Prospect Place to the corner of Prospect and 5th Avenue.**

As we hit the bottom of the slope, we are only one block away from Park Slope's western border, 4th Avenue, which is also home to the modern-day equivalent to the Brooklyn Bridge: the subway lines, which allow easy commutes for Brooklyn residents who work in Manhattan. In the nineteenth century, however, it was 5th Avenue—lined first with horse-drawn carriages and later with trolleys and shadowed by the grids of the elevated trains, which went up in 1889—that served as the Lower Slope's main transportation artery. From the beginning, well before 7th Avenue was developed as a commercial artery, 5th Avenue was lined with shops, pharmacies, theaters, and offices. In the years following the Civil War, the "least well paid" members of Manhattan's middle class also made the lower Park Slope area their neighborhood, since this was where they could afford their own homes. Additionally, many of the streets between 4th and 5th avenues were lined with houses designed to meet the needs of the working class, many of whom worked in factories off the Gowanus Canal, a few blocks to the west of Park Slope.

➤ **Turn left on 5th Avenue and walk one block south, to the corner of 5th and Park Place.**

Farther down on 5th Avenue, at the intersection of 3rd Street, is Washington Park, where the Brooklyn Dodgers practiced in the 1880s. At the turn of the century, 5th Avenue, especially the area around Union Street, was known as an Italian neighborhood, including Italian bakeries, groceries, and the Mazzini Democratic Club, which promoted Italian candidates for state office.

As you gaze at 5th Avenue today, two dynamics become immediately apparent. First, churches with signs in Spanish, Mexican restaurants, and the Arabic community centers all attest to the remarkable ethnic diversity of the Lower Slope. At the same time, the appearance of photo galleries, organic-food stores, and pricey and well-reviewed new gourmet restaurants point increasingly to a process of gentrification which has caused people to describe 5th Avenue as the "new Smith Street," referring to the inundation in recent years of Manhattan-quality restaurants and boutiques in nearby Boerum Hill and Cobble Hill.

CONTROVERSY OVER THE DISPLACEMENT FREE ZONE AND GENTRIFICATION

The gentrification process underway in Park Slope—and in many areas of Brooklyn and Manhattan for that matter—does not always make everyone happy. Especially disgruntled are long-term residents, many of them senior citizens, who can no longer afford the sky-rocketing rents. The Fifth Avenue Committee (FAC), a nonprofit community organization formed in 1978, organized a response in 1999 by creating the Displacement Free Zone. Low-income residents of the area between Flatbush Avenue and 20th Street and between 6th Avenue and 3rd Avenue who are forced to contend with a rent hike they cannot possibly afford are offered assistance by FAC. FAC is especially drawn to cases in which the landlord has other economic options.

Though FAC realizes that the neighborhood's unregulated housing legally permits landlords to raise rents, it will use moral persuasion to attempt to convince the landlord to modify the rent increase. The goal is to communicate that there is a higher value than the market—the neighborhood's ethnic and economic diversity—that is worth fighting for. And to carry out this principle FAC enlists creative tactics, such as sending letters signed by 12 clergy members to landlords or busing 80 angry residents to picket the Long Island residences of other landlords. Recently, FAC has raised awareness of the issues by holding carnivals—with 140 neighbors in attendance—in front of properties in question. FAC members readily admit that they expect to lose the cases that go to court, but they hope their efforts will deter future rent-raising landlords from buying properties in this zone.

➤ **Turn left on Park Place and walk to 6th Avenue. Turn right on 6th and walk to the corner of Sterling.**

Stop at St. Augustine's Church, 116 6th Avenue. In the late nineteenth century, the majority of Park Slope's residents were American-born citizens of German, English, or Scandinavian descent, and most of them were Protestant. By 1888, when plans were laid for this Victorian Gothic church, there were 18 Protestant churches in Park Slope. Thus, in building St. Augustine's, the neighborhood's first Catholic church, the congregation wanted to make a strong impression and so hired the well-established Parfitt Brothers to design the church. Their hopes and expectations turned out marvelously, as this mottled sandstone, elaborately carved church sports a magnificent red-tile roofline, complete with a verdigris copper statue of Gabriel. It inspired the 1893 *Guide to Brooklyn and Long Island* to describe the church as "one of the most notable Catholic sanctuaries in the country." On the inside, stained glass and sculpture work—"Queen Victoria's best" according to the American Institute of Architects (AIA)—greet the current parishioners, Catholics who attend Masses in English, Spanish, and Creole. Note that the building is best appreciated from the southeast corner of 6th Avenue and

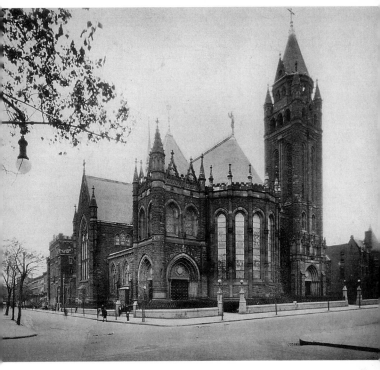

St. Augustine's Church, the first Roman Catholic church in Park Slope, described in the 1893 **Guide to Brooklyn and Long Island** as "one of the most notable Catholic sanctuaries in the country." Photo courtesy of the Brooklyn Historical Society.

Sterling, where one can more clearly see the scope of the roofline.

> **Walk east on Sterling. Stop about three-quarters of the way up the block.**

One of the most tragic events in Park Slope history unfolded on Sterling Place, on December 16, 1960, as a United Airlines DC-8 crashed onto the street, killing not only the 77 passengers aboard but also 8 people on the ground. The United Airlines aircraft had collided with a smaller TWA flight carrying 51 people above Staten Island and was trying to make an emergency landing, either at LaGuardia or Prospect Park, when it crashed here, its nose landing at the intersection of 7th Avenue and Sterling. The fires that ensued damaged many of the buildings on the street and destroyed the ironically named Pillar of Fire Church. Several memorials to this crash site exist in Park Slope. One of these is at Methodist Hospital on 7th Avenue and 5th Street, where a plaque holds the pocket change of 11-year-old Steven Baltz, who survived the initial crash but died the next day from severe burns.

➤ **Continue along Sterling. At the corner of 7th Avenue, turn right. Look at the row of homes across the street, to the east.**

Stop at the Lillian Ward Mansion, Nos. 21–27 7th Avenue, between Sterling and St. John's Place. Though most twenty-first-century passersby have never heard of Lillian Ward, an opera star, many have stopped to gaze and admire her home, on the corner of 7th and Sterling. The Romanesque Revival design of this 1887 home used various colors, details, and materials—including brick, brownstone, slate, and terra cotta—to create this striking corner mansion. What is most notable is the corner oriel with curvilinear peaked roof. Note also the band of terra-cotta tiles adorned with sunflowers. This was a common motif in Victorian-era homes. Inside are parquet floors, stained-glass windows, and several fireplaces. This home, together with the three homes to the south, was built by Lawrence B. Valk. The row presents uniformity with regard to color and texture, but it is the corner home that commands the most attention.

➤ **Continue on 7th Avenue, to the corner of St. John's Place.**

The intersection of St. John's and 7th Avenue presents a Protestant churchgoer with three intriguing choices for worship. The Gothic Revival church on the northwest corner of the intersection is the Grace United Methodist Church, designed by the Parfitt Brothers in 1882. On the southwest corner of the intersection stands the Memorial Presbyterian Church, built in 1882 by Pugin & Walter and housing Tiffany stained-glass windows.

> **Turn right and walk along St. John's Place.**

The oldest of the three churches, and the first church in Park Slope overall, is St. John's Episcopal Church, for which the street was renamed in 1870, replacing the old street name of Douglass. Though today the brownstone-lined St. John's Place has a decidedly urban residential air to it, when the Victorian Gothic chapel and rectory were built in 1869, they overlooked a grassy hill unsullied by construction. It was precisely this country feel that attracted members of a congregation based in downtown Brooklyn. The congregation brought with it the beginnings of a lending library, which would eventually be donated to the Brooklyn Public Library. Edward Potter, who designed the church and rectory, used random, rough-faced, ashlar sandstone and featured pointed-arch windows and doors.

> **Double back to the corner of St. John's and 7th and turn right on 7th. Walk one block to the corner of 7th and Lincoln.**

This red-brick corner mansion with brownstone trim was designed by S. F. Evelette for oil-cloth magnate William M. Brasher in 1881. As Park Slope became increasingly attractive, the wealthiest of the newcomers set their sights on corner lots on which to build free-standing mansions. Whereas today many of Park Slope's wealthiest residents have earned their money in computers, stocks, or law, in the late nineteenth and early twentieth centuries, the money that built the neighborhood's most lavish mansions came from chewing gum, baking powder, hot dogs, paper, cleaning powder, and, here, oil cloths. Though originally built for the use of a single family, by 1924 it was used by the Brooklyn Masonic Lodge, and by 1944 it had become the permanent home for the Brooklyn Conservatory of Music. In addition to offering lessons to more than 2,000 students of all ages, the conservatory also hosts many concerts and is considered one of the oldest and largest community music schools in the country.

Glance across the street to Ozzie's Coffee House. Coffee, tea, and assorted pastries are for sale as one might expect of any coffee house. But unlike other coffee houses, the interior maintains the traces of its previous occupant: a drugstore. The display cases and the cabinets are adorned with gilt-lettered signs indicating "prescriptions" and other drugstore services.

➤ **Cross 7th Avenue and walk east on Lincoln Place to the corner of 8th Avenue.**

Lincoln Place between 7th and 8th was developed mostly in the mid- to late 1880s, after the opening of the Brooklyn Bridge. The design most commonly employed on the south side of the block is the familiar Neo-Grec, but this time with a twist. The Manhattanites who settled here were in search of something grander than the two-sided bays that adorned the Neo-Grecs on the Lower Slope, and so their designers built their houses with three-sided bays. Also note the increased use of ornamentation around the windows and doors. By the 1880s, brownstones in Manhattan were priced at $60,000, while similar structures in the Upper Slope could be had for half the price.

On the north side of the street is the acclaimed Berkeley-Carroll School, an independent, nonsectarian, coeducational day school that enrolls 800 students. Founded in 1887 by Reverend Alfred C. Roe, it was originally named the Prospect Park Collegiate School for Girls. By 1896, the school had gained the funds and enrollment necessary to hire the architectural firm of Walker & Morris, which developed this Neo-Jacobean, eclectic style with brick and stone trim. The gym was built in 1937–38. The new building was built in 1992 to blend in with the original campus, which it did so well that the Landmarks Commission gave the school its Contextual Architecture Award that year.

➤ **Turn left on 8th Avenue and walk a few steps to 22 8th Avenue.**

Standing on the west side of 8th Avenue between St. John's Place and Lincoln Place, one's first inclination is to turn to face the majestic corner structure across the street. Fight this urge and concentrate for a moment on the row of Neo-Grec homes in front of you. What distinguishes this row from the rows of Neo-Grecs we just passed on Lincoln Place is that No. 22 once served as the home of William Jay Gaynor (1849–1913), mayor of New York City between 1909 and 1913. A vestige of his presence is evident in the City Hall Park mayor's lamps that adorn the doorway. A remarkable character, Gaynor daily braved the elements to walk the four miles down Flatbush Avenue and over the Brooklyn Bridge to City Hall. It was this tenacity perhaps that allowed Gaynor to fight the powers at Tammany Hall. Gaynor, one of New York's most independent mayors, appointed officials without Tammany's consent, eliminated useless positions, and introduced additional fiscal reforms. His activities aroused passions; a disgruntled former city worker shot him in 1910, but he survived.

Mayor's lamps adorn the front of 22 8th Avenue, indicating it was once the home of William Jay Gaynor, mayor of New York City from 1909 to 1913. Gaynor walked the four miles from his house here to City Hall in Manhattan daily. Photo courtesy of the Brooklyn Historical Society.

In many ways, Gaynor is even more important for his work within Brooklyn. At various turns a journalist, lawyer, and justice of the State Supreme Court, Gaynor was also active in the political and social circle that revolved around the Montauk Club, the glorious building that first caught your eye. Here, Gaynor gave an inspiring speech in favor of consolidation with Manhattan that stirred Brooklyn's mercantile and political leaders to form the Brooklyn Consolidation League in 1893. In turn, the propaganda work of this league—they distributed over 2 million pieces of literature—proved integral to Brooklynites' vote to merge with New York. Gaynor and the league persuaded reluctant voters of the importance of merging with New York by emphasizing the need for additional revenue and resources to deal with Brooklyn's incredible growth in the years following the completion of the Brooklyn Bridge.

The Montauk Club is considered the crown jewel of Park Slope. This brown, orange, and red brick and terra-cotta mansion takes after a Venetian palace, the Ca D'Oro. But though its designer, Francis Kimball (1845–1919), did indeed style his 1891 structure in the Venetian Gothic manner, complete with balustraded balconies and traceried openings, he used other techniques to achieve a distinctly American, particularly Brooklyn, theme. Named for the Montauk Indians that originally inhabited the eastern part of Long Island, the building depicts the story of the Montauks in its third-floor frieze, which winds around to the Lincoln Place side of the building. Additionally, above the second-floor arch, a frieze depicts the founders of the club decked in top hats laying the cornerstone of the building in 1889. Architects have noted the striking manner in which Kimball employed traceried openings, balconies, and wall openings to create strong contrasts between solids and voids.

The main doorway was designed for the club members —prosperous Brooklyn men and their guests. A center for political activity, the club hosted presidential candidates such as Grover Cleveland, Theodore Roosevelt, and Herbert Hoover. In more recent history, the Montauk Club

The 1891 brick and terra-cotta Montauk Club might seem more at home in Venice than in Park Slope. The third-floor frieze depicts the story of Long Island's Montauk Indians, and on the second floor another frieze depicts the founders of the club decked in top hats and laying the cornerstone of the building in 1889. Over the years, the club has hosted Grover Cleveland, Theodore Roosevelt, Herbert Hoover, Dwight D. Eisenhower, John F. Kennedy, and Robert Kennedy. Photo courtesy of the Brooklyn Historical Society.

hosted Dwight D. Eisenhower, John F. Kennedy, and Robert Kennedy. The doorway adjoining the main entrance was intended for members' wives. In the late nineteenth century, this was a progressive move, for, although women did not qualify as members, the club was one of the first of the nineteenth-century clubs in Brooklyn to open its facilities to women. A chivalrous rationale for the separate doorway (which funneled the women past the men's drawing room on the first floor to the third-floor dining room) was to protect women from the cigar smoke that filled that dark-paneled drawing room. A less gallant rationale was that the men did not wish to be bothered by their wives.

Today the Montauk Club is "a private club open to all." The club offers a wide array of services and events, ranging from etiquette classes for children to music series and cigar nights for their parents. The club also hosts a "Brooklyn Book Connection" evening. The two top floors are cooperative apartments, and the basement (bowling alley and all) is home to a realty office.

The homes situated between 8th Avenue and Prospect Park West (formerly 9th Avenue) were built after the completion of the Brooklyn Bridge and were designed to attract wealthy Manhattanites. By the 1890s, 8th Avenue vied with Prospect Park West as the premier Park Slope street, with the most elegant homes and the most distinguished residents. We are almost at the height of the slope, and the wider lots here allowed for bigger-scale houses than the side streets. Here, too, we will see more variety of styles and use of color both in the traditional row houses and especially in the detached, free-standing homes.

The residents of the upper part of the Slope seemed to consider themselves above the rest of the Slope—both literally and figuratively. A 1903 diarist recounts the special atmosphere of the Upper Slope: "We do not journey below 7th avenue and we instruct the servants to go about their shopping in other places. Here on the hilltop the breezes are fresh. We look over the farms and orchards and take our walks in the park. On Sunday a group of us visit the museum and rest by the fountain in the Grand Army Plaza. There surely can be no finer place of residence in the whole city."

➤ **Walk south along 8th Avenue.**

The mansion on the corner of Berkeley and 8th Avenue (Nos. 52 and 54 8th Avenue) is a perfect place to consider the "rebellion" from brownstone that erupted in the late 1880s and the 1890s. When Manhattan jeweler Henry Beguelin purchased this lot in 1886, he brought a Manhattan architect, F. Carlos Morry, who wove Queen Anne and Romanesque Revival elements into the single-family design. The varied materials include Euclid stone at the basement and parlor floor, red brick for the two upper stories, red Spanish tile on the roof, and terra cotta for decorations throughout the building. The house is noted for the corner bay that runs the full height of the building, as well as for the semicircular curved window and intricate wrought-iron work.

In 1914 a fire from a Christmas tree forced reconstruction, and it was decided to divide the mansion into a two-family home. In recent years, it was further divided into apartments. Similarly, the Romanesque Revival and Queen Anne house on the corner of 8th and Union was originally designed in 1897 as a single-family home for a Mrs. M. V. Phillips, and in the 1930s it was converted into a bridge club and restaurant. Now, it too is an apartment building.

➤ **Walk to the corner of 8th and Union.**

Though in the 1880s it was the opportunity to own homes rather than settle for apartments that lured Manhattanites to the Slope, by the 1910s and 1920s, apartment buildings began to dot the neighborhood. In fact, many of the apartment buildings that line 8th Avenue and Prospect Park West were built after the original mansions were torn down. The reason for this shift is two-fold. Mansions were costly, not only to buy but more importantly to maintain. Who could afford the servants that went hand in hand with such living? A more attractive option for glamorous living lay in the easy-to-maintain luxury apartment. And for the wealthy who could afford mansion living, the purchase of an automobile offered the option of country living and much more space to build the dream mansion. Second, by the mid-1910s the subway was bringing in a more working-class population, which was content to live in the boarding houses and apartments that the former mansions were being converted into.

Today, prime real estate lies also in apartment living. Witness the new Shinnecock condominium high-rise that looms over the Slope on Union Street. In September 2001, the *New York Times* listed projected prices ranging from $717,000 for a two-bedroom unit to $2 million for a triplex penthouse with private roof terrace. Residents will revel in details such as limestone-finished bathrooms and cherrywood cabinets in the kitchen. Neighbors, however, are less than thrilled. Residents of the surrounding lots led a fight to halt construction, arguing that the building's height would block their views. But because the Shinnecock is not within the designated historic district, the neighboring residents were unable to limit the height of the building. When asked by a *New York Times* writer about the conflict, an associate broker with Harbor View Realty, the agency that is handling sales, remarked that though it will block its neighbor buildings' views, it will offer "great views for the people who live in the building."

➤ **Continue south along 8th Avenue. Turn left on President Street and walk a third of the way up the block.**

The Neo-Grec house at 916 President Street placed its nineteenth-century resident, Mrs. Van Mater Stilwell, in the ranks of Park Slope's upper class. However, Stilwell's alias, Laura Jean Libbey, adorned the title pages of millions of dime-store novels that found their way onto pushcarts in working-class neighborhoods like the Lower East Side and eventually into the pockets of working girls' coats. In the 1890s Stilwell wrote more than 60 books, selling 10–15 million copies. Her romances were so popular that they influenced turn-of-the-century magazine stories and, later, serial motion pictures as well. As historian Nan Enstad details, working-class girls virtually ate them up (they would read them on the shop floor during their lunch breaks) and even adopted the names of Libbey's heroines: hence, a "Malke" or a "Sofia" became "Leonie" or "Rosebud."

➤ **Double back on President to 8th Avenue. Turn left and walk to the corner of Carroll and 8th. Turn left again and walk to the entrance of the corner home.**

In 1888 Thomas Adams, "chewing gum king" and inventor of the Chiclet and its automatic dispenser, hired C. P. H. Gilbert to design this sprawling double home, considered the finest example of Romanesque Revival residential architecture in the city. Sandstone, terra cotta, salmon-colored brick, and a brownstone base serve as the dominant materials for the home, which boasts a deep entrance arch, stained-glass windows, and a polygonal tower and is capped by an octagonal-tile roof. The *AIA Guide* highlights the Carroll Street arch, which is supported by Romanesque-capped columns and incised with naturalistic bas-reliefs.

Now divided into apartments, the building provides the setting for Park Slope's most famous ghost story. When built, it was the first residence in the neighborhood to have an elevator. One summer, when the Adams family was away in the country, the family's servants got trapped in the elevator and died. Their spirits, however, have not left the home, and residents of the building have been known to complain of Irish-accented pleas for help.

On the southwest corner of 8th and Carroll, the ghost of Coney Island restaurant-owner Charles Feltman probably laments the construction of the 1950 apartment building that necessitated the destruction of his Romanesque Revival townhouse. Whereas his neighbor was known for the Chiclet, Feltman was associated with the invention of the hot dog at his Coney Island establishment.

➤ **Walk along 8th Avenue one block to Montgomery Place and turn left.**

Named for war hero Richard Montgomery, who died in the Battle of Quebec, this block with some of the finest homes in New York was built between 1887 and 1892. Investor Harvey Murdock hired C. P. H. Gilbert, a young architect who worked primarily in Park Slope in the 1880s and 1890s. By the turn of the century, Gilbert worked in Manhattan, designing 5th Avenue mansions in his distinctive Neo-Tudoresque style and in other styles for noted financiers and other businessmen. Perhaps the most well known is the mansion he designed for Felix Warburg on 5th Avenue and 92nd Street, now home to the Jewish Museum. But in no street in Brooklyn is Gilbert's work more concentrated or celebrated than on Montgomery Place. Encouraging him to avoid a standard look, Murdock commissioned Gilbert to design 20 out of the 46 lots. The result is breathtaking. The *AIA Guide* extols the "symphony of materials and textures," and it is generally agreed that Montgomery Place is one of the finest examples of urban row house architecture in the country.

The mansions of Montgomery Place, most built between 1887 and 1892, are perhaps the finest examples of urban row house architecture anywhere in the country. Image courtesy of the Brooklyn Historical Society.

➤ **Walk back along Montgomery to 8th Avenue. Turn left on 8th and walk to the corner of Garfield Place.**

On St. John's we beheld the first Protestant church and on Sterling, the first Catholic church. Here we see the third major religious group to establish a place of worship in the Slope: the Jews. In 1909, Beth Elohim, a Reform congregation that had been formed in downtown Brooklyn in the 1860s, hired the firm of Simon Eisendrath & B. Horowitz to construct this Neoclassical temple, which the *AIA Guide* describes as a "domed Beaux-Arts limestone extravaganza." After the Columbia Exposition in Chicago in 1893, architects heralded a move to classical styles, from Greek and Roman to Renaissance. This trend is evident in the design of the Neoclassical synagogue and in other institutions and homes built in Park Slope at the time. The temple is molded in the shape of a pentagon, symbolizing the five books of Moses. Across Garfield Place is the congregation's 1928 temple building, with an Art Deco Moses holding up the Ten Commandments.

➤ **Turn left on Garfield and walk to Prospect Park West. Turn right on Prospect Park West and walk to 1st Street.**

On August 27, 1776, 1st Street, then called Port Road, was the scene of one of the earliest Revolutionary War battles, the Battle of Long Island. Here, American forces fled from the 20,000 British troops that had landed in Gravesend, Brooklyn, several days before. General John Sullivan led his American forces down Port Road and away from the approaching British forces. Many of the men who traveled down Port Road survived, in large part because another group of men, led by General William Alexander Stirling, had diverted a large contingent of British troops by holding their positions by the Vechte-Cortelyou house, now known as the "Old Stone House" on present-day 5th Avenue and 3rd Street. As the Park Slope Landmarks Commission reports, this stand "prevented the British pincer from closing and trapping" the American troops traveling down the Port Road.

➤ **Cross 1st Street and stop in front of the corner mansion.**

When paper-magnate Henry Hulbert (1831—1912) commissioned Montrose Morris to design this light-gray-limestone Romanesque Revival mansion in 1892, such was the development of Brooklyn that the back porch commanded a panoramic view of the harbor. Alas, the view is no longer unobstructed, and the "splendid isolation" that drew Hulbert to the area is no more; still, the polygonal towers, grand entranceway, and gorgeous ornamentation that combines Romanesque and Byzantine motifs still manage to impress the passersby. When first designed, the structure served as a "double home": on the north end were Hulbert and his wife, and on the south end were Hulbert's son-in-law and business partner and his daughter. For many years this was home to the Brooklyn Society for Ethical Culture; today it serves the rapidly expanding Poly-Prep School.

➤ **Walk down Prospect Park West a few more steps to the neighboring mansion, 53 Prospect Park West, the Brooklyn Society for Ethical Culture Meeting House.**

In 1900 the two lions flanking the entrance to this mansion greeted William Childs, the originator of Bon Ami cleanser (hint: when around true Brooklynites, make sure to drop your French accent when mentioning this cleanser: "Ba-NA-mie"). Childs enlisted William B. Tubby to design the red-brick Neo-Jacobean home, as well as the Italian-provincial-style home across 2nd Street at 61 Prospect Park West, as a wedding present for his daughter, Mary. In 1907 additional work on the home by Tubby resulted in the splendid morning room, complete with Tiffany stained-glass windows and space below for a billiards room.

Like so many of Park Slope's mansions, this too has a public use, as it serves as the home for the Brooklyn Society of Ethical Culture. A religious humanist movement, the society dates to 1876, when Felix Adler turned his back on a junior rabbi position at Manhattan's prestigious Temple Emanu-El to start a nonsectarian movement that championed Enlightenment ideals of universalism and progress. In addition to edifying lectures, the movement was concerned with social issues of the day and fought hard for tenement reforms, child labor laws, and the spread of settlement houses. Today, the Brooklyn branch is "dedicated to improving the ethical quality of relationships in personal lives and in the world" and, to that end, has regularly scheduled meetings and events and works on issues ranging from environmental affairs to family and children's issues.

➢ **Continue south along Prospect Park West for a few blocks, to 4th Street. Cross Prospect Park West and enter the park.**

The Italianate villa at this spot, Litchfield Manor, was built by the renowned architect Alexander Jackson Davis in 1857, well before the neighborhood was known as Park Slope. At the time, the area was composed of several tracts of land—some of it farmland, most of it undeveloped—that had been in the hands of several Dutch and Huguenot families. But the man who lived in this house, Edwin Clark Litchfield, an attorney who made his millions in the railroad business, had the idea of Park Slope firmly rooted in his imagination. Indeed, if one person could be heralded as the founder of Park Slope, it would be Litchfield. Unfortunately, the man with the vision was unable to witness the materialization of his ideas.

What happened? In the 1860s, Litchfield was one of the prime backers of Brooklyn's plan to create Prospect Park. Litchfield, who by the 1850s had purchased all the land between present-day 1st Street and 9th Street and from the Gowanus Canal to 10th Avenue, viewed the park as a perfect magnet for potential residents. But after the Civil War, the plans for the park's development changed. The original plans drawn up by Egbert L. Viele in 1858 were discarded in favor of a more ambitious design by Frederick Law

Litchfield Manor was built in the mid-nineteenth century, long before the neighborhood was known as Park Slope. Edwin Clark Litchfield was a prominent booster of the idea of Prospect Park and once owned many acres here. Unfortunately, when the park was laid out, it included the land under his mansion, and Litchfield was forced to sell to the city. His mansion became the home of the Prospect Park administration. Photo courtesy of the Brooklyn Historical Society.

Olmsted and Calvert Vaux. While under Viele's plan 10th Avenue was to serve as the western boundary of the park, Olmsted and Vaux's plan expanded the park to 9th Avenue (today's Prospect Park West). In short, Litchfield's mansion was now in the jurisdiction of the park/city, and he was forced to sell it to the city of Brooklyn for $552,000. Litchfield was able to rent his own mansion back at a rate of $2,500 per year, but by 1882 he had left Brooklyn for Paris. What had once been the center for Civil War–era Brooklyn high society became the offices of the park administration.

Spend more time walking in the park with our Prospect Park chapter or return to Prospect Park West and walk to 9th Street. Turn right and walk one block to 8th

Avenue where you can get onto the F train at its 7th Avenue stop. The 7th Avenue stop stretches from 8th Avenue, where you're standing, to 7th Avenue down the slope of 9th Street.

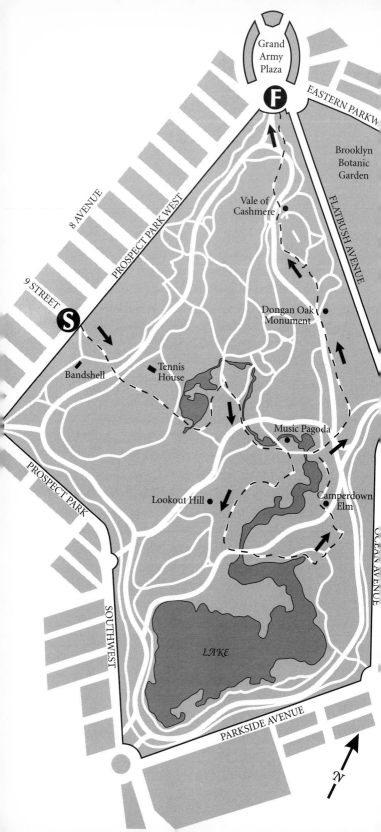

Grand
Army
Plaza

F

EASTERN PARKW

Brooklyn
Botanic
Garden

FLATBUSH AVENUE

8 AVENUE

PROSPECT PARK WEST

Vale of
Cashmere

9 STREET

S

Dongan Oak
Monument

Bandshell

Tennis
House

Music Pagoda

Lookout Hill

Camperdown
Elm

OCEAN AVENUE

PROSPECT PARK

SOUTHWEST

LAKE

PARKSIDE AVENUE

N

7 PROSPECT PARK

"Landscape Painted by a Skilled Hand"

➤ **Start: One block east of the 8th Avenue exit from the F train's 7th Avenue stop.**

BROOKLYN'S PRIMARY natural oasis —Prospect Park—is considered by many to be the greatest urban park designed by nineteenth-century masters Frederick Law Olmsted and Calvert Vaux. Prospect Park covers 526 acres and features long meadow vistas, numerous water pools connected by streams and waterfalls, and Brooklyn's only remaining forest.

In the mid-nineteenth century, the City of Brooklyn watched as Central Park was created across the river in Manhattan. Envious, Brooklyn followed suit, encouraging the New York legislature to pass an act supporting a park, issuing bonds to fund the land purchase, and creating a board of park commissioners. The commissioners, echoing the movement for public parks that Central Park had created, noted, "The intense activity and the destructive excitement of business life as here conducted, imperatively demands these public places for exercise and recreation." The result was what Clay Lancaster, quoting eleventh-century painter Kuo His, described in his classic 1967 *Prospect Park Handbook* as a "landscape painted by a skilled hand."

The land Brooklyn bought for the new Mount Prospect Park unfortunately straddled both sides of the city's major road, Flatbush Avenue. The commissioners first hired civil engineer and West Point graduate Egbert Viele to design the park. Perhaps not coincidentally, Viele had been the original "chief engineer" of Manhattan's Central Park, where his uninspiring design was rejected in favor of Olmsted and Vaux's Greensward Plan. Viele's 1861 plan for Prospect Park proposed a series of pedestrian bridges to connect the bisected park land, in which, he wrote, "people of all classes, escaping from the flare, and the glitter, and turmoil of the city, might find relief for the mind, and physical recreation."

Thankfully, the onset of the Civil War prevented Prospect Park's construction (although Central Park was built right through the war) and gave the commissioners time to reconsider Viele's plans. In 1865 they turned to Calvert Vaux to survey the park lands. Vaux proposed selling the land east of Flatbush and purchasing additional property to the south and west to create a single large expanse. His much better plan was accepted, although it took a few years to buy the land to the southwest, called "rather expensive lots" by Vaux. Vaux's success must have come as quite a blow to Egbert Viele. He had now lost two major projects—Prospect Park and Central Park—to Vaux and Olmsted!

Next, Vaux convinced his former partner, Frederick Law Olmsted, to return from California, where he was living at Yosemite Valley, managing a gold mine, and trying to salvage his failed Marisopa Estate project. Vaux wrote numerous letters over the course of six months entreating his colleague to return east and take on this fantastic opportunity. In July 1865, Olmsted agreed to collaborate with his old partner on a park that offered him the freedom to work without the interference of the "infernal scoundrels" that had interfered with Central Park.

Prospect Park had many advantages for the designers that Central Park lacked, and the result was that Vaux and Olmsted were able to create an even more beautiful park. For example, the Brooklyn land had no giant rectangular reservoir (now Central Park's Great Lawn) sitting in its middle, nor did it need roads cutting across it. As a result, Olmsted and Vaux could create the huge undulating and uninterrupted Long Meadow. And the absence of Manhattan schist sticking up throughout the park allowed for better vistas and a larger lake.

Vaux and Olmsted's 1866 plan called for three distinct "regions" in the park, as summarized by the commissioners:

> first, a region of open meadow, with large trees singly and in groups; second, a hilly district, with groves and shrubbery; and third, a lake district, containing a fine sheet of water, with picturesque shores and islands. These being the landscape characteristics, the first gives room for extensive play grounds, the second offers shaded rambles and broad views, and the third presents good opportunities for skating and rowing.

Think about today's park in relation to the above description. The "open meadow" is now called Long Meadow. The "hilly district" contains a valley, brook, and ravine and includes Lookout Hill. Finally, the "lake district" has a 60-acre lake and other narrow bodies of water. Clay Lancaster, in his *Prospect Park Handbook*, likens Prospect Park to a Chinese landscape: "The Chinese term for 'landscape' is composed of two words, shan and shui. The first means 'hill' and the second 'water.' Prospect Park is a perfect example of that nineteenth-century park landscaped for the appreciation of the public."

➤ Enter the park at Prospect Park West and 9th Street, one block east of the 8th Avenue exit from the F train's 7th Avenue station. As you exit the station, walk east one block along 9th Street to Prospect Park West.

Standing squarely in front of the 9th Street entrance to Prospect Park is an imposing monument to Marie Joseph Paul Yves Roch Gilbert du Motier, also known as the Marquis de Lafayette. Having given financial support to the Continental army during the American Revolution, Lafayette was greatly respected by New Yorkers. In August 1784, he became one of the first European statesmen to visit New York following the Revolution. He also made a profound impact on the city with his second visit, 40 years later, in 1824. Returning once again a year later, the Marquis ventured to Brooklyn, where he met the six-year-old Walt Whitman.

The Lafayette Monument was designed by Daniel Chester French (who designed the Lincoln sculpture in the Lincoln Memorial in Washington, DC) and sculpted by Augustus Lukeman. It was dedicated by Marshall Joseph Joffre, France's military commander of forces along the western front during World War I, as a symbol of the strong ties between France and the United States. The dedication ceremony took place on May 10, 1917, only a few weeks after America had formally entered the war and a full month before General John J. Pershing landed his American Expeditionary Forces in France. The timing is curious in that it takes months (if not years) to design, finance, and plan such sculptures. While the Lafayette Monument can be viewed as a symbol of friendship, it also reflects the desire of some Americans to join the war effort sooner.

➤ Walk into the park, keeping the barbecue area to your left and the bandshell to your right.

The bandshell is a 1939 addition to the park by then–parks commissioner Robert Moses. It was designed by Aymar Embury, who also helped design the zoos in Prospect and Central parks. Like Central Park's earlier bandshell, this one has witnessed the changing approaches to recreation in New York City's public parks. Before there was a bandshell, parkgoers practiced archery and hockey here. With the popularity of ballroom dancing, the bandshell got a lot of use in the 1940s and 1950s. Lately, it is a place for concerts, including the one at which Curtis Mayfield (who had a long and brilliant career but is perhaps best remembered for his Grammy-nominated soundtrack to *Superfly,* as well as for the anthem "People Get Ready") was tragically injured when a light tower fell on him in 1990, leaving him a quadriplegic. Since 1979, Celebrate Brooklyn! concerts and movies have been held here, and it serves as a performance space similar to the Rumsey Playfield's Summer Stage in Central Park, which coincidentally sits behind the rarely used Naumberg Bandshell.

The barbecue area and even the bandshell are controversial because they are examples of what historians call "contested spaces." Put less pompously, different people want to use the park for different things, and they disagree about what is appropriate in a public park. This conflict is as old as the park. Barbecuing is prohibited in some city parks, notably Central Park, but it is allowed in certain areas in Prospect Park. Some parkgoers and residents near the park complain about cooking smells and the garbage that some barbecuers leave behind, just as some parkgoers like to listen to music at the bandshell and others find it intrusive. The key for Prospect Park and for any park is to satisfy all its constituencies as best it can in a place like New York.

As you approach the road known as West Drive, note the lack of an underpass for pedestrians. As we will see

Out for a drive in Prospect Park in an 1899 auto. Photo courtesy of the Brooklyn Historical Society.

throughout the park, Calvert Vaux designed a vast series of bridges, allowing walkers to travel unobstructed. This awkward crossing, managed by a modern traffic light, is in itself part of the story.

The terrain we have just crossed was part of the "very expensive lots" that Vaux proposed purchasing with funds generated by selling the land east of Flatbush, which Egbert Viele wanted to connect by pedestrian overpasses. This land, about 12 acres, was purchased for $1.7 million in 1869 from Edwin Clark Litchfield (discussed in our Park Slope and Green-Wood Cemetery chapters) and Hugh McLaughlin, the political boss of Brooklyn's Democratic Party. The heavy cost for these acres, coupled with the depression of 1873, left the park commissioners without the funds to properly develop the land. They had spent over $4 million on land and almost $5 million improving it. It wasn't until the 1880s, long after Olmsted and Vaux had moved on to other projects, that this area was developed, so it never got a Vaux-designed pedestrian bridge and instead has a traffic light.

➤ **Cross West Drive and continue straight along the path into the Long Meadow.**

As you begin your descent into the Long Meadow, take note of the Neoclassical Tennis House partly obscured by the trees to your left. Built in 1910, by the firm of Helmle, Huberty & Hudswell, it originally served as a locker facility and storage space for lawn-tennis equipment. Lawn tennis was hugely popular in the 1890s, and the Long Meadow was covered with about 300 courts. Tennis House, with its classical colonnade and arched Guastavino-tile ceiling, was built after the craze had begun to wane, so it didn't get much use for its intended purpose. It has since been restored to its original glory and is now home to the Brooklyn Center for the Urban Environment. The structure is often mistaken for a McKim, Mead & White building. In fact, its architect, Frank Helmle, was associated with the McKim partnership before starting his own architectural firm.

The Long Meadow, almost a mile long and covering nearly 90 acres, is the largest open meadow in any New York City park. The baseball fields to your right were not part of the original design but were added by Robert Moses in the late 1950s, quite in contrast to Vaux and Olmsted's rustic vision. Olmsted repeatedly warned about encroachments to the parks that he and Vaux designed, urging that a park be seen as "a single work of art." He even went so far as to publish in 1882 a pamphlet titled "The Spoils of the Park," in which he decried the degradation of the work "to which I had for years given all my heart, to which I had devoted my life." Nonetheless, keeping Prospect Park as an unchanging work of art is not the same as keeping the *Mona Lisa* as an unchanging work of art. The park is a living thing, a contested space in which New

Capturing the early-twentieth-century craze of lawn tennis on Prospect Park's Long Meadow. The Long Meadow is now more commonly a site for baseball in summer and dog walkers year round. Image courtesy of the Brooklyn Historical Society.

Yorkers often forget the vision of its designers. And so, once every spring the annual Little League parade concludes on these fields, after the uniformed youngsters march through Park Slope.

As you stand in the Long Meadow, note the scale of the surrounding trees in relation to the buildings outside the park perimeter. Unlike Manhattan's Central Park, here in Brooklyn the park is not framed by high-rise buildings. While there are a number of taller structures, especially along Prospect Park West, the park has retained its nineteenth-century feel with uninterrupted vistas. The tops of the distant trees climb to the sky and not to the middle of an apartment house.

As you walk the width of the Long Meadow, sloping downhill slightly, and approach the Upper Pool (formerly Swan Boat Lake), note the unique "Dog Beach" to your left. This small swimming area opened in August 2002 as part of the lake's renovation efforts. Created by the partnership of the Prospect Park Alliance and the Fellowship in the Interests of Dogs and their Owners (FIDO, for short), this swimming area demonstrates yet another way in which Prospect Park is used by a variety of groups. FIDO simultaneously encourages dog owners to respect the park while advocating for dog owners with city officials. Bring your dog for a swim.

Swan Boat Lake was named for the pedal-boats that used to be rented on the water. These multiseat pedal-boats offered tours around the lake. Each one had a large decorative swan in the rear of the boat to hide the bicycle-like contraption that powered them. These "swan boats" and the Swan Boat House that used to stand next to the water are long gone.

➤ **Continue walking straight, with the Upper Pool and Dog Beach to your left. Take the path that leads around the Upper Pool and into the woods.**

As you stroll around the Upper Pool, you will come to a rustic wooden bridge. This is a re-creation of the original Olmsted and Vaux crossing, with some hidden steel tie-rods inside. In fact, this whole area was only reopened to the public in 2002, after years of restoration efforts to return it to its original beauty.

While standing on the bridge, note the small body of water to your right. This is Fallkill Pool, the beginning of the water system that runs throughout the park. *Kill* is an often misunderstood word in the New York area. It is the Dutch word for waterway and appears throughout what was former New Amsterdam and New Netherland. Recently, People for the Ethical Treatment of Animals (PETA) requested that the town of Fishkill change its name because it implies killing fish. "Fishkill" actually means "fish stream."

The steep cliffs and thick forest of the ravine and Ambergill Falls represent the Adirondack Mountains. This nineteenth-century stereocard depicts the original rustic shelter. Note the Victorian women with a parasol on the far left. A re-creation now stands in its place. Image courtesy of Big Onion Walking Tours.

Following the Fallkill Bridge, the path will fork. Continue to your left, keeping the Upper Pool on your left side. The path will come to an end just beyond the pools. Turn right and continue, downhill, into the ravine.

Unfortunately, the paths that run through the ravine are open only on weekend afternoons between April and November. It is still undergoing restoration under the guidance of the Prospect Park Alliance, although it may be open longer hours in the future. If you listen closely, you can hear the water rumbling over the falls. Olmsted was greatly affected by his time at Yosemite, as well as by the trip he and Vaux took to the Adirondacks. The rugged wooden bridges and the fast-moving water through the ravine reflect these influences. Deep within the ravine, on a hilltop, stood a rustic shelter. It has since been rebuilt. The stereograph image that accompanies this chapter is of that original shelter.

The Prospect Park Alliance is using archival photographs and the writings of Vaux and Olmsted to re-create the nineteenth-century landscape. According to these photographs, there was a significant waterfall somewhere within the ravine. Unfortunately, with soil erosion and the shifting of many of the boulders, it is hard to place exactly where it was.

LOST PROSPECT PARK AND THE PROSPECT PARK ALLIANCE

Another structure that has been lost in Prospect Park is the dairy. Until 1935, the dairy stood on the other side of the rustic shelter, on the far side of the ravine from where you're standing. Prospect Park's dairy, designed by Vaux, was similar in design to his dairy in Manhattan's Central Park, now restored as a Central Park visitors' center in the middle of the park at 64th Street. Prospect Park's dairy had two gabled wings, public rooms with fireplaces, and living quarters for a family that supervised it. Both dairies served the same purpose, to shelter some of the cows and sheep that grazed in nearby meadows and to give fresh milk to visitors. Milk was tasty as well as symbolically representative of purity and wholesomeness in a century when city residents regularly suffered from dysentery, cholera, and other diseases. In Prospect Park, the animals grazed on the Long Meadow; and in Central Park, on the Sheep Meadow.

Like Central Park, which has been renovated and restored with the funds and labor of the private Central Park Conservancy, Prospect Park has also been restored over the past two decades. The Prospect Park Alliance is a private group that partners with the city to restore the park. Over the years, the partnership has rebuilt rustic shelters and waterways, renovated buildings, and done extensive landscaping work. Visitors to the park can thank—and donate to—the Alliance, but it is also good to remember that it was the city's neglect of its parks during the fiscal crisis of the 1970s that let them spiral into decrepitude. That private groups were forced to take over what had been seen and treated by the city as a public good is both a testament to citizen involvement and a disgrace to the city for its neglect. Hopefully, the future will see all parks taken care of as well as Prospect Park and Central Park are today.

➤ **Walk to Nethermead Arches. Continue under the Arches. The Binnenwater will be to your left, the Nethermead to your right.**

The Nethermead Arches are classic Calvert Vaux. The triple-arched bridge allows pedestrians, horses, and the Binnenwater to pass unobstructed below as vehicles pass above on Central Drive. The Arches also serve as a boundary between the wooded areas we are leaving and the Nethermead.

The Nethermead is the center of the park, a gently rolling meadow uniquely isolated from the rest of the park, quite unlike Long Meadow. The name comes from Old English: *nether*, meaning "lower" or "beneath," and *mead*, meaning "meadow."

➤ **Continue walking with the Binnenwater to your left, into the tree grove and past the Music Pagoda.**

The large Music Pagoda to your left was originally built in 1887. Upon completion, it was the musical focal point of the park, supplanting Vaux's 1874 Concert Grove Pavilion (see below). For many years, the Edwin Franko Goldman brass band held concerts here, and in the 1960s it was used for a series of stage performances. The original structure burned down in 1968. The current pagoda opened in 1971 and was immediately used to stage an anti–Vietnam War concert.

➤ **After you pass the Music Pagoda, continue through the trees; at the fork in the path, head to your right. Continue walking along with the Nethermead on your right and the woods on your left. Proceed to the far end of the Nethermead. Lookout Hill is ahead of you.**

Lookout Hill is one of the most isolated parts of Prospect Park. At approximately 190 feet above sealevel, it provided tremendous views in the nineteenth century. It was said that on a clear day one could see New Jersey and beyond. Olmsted and Vaux envisioned this area to be a focal point of the park, including a large carriage court with a 100-foot-long terraced platform and refreshment stand. Atop Lookout Hill was to be a tall observation tower for panoramic sightseeing. None of these plans were brought to fruition, but you can still climb up the hill, which is one of the prime bird-watching areas in the park.

Before continuing past Lookout Hill, you may want to take a detour to your right, over to the Friends Cemetery. If you cut across the southern end of the Nethermead over to Center Drive and then walk to your left (southwest) about fifty yards, you will come to the fence around the cemetery. This small Quaker cemetery was officially established decades before the development of Prospect Park, and burials began here in the 1820s. Less than half of the original cemetery land remains as private property of the Society of Friends of Manhattan; the rest was taken for the park. Keeping within the Quaker tradition, all persons, regardless of wealth or fame, are buried with simple grave markers. The actor Montgomery Clift, star of *From Here to*

Eternity, *Red River*, *A Place in the Sun*, and *Judgment at Nuremberg*, was buried here after his July 1966 death at the age of 46.

As the Nethermead comes to an end and you approach Wellhouse Drive, which is closed to traffic, note the white granite memorial tucked away near the trees to your right. This often-missed monument was created by Stanford White and erected in 1895. Officially called the Maryland Society Battle Monument, it commemorates the Maryland volunteers who fought under the leadership of Lord Stirling during the Battle of Brooklyn in August 1776. It was roughly on this spot that the volunteers rallied before marching to the southwest, into what is now Green-Wood Cemetery.

➤ **Upon reaching Wellhouse Drive, cross it and turn left. Walk across Terrace Bridge.**

Terrace Bridge was Calvert Vaux's last park project. Built in 1890 from steel and brick, the bridge began to receive its badly needed restoration in 2004. From the bridge, looking through the trees to the right, you can see the only lake in all of Brooklyn.

➤ **As you leave the Terrace Bridge, take the wide dirt path to your right. After a few feet, the path becomes paved, first with concrete tile then with tar. This path takes you to Wollman Rink (on your right) and the Lincoln monument (on your left).**

Visitors used to skate right on the lake, but all that changed when Robert Moses built Wollman Rink in 1960, dramatically altering the lake, destroying the small Music Island, and filling in part of the water. The rink is 26,600 square feet of raw concrete surrounded by an unattractive chain-

The Terrace Bridge as it appears from the shore of Prospect Park Lake. Image courtesy of Big Onion Walking Tours.

link fence. It is well used by both bladers and skaters but is an aesthetic embarrassment, like much of what Robert Moses wrought. There has been talk for years of moving the rink or at least changing the fence. Alas, this isn't Central Park, and we don't have Donald Trump to do it for us.

Perhaps Wollman Rink would be less visually jarring if it weren't situated directly next to the only formal aspect of Prospect Park. Standing directly opposite Wollman Rink is a powerful statue of Abraham Lincoln. Dating back to 1868, this is one of the oldest statues in the park. It depicts Lincoln holding the Emancipation Proclamation. He is flanked by two bronze eagles. The statue was commissioned by the War Fund Committee of Kings County, an organization that raised money to support the Union during the American Civil War. It was sculpted by Henry Kirke Brown, who also did the statue of George Washington on horseback in Manhattan's Union Square Park, as well as many prominent grave markers in Green-Wood Cemetery. Originally standing in Grand Army Plaza, the Lincoln monument was moved here in the 1890s. Lincoln must have had a lovely view of the lake before Moses blocked it.

The Lincoln statue stands at the entrance to the Concert Grove, the only formal section in the park. Busts of composers and writers, not part of the original park plan, were placed here in the late nineteenth century.

CONCERT GROVE SCULPTURE

There are five busts scattered throughout the Concert Grove. Three of them were donated by the German Singers of Brooklyn after they won the national saengerfest. These three are the 1897 bust of Wolfgang Amadeus Mozart, done by sculptor Augustus Meuller; Henry Baerer's bronze of Ludwig van Beethoven, from 1894; and the 1909 bust of German composer Carl Maria von Weber, done by Chester Beach. Note that the Mozart and Beethoven busts were donated to the **City** of Brooklyn while the von Weber bust was presented to the **Borough** of Brooklyn. This is yet another reminder of the consolidation of New York City that took place on January 1, 1898. (See chapter 1 for more on the union of New York and Brooklyn.)

The fourth sculpture is a bust of Irish poet Thomas Moore, from whose poem the park took the name for the Vale of Cashmere, which we will see later on our tour. Dedicated in 1871 to commemorate the 100th anniversary of his birth, it was presented to the City of Brooklyn by the St. Patrick Society.

The final bust is the least known. It is of the nineteenth-century Norwegian composer Edvard Grieg. Grieg was sculpted by his countryman Sigvald Absjornsen and was donated by the Norwegian Society in 1914. Brooklyn was home to the largest Norwegian community in New York City at that time.

There is a sixth bust standing just outside the grove. Just across East Drive is the 1871 Washington Irving memorial. Donated to the park by congressman Demas Barnes, it was sculpted by James Wilson Alexander MacDonald. MacDonald is also responsible for one of our favorite statues in Manhattan's Central Park, that of forgotten poet Fitz-Greene Halleck.

➤ **Continue behind Lincoln and into the formal Flower and Composers Garden. Walk through the grove to the Oriental Pavilion.**

The Oriental Pavilion, officially christened the Concert Grove Pavilion, was designed by Calvert Vaux in 1874. It is a wonderful Victorian structure, combining elements of English garden architecture with Moorish, Romanesque, Chinese, and Egyptian styles, which is why nineteenth-century observers called it "Oriental." The pavilion served as a covered listening area for concerts, although its acoustics were better across the water of the lake than on land, which led to the construction of the Music Pagoda further inland. Alas, the original pavilion was destroyed in 1974, when the 25-year-old snack bar (installed by none other than Robert Moses) burned it to an iron shell. After being fenced off for more than a decade, the pavilion was completely restored, without the snack bar.

➤ **Continue walking, with the pavilion on your right, toward the Cleft Ridge Span (bridge under roadway). Pass under the bridge into the Breeze Hill area.**

Prospect Park has had more than its share of economic hardships. As we have seen throughout the park, the fiscal crisis of the 1970s left many areas neglected and destroyed. Some 30 years later, there are still areas in Prospect Park awaiting revival. In fact, as this chapter is being written, the city is facing the worst economic conditions since that time. We can only hope that this fiscal crisis will be shorter and less devastating to our parks and our city.

The park ran into financial difficulties even before completion. In the early 1870s, as the depression of 1873 was looming ahead, the park commissioners began to run out of funds. Calvert Vaux, in building the Cleft Ridge Span, found a way to balance a shrinking budget with the maintenance of his high artistic standards.

Rather than build the bridge from hand-cut stone, Vaux employed the newly developed Beton Coignet cast concrete. This process, created by Frenchman François Coignet in the 1850s, used wooden molds to shape very detailed slabs. This is the first time the Coignet process, a forerunner of terra cotta, was used in the United States.

➤ **As you pass under the span, the path will fork; stay to the right. Immediately after the fork, take note of the odd tree surrounded by an iron fence to your immediate right.**

This odd-looking tree is the very rare Camperdown Elm (*Ulmus glabra camperdownii*). The tree hails from Camperdown House in Scotland. A genetic anomaly was discovered within a single Scotch elm in that it lacked the gene for negative geotropism, preventing it from "knowing" how to grow up instead of down. A series of cuttings were made from the original tree, and one was donated to Prospect Park in 1872. The cutting was grafted onto the trunk of a normal Scotch elm and, 130 years later, here is the result!

Like so much in Prospect Park, the Camperdown Elm was ignored and neglected. Brooklyn poet Marianne Moore, who had written a poem about the elm in 1967, helped rally neighbors to save the tree. The plan was a success. Closely examine the tree. You will notice the cables that hold the heavy branches together. Marianne Moore wrote one of her most famous poems, "The Camperdown

The 1905 Beaux-Arts boathouse, which has been newly renovated as the first urban Audubon Center in the nation. Photo courtesy of the Brooklyn Historical Society.

Elm," about this tree, which she called "our crowning curio." The poem begins,

> *I think, in connection with this weeping elm,*
> *of "Kindred Spirits" at the edge of a rockledge*
> *overlooking a stream.*

➤ **Continue past the elm to Audubon Center Boathouse.**

The Beaux-Arts boathouse was built in 1905 by the same firm that built the Tennis House—Helmle, Huberty & Hudswell—from a design that evokes the lower floor of Sansovino's Library of St. Mark in Venice. It replaced a wooden building that stood adjacent to the current site. The terra-cotta-faced building was extremely popular with parkgoers. The city had actually planned to destroy the boathouse in the 1960s, but Marianne Moore, as Jacqueline Kennedy Onassis did with Manhattan's Grand Central Terminal, led the charge to save this elegant site. As Jackie O's actions helped revitalize the Municipal Art Society, Moore's led to the creation of the Friends of Prospect Park.

After years of neglect and a blundered renovation, the restored boathouse opened in April 2002 as the first urban Audubon Center in the nation. Its two floors of exhibits highlight the importance of Prospect Park for the annual aviary migration. With more than 240 recorded species of birds sighted within the park, the Center houses numerous activities for those interested in bird watching and the environment. The boathouse also houses the park visitor center, a café, and restroom facilities. The Center is open Wednesday through Sunday and admission is free. For more information about activities, call (718) 287-3400.

➤ **Continue past the boathouse until the path you are on ends. Take a slight detour to the left, onto the wooden Binnen Bridge, which straddles Binnen Falls.**

As you continue to the far side of the boathouse, gaze across the Lullwater at Lullwater Bridge, the finest bridge in Prospect Park. The bridge was installed around 1905, replacing the original rustic stone and wooden one built by Olmsted and Vaux. Instead, Lullwater Bridge is cast iron and is reminiscent of the Bow Bridge in Central Park.

The Lullwater is a serpentine body of water that connects the flowing water of the ravine with the lake. In fact, as you step up onto the rustic wooden bridge that straddles the waterfall, if you gaze straight ahead, you will see the Music Pagoda and Nethermead in the near distance.

➤ **Turn back around and walk in the opposite direction. The path will travel under the East Wood Arch and to the carousel.**

Passing through the East Wood Arch, we are leaving the formal aspects of Prospect Park and moving back into more-rustic terrain. The arch was erected in 1867, one of the first designed by Vaux.

The carousel is a wonderful composite of two old Coney Island carousels built by Brooklynite Charles Carmel and restored in the 1980s by the Prospect Park Alliance. The carousel runs on weekends and holiday afternoons between April and October.

Directly behind the carousel is the Lefferts Homestead, the park's oldest structure. The original house was burned by the Pennsylvania riflemen during the Battle of Brooklyn in 1776, in an attempt to harass and distract the advancing British. The "new" house was built in 1777 by Peter Lefferts, a farmer of Dutch heritage. It was granted to the city and moved to the park from its location on Flatbush Avenue between Maple and Midwood streets after the last family member moved out in 1918. The homestead is used as a children's museum, focusing on Dutch, African, and Lenape Indian heritage and life in the early nineteenth century. The Lefferts Homestead is a member of New York City's Historic House Trust.

➤ Return to the main path and continue to your right. Walk with the main park drive (East Drive) on your left. You will soon approach the rear of the small Prospect Park Zoo.

Notice that as the path begins to ascend into the woods, the roadway cuts through a small valley. This was the Flatbush Pass, now known as Battle Pass. It was here that Continental General Sullivan commanded the center of the American line during the Battle of Brooklyn. The area around you was the center of fighting during this stage of the battle. The direction you are walking is roughly the same route taken by the British and Hessian troops.

Nineteenth-century lithograph of the Battle Pass site where General Sullivan commanded the center of the American line during the Battle of Brooklyn. Image courtesy of the Brooklyn Historical Society.

The monument, nestled in the trees to your right, with the bronze eagle atop the squared stone column marks the location of the Dongan oak, a large white oak tree that was the border marker between the villages of Brooklyn and Flatbush. The Continentals felled the oak across the pass to slow the advancing enemy.

➤ Follow the footpath up the hill. At the crest of the hill, below and to the left is Nellie's Lawn. Walk across the grass toward East Drive, keeping the trees and foliage to your close left. As you approach the road, look for the Battle Pass marker affixed to a large boulder.

This marker indicated the position and direction of the American defensive line. There is another marker across East Drive. It is virtually identical to the one before you. Should you choose to cross East Drive to have a closer look, please be careful.

➤ **Turn approximately 90 degrees to your right and walk the length of Nellie's Lawn to the run-down Vale of Cashmere.**

The Vale of Cashmere is an odd formal garden nestled into the woods. It was not part of the original design but was added in the late nineteenth century and is now heavily overgrown, with the fountain and water pools clearly in need of revitalization. The fountain was crafted by Frederick MacMonnies and includes a statue of a young naked boy holding a duck, surrounded by a half-dozen turtles spouting water. A curious statue indeed for the Victorian era, it clearly had its admirers, since it was stolen in 1941. The MacMonnies statue was popular enough that a replica can be viewed in Manhattan's Metropolitan Museum of Art.

Walk through the Vale of Cashmere, and on the far left side, take the footpath up the hill. The footpath will cross East Drive (with crosswalk/light) to the southern end of the Long Meadow. Continue along the path that skirts along the left side of the vale and climb the stairs on the far left side. Cross East Drive at the traffic light and continue to your right along the edge of the Long Meadow to Endale Arch. As you approach Endale Arch, have a look to your left and admire the double-entranced Meadowport Arch across the meadow.

➤ **Walk under Endale Arch.**

The banded-stone Endale Arch was originally called Enterdale Arch (as in "enter the dale") by Vaux and Olmsted, since it was a primary entry point for the Long Meadow. The view looking back through the arch into the Long Meadow is fantastic.

The Grand Army Plaza arch, a triumphal entrance to Prospect Park built to commemorate the victory of the Grand Army of the Republic in the Civil War. Photo, by Abraham Elfenbein, 1938, courtesy of the Brooklyn Historical Society.

➤ **Once through Endale Arch, bear to your left and walk toward the outskirts of the park at Grand Army Plaza.**

As you exit Prospect Park, immediately to your left is the 1891 Frederick MacMonnies–designed statue of the "father" of the park, James S. T. Stranahan. Stranahan (1808–1898) hailed from Peterboro, in northwestern New York State, and moved to Brooklyn in 1844. He became rich from his numerous business ventures and later served in the state assembly, ran unsuccessfully for mayor of Brooklyn, and was elected to the U.S. Congress in 1854. Between 1860 and 1882, as president of the Brooklyn park board, he oversaw the creation of the park we have just explored. Stranahan firmly understood the relationship of Brooklyn to its neighbor across the East River. He was a powerful promoter behind the Brooklyn Bridge and a vocal supporter of the 1898 consolidation of New York City. Like many great Brooklynites, Stranahan is buried in Green-Wood Cemetery (see our Green-Wood tour).

You are passing through the McKim, Mead & White–designed entrance to the park, with its giant pillars. Directly in front of you is Olmsted and Vaux's Grand Army Plaza. Originally a simple space with a small fountain, the plaza was graced by a giant triumphal arch called Soldiers' and Sailors' Monument in 1892, designed by John Duncan, who also did General Ulysses S. Grant's tomb in Manhattan. The arch, in turn, was topped four years later with the Frederick MacMonnies sculptures of Columbia, representing the United States, winged victory figures, and the Army Group and Navy Group figures. To come from the pastoral park in which nature was shaped by humans to the plaza in which nature was also shaped, but entirely differently, is a humbling experience.

➤ From here you can walk to the Grand Army Plaza stop on the 2 and 3 trains just a few blocks toward Manhattan on Flatbush Avenue.

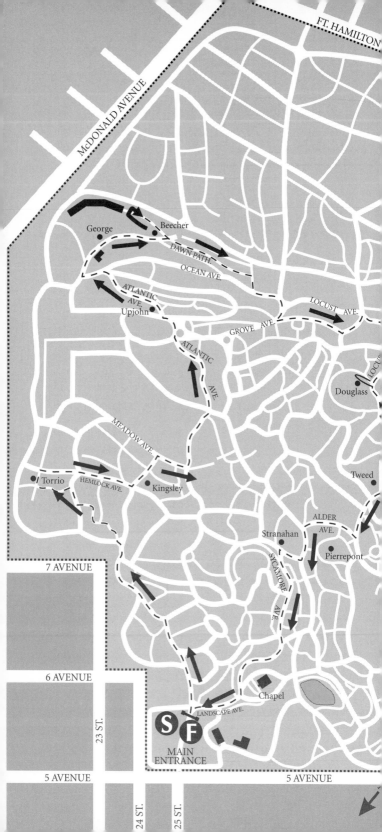

8 GREEN-WOOD CEMETERY

Brooklyn's Great Victorian Legacy

➤ **Start: Take the R train to the 25th Street station and exit at 4th Avenue. Walk one block to 5th Avenue to the entrance to Green-Wood. A word of caution: This is a very long walk that could take upward of three hours. Green-Wood Cemetery closes at 4:00 p.m. sharp. Please plan your visit accordingly.**

GREEN-WOOD CEMETERY is approximately 6 avenues deep and 17 blocks wide. It covers 478 acres, just 50 acres smaller than neighboring Prospect Park. Our walk explores the history, architecture, and people of this great urban treasure, with an emphasis on the many Brooklynites buried within. Not all the personalities on our tour are Brooklynites, but all directly or indirectly affected our city. Also, this tour is far from all-inclusive. Due to the vast size of the site, and the space constraints of this book, not everyone could be included. Green-Wood does maintain a computer database with all persons cross-referenced with location. Public access to the terminal can be found in an alcove at the entrance gates.

Green-Wood Cemetery was chartered in Brooklyn on April 18, 1838, only after being rejected by neighboring

Manhattan. Brooklynite Henry Evelyn Pierrepont (1808–1888) first proposed a sprawling garden cemetery to alleviate Manhattan's rapidly filling churchyard cemeteries. It was rejected primarily as a waste of valuable real estate on the small island of New York City. Pierrepont, who was at the time one of the city leaders charged with creating a street plan for the newly established, and rapidly expanding, City of Brooklyn, saw an opportunity to fulfill his dream. Green-Wood Cemetery is a crucial part of Pierrepont's vision of Brooklyn as the great European-style American city. He envisioned Brooklyn having wide avenues, splendid public plazas, and a grand garden cemetery.

Working with prominent Brooklyn families such as the Wyckoffs, Deans, Sacketts, Schermerhorns, and Bergens, Pierrepont secured the purchase of 200 acres, here, along the hills of Gowanus. Pierrepont then hired David Bates Douglass to design the cemetery. Douglass's story and his achievements are discussed later on our tour. The first burial took place on September 5, 1840. Although considered an aesthetic success from the beginning, many were unwilling to leave traditional church graveyards for a garden cemetery that was both distant and so very new in concept. Only 352 internments took place during the first three years. But in 1844 a dramatic change occurred: 354 persons were buried in that year alone, and lot sales reached $20,000. This tremendous increase was caused by three factors: First, the growing acceptance of nondenominational burial made Green-Wood's nonaffiliation with any church acceptable; second, an easing of the financial effect of the depression of 1837 gave people more disposable income; and third, the relocation of former senator, governor, and mayor DeWitt Clinton's casket from Albany to Green-Wood showed that the wealthy classes had accepted the place.

As a nineteenth-century garden cemetery, Green-Wood served many roles beyond a place of burial. The lush foliage, artistic grave markers, and scenic views were also designed for quiet contemplation. Image courtesy of Big Onion Walking Tours.

By 1855, just 15 years after the first interment, 45,576 persons had been buried here, and over 100,000 local people and tourists were visiting annually. Since that time, the cemetery has expanded to 478 acres by purchasing neighboring land. There are an estimated 600,000 people buried here today.

A GARDEN CEMETERY

What is a garden cemetery? The garden cemetery emerged from the English landscape garden movement of the early eighteenth century. Landscape gardeners altered and tamed the countryside to make it picturesque, so that it literally looked like a picture.

Victorian garden cemeteries were strongly supported by ministers and religious liberals, who argued that such cemeteries could be catalysts for civic virtue. Supporters urged the young to visit and take away life lessons from the biographies of famous or accomplished people buried there. At the same time, visitors would come to understand the shortness and unpredictability of life. They were to return home with a new resolve to work hard and to do good. The cemetery was as much a civic space as a place for burial. And, in some sense, when we visit a cemetery today, we are engaged in similar reflection on those whose lives we encounter.

Cemeteries in the Victorian age were also romantic. They served as a place to mourn, not just for a passed loved one but also for a lost rural ideal. America in the mid-nineteenth century was a nation undergoing tremendous change. Many older Americans longed for the days of their youth—a time before mass immigration, modern political parties, enormous urban centers, and technological advancements such as the railroad and telegraph. The garden cemetery allowed for the nostalgia of days gone by.

We start our tour at the dramatic Gothic Revival gates designed by renowned Brooklyn architect Richard Upjohn. These gates were built between 1861 and 1863, by which time Green-Wood was an established success and its trustees wished for an imposing entrance.

Gothic Revival architecture was one of the dominant styles of the Victorian era, an age of great romanticism. The period saw the construction of buildings that appealed to the imagination by stressing mystery, illusion, and nostalgia. Turning away from the rational and intellectual lines of Greek Revival, this new movement replaced the old geometry and balance with texture, color, and a complex and lively asymmetry. The Gothic Revival style reflects and celebrates the inherent irregularity of nature itself. This style was a perfect match for Green-Wood Cemetery and its vision of pastoral contemplation.

The entrance gates are a splendid example of Gothic Revival architecture. The center tower stands 106 feet tall and is flanked by two 90-foot-tall peaks. While the towers are symmetrical, they are counterbalanced by office wings that are constructed of differing shapes and sizes. The gates are made of red sandstone, from Belleville, New Jersey, which is the same building material Upjohn used for Trinity Church. Take special note of the tremendous array of details and architectural elements throughout the gates. They contain, among other things, steep and colorful slate roofs, stone trefoils and quatrefoils, cast-iron bannerets, a variety of columns, open gables, and detailed finials.

Embedded within the gates, above the entranceways, are four reliefs. Carved by John M. Moffitt in Nova Scotia yellow sandstone, they symbolize rebirth and resurrection. They are titled "Come Forth," "The Dead Shall Be Raised," "I Am the Resurrection and the Life," and "Weep Not." Higher up on the gates are smaller reliefs of Faith, Hope, Memory, and Love. In 1966 the Green-Wood Cemetery main gates were designated a New York City landmark.

There are public restrooms within the gates, on your left, behind the office.

➤ **Walk through the gates and take about 20 steps forward.**

The grave of Joseph Alfred Perry (1807–1881) is the first one you see upon entering Green-Wood Cemetery. Located directly in front of you, directly opposite the main gates, Perry can be credited with laying the foundation for Green-Wood's success. Related to founder Henry Pierrepont through marriage, Perry managed the cemetery for more than four decades, beginning in 1842. While maintaining the vision of Pierrepont and Douglass's garden cemetery, Perry oversaw the expansion from the original 175 acres to more than 450. He was also instrumental in having the body of DeWitt Clinton moved from Albany to his resting place in Green-Wood.

Walk to your left along Battle Avenue to Bay View Avenue. Bay View Avenue is the first intersection on the left side of Battle Avenue. On the far side of the intersection is a tall obelisk commemorating the Brooklyn Theatre Fire of 1876. This large monument was erected by the City of Brooklyn to memorialize the 278 people who lost their lives during the fire on December 5, 1876. Buried here are 103 of the victims.

Theater was a main source of entertainment for nineteenth-century America. One of the more prominent theaters, the Brooklyn, was located in downtown Brooklyn, at the intersection of Johnson and Washington streets. More than a thousand patrons had gathered on a Tuesday evening to watch the stage star Kate Claxton appear in the very popular *Two Orphans*.

As the play was ending at approximately 11:00 p.m., someone told Claxton that a kerosene lamp had ignited a small fire amid the scenery backstage. Since the actors were unsure what to do, Claxton supposedly whispered, "Go on, they will put it out, if we say anything there will be panic, go on." The fire could not be quashed, and it started to burn out of control. As the audience learned of the fire, Claxton tried to reassure the crowd, saying, "We are between you and the flames." Nonetheless, patrons fled in panic, clogging the few narrow exits. Within half an hour the roof of the building collapsed. In the end, 278 lives were lost.

Kate Claxton was found the next morning, dazed and burned, wandering in Manhattan, near City Hall. She claimed she could not recall how she crossed the river, and this was years before the Brooklyn Bridge was completed, so she likely crossed by ferry. She was thereafter known as "Kate Claxton of the Big Brooklyn Fire."

The City of Brooklyn arranged for a mass grave in Green-Wood for those families that could not afford burial

The Brooklyn Theatre in the aftermath of the 1876 fire that killed 278 people, 103 of whom are buried in a common grave in Green-Wood Cemetery. Photo courtesy of the Brooklyn Historical Society.

and for the unidentified bodies. Cemetery workers dug a 7-foot-deep crescent-shaped common grave, and 103 donated coffins were arranged with heads facing the center. Over 2,000 mourners attended, accompanied by song, speeches, and flowers.

➤ **Continue walking along Battle Avenue, up the hill and around the bend.**

On your left, at the intersection of Battle and the other end of Bay View Avenue, is a magnificent pyramid. While not erected in honor of a Brooklynite, this is a wonderful example of Green-Wood's vast array of artistic monuments. Albert Parsons (1847–1933) was a Christian by religion and an Egyptologist by profession. There are a number of pyramids in Green-Wood, but none as extravagant. The symbol above the entry is also common here; it is the sign of Osiris. However, the rest is unique. The entry is flanked by Mary, Joseph, and the baby Jesus. On the door is a fantastic set of zodiac symbols, and, of course, there is that great stone sphinx!

After a sharp curve to the right and a short but steep climb, Battle Avenue reaches a plateau at the intersection of Fern Avenue. Continue walking straight and climb the short set of stairs directly in front of you.

As you reach the top of the stairs, you are climbing the crest of the highest natural point in Brooklyn, Battle Hill. The granite column before you is called the Soldiers' Monument. Erected in 1869, just four years after the end of hostilities, it commemorates the New Yorkers who served the Union during the Civil War. The monument honors the 148,000 New York men who fought "in aid of the war for the preservation of the Union and the Constitution." It is curious that this monument, located in Brooklyn, remembers the men of New York, since New York at the time meant Manhattan. Although situated outside New York City, Green-Wood was considered an appropriate place for citywide monuments.

Take note of the grim and realistic reliefs that grace the column. They depict the pain and agony of warfare. Surrounding the monument are four life-size soldiers. Both the reliefs and the soldiers were rebuilt by the Green-Wood Historic Fund.

CITYWIDE MONUMENTS IN GREEN-WOOD CEMETERY

Green-Wood Cemetery was in a unique position during the nineteenth century, as it offered a nonsectarian setting that was both public and private space. Being separate from any particular religion, it enabled civic memorials to be built before they were really in vogue. We have already seen two large-scale monuments on our tour, the Brooklyn Theatre Fire memorial and now the Soldiers' Monument. There are numerous others throughout the cemetery, from both Brooklyn and New York.

Green-Wood has two different firemen's memorials. The first, built in 1848, remembers the volunteer fire fighters of New York City. It stands in the southwest section of the cemetery, off Orchard Avenue. It is a tall squared obelisk with a fireman holding a small child. The base is covered with fire-fighting symbols, including hydrants, hoses, hats, and the symbol of the City of New York. The second firemen's memorial stands on Border Road, not far from the Eastern Gate and along the eastern edge of Green-Wood. This one is for the Brooklyn Fire Department. The two departments became one with the consolidation of New York City in 1898. One of the stated goals for these two official firemen's memorials was to encourage firemen themselves to seek burial at Green-Wood. This plan had moderate success, since there are a number of individual firemen here.

Also located in Green-Wood are a series of monuments remembering individuals lost during tragedies. For example, one site commemorates two people lost when the S.S. **Lusitania** was sunk on May 7, 1915. The memorial reads, in part, "In memory of Allen Donnell and Loney and Catherine Wolfe Brown, his wife, who lost their lives on the S.S. **Lusitania** May 7, 1915. Their bodies were not recovered." There are also a number of memorial sites for people who died outside the Brooklyn area before modern transportation allowed bodies to be properly moved after death.

There are more than 70 individual victims of the September 11, 2001, World Trade Center tragedy buried in Green-Wood Cemetery. At this time, there is no large-scale or public monument planned.

➤ Walk around the Soldiers' Monument and look for a low white gravestone whose only inscription is "Grandmother." It is near granite cemetery marker No. 18495.

This is the grave of Elizabeth Tilton (1834–1897). Elizabeth had been married to Theodore Tilton and was a schoolteacher for the Reverend Henry Ward Beecher of Plymouth Church in Brooklyn Heights. She and Beecher had an affair that was exposed by Victoria Woodhull (see our Downtown Brooklyn and Brooklyn Heights tour for the complete story). Theodore sued Beecher for "alienation of affection," and the story became national news. Beecher was able to claim victory with a hung jury. But what happened to the Tilton family after the "Trial of the Century"? The family was torn apart. Theodore left the United States in 1883 and spent his life in Paris. Elizabeth was ostracized by everyone except her daughter and a few religious friends. She died alone and blind in 1897. Her marker simply reads "Grandmother" in an attempt to keep tourists from invading Elizabeth's final resting place.

➤ Continue walking along Battle Path toward the statue of Minerva, about 50 feet away.

Minerva and the Altar to Liberty was sculpted by F. Wellington Ruxell and unveiled in 1920. In Roman mythology, Minerva (known as Pallas Athena by the Greeks, who built the Parthenon in her honor) sprang fully formed from Zeus's head, clad in armor. She was the goddess of battle and protector of civilized life, the inventor of the bridle, and the one who first tamed horses for the use of humans. She also carried Zeus's thunderbolt for him. *Minerva* was unveiled on August 27, 1920, the 144th anniversary of the Battle of Long Island, which was fought on this spot in late August 1776.

Governor Alfred E. Smith at the dedication of **Minerva and the Altar to Liberty** in Green-Wood Cemetery in 1920. The statue commemorates the Battle of Brooklyn, which was fought on this spot, among others in Brooklyn, in late August 1776. Photo courtesy of the Brooklyn Historical Society.

This battle was the first for the Continental Army following the Declaration of Independence some seven weeks prior. During the engagement, 2,000 American troops under General William Stirling battled General James Grant's British force, which was three times larger. Much of the fighting occurred across the ridge where you are now standing—hence the name Battle Hill. It is said that atop this hill a group of American riflemen were surrounded, shot, and buried where they fell.

The Greek Revival tomb directly behind Minerva is that of Charles M. Higgins (1854–1929). A Park Slope,

Brooklyn, businessman, he was the inventor of India ink. It was Higgins's ambition to build a memorial to the first large battle for American freedom, and he led the movement to erect the statue of Minerva. As you look down the hill that you are now on, note that you are now at the highest natural point in Brooklyn, 216 feet above sea-level. If you stand directly in front of Minerva, you will also see that her left hand is raised in salute to the Statue of Liberty standing due west in New York harbor. The Statue of Liberty is waving to Paris. Brooklyn has the good fortune of standing in the way!

➤ **Facing the front of Minerva, continue along Battle Path, to your left, around the Higgins tomb. As you curve around, you are now behind the Litchfield plot, which is on your right.**

Edwin Clark Litchfield (1815–1885) was a prominent Brooklyn lawyer and businessman. Along with his brother, Electus, he developed Brooklyn's street railways and the Gowanus Canal and acquired a significant tract of land from the Cortelyou estate, which the Litchfield brothers developed into Park Slope. Litchfield also played a prominent role in the creation of Prospect Park. In fact, in 1892, after his death, the family estate was converted into the Parks Department building within the park. It has been renamed Litchfield Villa to honor its benefactor.

Litchfield had great vision. Many of his Brooklyn contemporaries were still looking to Manhattan as a place to make a fortune. Litchfield, in the tradition of the Pierreponts, turned his back on Manhattan, and he profited quite well as his home town became the third-largest city in America.

> ➤ Continue walking along Battle Path, which will curve to the left and end on Garland Avenue. As you step onto Garland Avenue, look slightly to your left and up the rise, to the rough-cut stone grave marker of Charles Ebbets.

Charles Ebbets (1859–1925) is the name most identified with baseball's Brooklyn Dodgers because of the stadium he built for them in Brooklyn in 1913. Ebbets joined the Dodgers staff in 1883 and held a number of positions. He sold scorecards, kept the books, clerked in the office, and was eventually promoted to the role of business manager. He became club president in 1898 and bought the team from owner Ned Hanlon in 1905. Ebbets is credited by some with inventing the rain check and with suggesting, long before there was a players draft, that teams with the worst records should draft first. In 1912, Ebbets announced he had purchased land in an area called Pigtown (in today's Bedford-Stuyvesant) to build a 30,000-seat steel and concrete stadium for his team. When the park was opened the next year, it was named "Ebbets Field" by a vote of sportswriters. Ebbets's Dodgers won pennants in 1916 and 1920.

Dodgers president Walter O'Malley moved the Dodgers to Los Angeles in 1957, and Ebbets Field was demolished in 1960 to be replaced by the Ebbets Field Houses and the Jackie Robinson Apartments. Columnists Pete Hamill and Jack Newfield spoke for many Brooklynites when they named the three most evil men of the twentieth century as "Hitler, Stalin, and Walter O'Malley."

> ➤ Turn to your right and walk along Garland Avenue to Canna Path, the first footpath on your left. Turn left onto Canna Path and walk up the hill to the simple gray granite grave marker that reads "Singstad Johansen."

This is the final resting place of civil engineer Ole Singstad (1882–1969). His name is fairly unknown, and his many projects are taken for granted every day by millions of New Yorkers. Singstad designed the Brooklyn Battery Tunnel, one of the longest continuous underwater tunnels in the world. Running 9,117 feet, construction started in 1940 and was finished in 1950, with a work stoppage of nearly five years because of World War II. Singstad also had a hand in building the Holland, Lincoln, and Queens-Midtown tunnels, as well as the mass-transit Hudson Tubes between Manhattan and Jersey City.

Singstad's neighbor to the right, by about 40 feet, is the amusement-park-ride inventor William Mangels. Mangels is not the most famous name currently associated with Coney Island, but his inventions can still be found in amusement parks. Mangels is credited with developing, in New Jersey, the first wave pool. At Coney he came up with the Whip and the Tickler, two rides that were immensely popular since they enabled men and women to bump against each other in a "semirespectable" setting.

There are numerous Coney Island legends buried in Green-Wood Cemetery. Some of the more famous include Charles Feltman, the inventor of the Coney Island Red Hot—better known as the hot dog; George C. Tilyou, creator and grand master of Steeplechase Park; and the political "Czar of Coney Island," John Y. McKane.

➤ Continue walking to the intersection of Canna Path and Canna Path. Yes, they have the same name. Turn right on Canna Path and walk to the end, which is the major road called Hemlock Avenue. As you step onto Hemlock, gaze to your left and notice the imposing granite mausoleum with the large angel standing on the very top.

This is "Little Johnny" Torrio or, as his colleagues called him, "Terrible Johnny." John Torrio was born in Italy in 1882 and came to America at the age of two. Raised in the Lower East Side, he became a prominent member of the Five Points Gangs and was boss of his own gang, the James Street Gang, which included one Alphonse Capone as a member. Torrio moved his outfit to Brooklyn in 1912 and ultimately ran the Chicago prostitution operations for his uncle, Big Jim Colosimo, whom he eventually deposed. Torrio tried to divide up Chicago's bootlegging business during Prohibition by dividing the city among a number of his rivals. This tense arrangement led to his attempted assassination on January 24, 1925. After his recovery, he passed leadership over to Capone, took his millions of ill-gotten dollars, and moved back to Brooklyn. He died of a heart attack in April 1957, while at his barber's.

➤ **Walk to your right along Hemlock Avenue. Turn left at the first major intersection onto Battle Path. Continue along Battle to the first right-side footpath, called Lake Path. At this intersection is a granite marker with a bronze plaque that reads "W. C. Kingsley."**

William Kingsley (1833–1885), a Brooklyn contractor, was one of the earliest proponents of building a bridge between Brooklyn and Manhattan. In 1865, at age 32, he employed engineer (and fellow Brooklynite) Colonel Julius Walker Adams to draw up a design with cost estimates for materials and labor. Adams estimated that the Brooklyn Bridge could have been built for approximately $5 million. This may have been so, if corrupt politicians had not gotten involved. In the end, the bridge cost $15 million.

Kingsley was active in Brooklyn politics and was a leader of the Democratic machine. His contracting company worked on several important public-works projects, including Prospect Park and the Hempstead Reservoir, but the Brooklyn Bridge project made him almost a million dollars alone, perhaps thanks to his association with Manhattan "Boss" William M. Tweed.

When the Tweed Ring was broken in 1873, it became known that Kingsley, a major stockholder in the Brooklyn Bridge Company and general superintendent of the building project, was being paid 15 percent of the total construction expenses, over $170,000 per year. According to the Bridge Company's records, this payment was made at Tweed's suggestion. Following the removal of Tweed, Kingsley's annual salary was renegotiated to a flat $10,000 per year. Without the salary change, Kingsley would have garnered some $1.755 million by the time the bridge was finished in 1883.

Kingsley's grave marker was cut from a granite stone taken from the Brooklyn Bridge itself. The bridge trustees placed it here to commemorate his role in making the Great Bridge a reality.

➤ **Remain on Battle Avenue until it ends at Meadow Avenue. Turn right on Meadow and continue a short distance until you get to Atlantic Avenue. Turn left onto Atlantic Avenue and walk to the next major avenue, Linden. Just before Linden Avenue, look to your left, set off a bit from the road, for a life-size statue of a boy, in uniform, holding a drum.**

This white-zinc statue of a Union army drummer boy memorializes Clarence Mackenzie (1848–1861), the first Brooklynite to die during the Civil War. Mackenzie was the 12-year-old drummer for Brooklyn's Thirteenth Regiment. He was killed in a "friendly fire" incident in 1861, while stationed in Annapolis, Maryland. Mackenzie is lo-

Ornate mausoleums and angels surrounding one of Green-Wood's many fountains. After Niagara Falls, Green-Wood was the second most popular tourist destination in nineteenth-century New York State. Image courtesy of Big Onion Walking Tours.

cated within the Soldiers' Lot area, a section donated by Green-Wood for Civil War soldiers and veterans.

➤ **Continue along Atlantic Avenue, past Linden, and walk through the intersection with Grove Avenue. This is a bit of a walk. The next major avenue will be Elm. On the far side of Elm and Atlantic is a columned marble structure that is both simple and elegant.**

This marble grave marker has lost much of its detail due to weathering. It is the resting place of architect Richard Michell Upjohn (1828–1903), son of the more prominent Richard Upjohn. Father and son lived at 296 Clinton Street in Cobble Hill, Brooklyn. Richard Upjohn designed many of the most beautiful churches in Brooklyn and Manhattan, including Trinity Church in Manhattan and Grace Church in Brooklyn Heights, as well as the A. A. Low mansion in the Heights. The two Upjohns worked together on the grand entry gates to Green-Wood Cemetery as well as on St. Paul's Church in Carroll Gardens, Brooklyn. Richard M. Upjohn is best known for his 1865–66 Christ Church in the Fieldston section of the Bronx.

➤ Continue walking along Atlantic Avenue until you come to a complex, four-way intersection. There will be two different forks to your right; turn to your left and walk toward the massive John Mackay mausoleum.

This landmark simply cannot be passed without a brief comment. Scotch-Irish immigrant John Mackay (1831–1902) arrived in America at the age of nine. He somehow moved to California and made a huge profit in the gold rush. By the age of 41, he held a controlling interest in the Comstock Lode, earning his company in excess of $150 million. He was a director of the Southern Pacific Railroad, oversaw the laying of communication cables between New York and Europe, and took on Jay Gould's Western Union land and telegraph monopoly. Mackay's massive tomb is unique. Not only is it bigger than many New York City apartments, it was built with electric light and heating.

➤ After leaving Mackay's tomb, continue along and make a right turn on Hillside Avenue. Walk past the Crestview mausoleum. As you approach the Hillside mausoleum, look to your left. Just about dead center of the mausoleum, halfway between the avenue and the building, is buried Henry George.

Henry George (1839–1897) struggled for the first half of his life in support of himself and his family. He established his political and economic legacy with the publication of his book *Progress and Poverty* in 1879. His critique of the emerging robber-baron capitalism and his proposed single-tax theory made his book the most influential economic treatise of the nineteenth century. After moving to New York City in 1880, he ran an unsuccessful independent campaign for mayor in 1886. He lost to the Tammany Democrat Abram S. Hewitt but received more votes than Republican Theodore Roosevelt. The election was one of the most heavily contested and closely watched mayoral races in the history of New York.

Henry George lived in two different Brooklyn locations. First at 70 Hancock Street in Clinton Hill, from the summer of 1883 until the spring of 1884; and then at 267 Macon Street in Bedford-Stuyvesant, between 1884 and 1886. We thus bestow upon Henry George the title of "Brooklynite."

➤ **Continue a short way along Hillside, looking to your right, up along the hill, for the grave of General Henry Warner Slocum.**

Slocum (1827–1894) was an 1852 graduate of the U.S. Military Academy at West Point. After serving four years, he resigned to practice law in Syracuse, New York, only to return to active duty in May 1861 to join the Union as a colonel of the 27th New York Infantry. Slocum was promoted to brigadier general of volunteers that August and then to major general the following summer. He fought in all the Virginia campaigns, from the first battle of Bull Run to Gettysburg. In 1863 he joined General Hooker's command in Tennessee and took part in the Battle of Chattanooga. He later commanded the Atlanta garrison and joined Sherman on his devastating "March to the Sea." General Slocum led the first Union troops into the city of Atlanta.

Following the war, Slocum moved to 465 Clinton Avenue in Brooklyn, where he resumed his law practice. He was a Democratic representative in Congress for three terms, and he served as president of the Brooklyn Board of Public Works and as a trustee of the Brooklyn Bridge. Slocum died on April 14, 1894, from heart failure following pneumonia. His funeral took place on April 17 and was regarded as a citywide day of mourning.

The name Henry Slocum is, unfortunately, associated with the steamer that was launched in his honor in 1891. The excursion vessel *General Slocum* burned and sank in the East River on June 15, 1904, killing at least 1,021 of its 1,331 passengers.

➤ **Continue walking along Hillside Avenue until you come to Dawn Path. Take a short detour, to the left, along Dawn Path. About 15 feet in, look to your left back up at Hillside Avenue above you for the large granite tombstone of Reverend Henry Ward Beecher.**

Henry Ward Beecher (1813–1887) was the best-known member of one of America's most powerful nineteenth-century families. The Beecher power came from their literary and religious pursuits rather than from the more traditional financial means. He was pastor at the influential Plymouth Congregationalist Church in Brooklyn Heights (see our Downtown Brooklyn and Brooklyn Heights chapter for more) and was brother to both writer Harriet Beecher Stowe (*Uncle Tom's Cabin*) and educational reformer/writer Catherine Beecher.

The Reverend Beecher had an affair with Elizabeth Tilton, whose grave we visited earlier, and was charged with adultery by her husband, Theodore, in 1874. Beecher was able to claim victory through a hung jury trial, but the lingering specter of impropriety diminished his influence. There is more than a touch of irony in that his tomb reads, in part, "He Thinketh No Evil."

Buried to the right of Beecher, under the large stone cross, is Benjamin Franklin Tracy (1830–1915). Tracy was awarded the Congressional Medal of Honor for his heroic actions during the Civil War Battle at the Wilderness. Following the war, he was U.S. District Attorney for the eastern district of New York and then, in 1881, served as defense counsel for Reverend Beecher during the adultery suit brought against him by Theodore Tilton. Tracy was President Benjamin Harrison's Secretary of the Navy between 1889 and 1893. He was also the chairman of the 1898 Consolidation Commission, which laid the groundwork for the cities of Brooklyn and New York to merge.

➤ **Turn back around and return the way you came. Remain on Dawn Path, crossing Hillside Avenue, for a long walk until it ends at Hill Path. Take a right onto Hill Path and walk a short distance to Cypress Avenue. Turn left onto Cypress and walk to the next major intersection. Five different avenues come together here, and there is a small grass circle in the middle of the roundabout. Walk to the far left side of the intersection and take a left onto Grove Avenue. Walk past the Catacombs and to where Oakwood comes from the right side and intersects Grove. Look to your left for the granite obelisk that reads "Webb."**

Eckford Webb (1825–1893) introduced shipbuilding to Greenpoint, Brooklyn, in 1850. His firm, Webb & Bell, built numerous schooners and other vessels, and shipbuilding quickly became the core industry for the neighborhood. The front of Webb's granite obelisk is adorned with a steamship in drydock. Stroll around to the back to view the memorial of his crowning achievement, building the caissons for the Brooklyn Bridge.

An engineering marvel, the caissons were massive wood and steel boxes that were sunk into the East River and that allowed workers to dig down to the bedrock that was deemed necessary to support the bridge's towers. The smaller caisson, the Brooklyn one, was 168 by 102 feet and used 111,000 cubic feet of lumber. It had a roof that was 20 feet thick and walls that were 8 feet thick at the top and sloped down to 2 inches thick with a steel cutting edge along the bottom.

➤ **Continue walking along Grove Avenue, which will gently merge (turning left) with Grape Avenue. Take your first right, onto Locust Avenue. A few yards past Euonymus Path, on your left, can be found actress Kate Claxton.**

Kate Claxton (1848–1924) was born Kate Cone in Somerville, New Jersey. She was first noticed as an actress when she appeared with the superstar showgirl Lotta Crabtree in Chicago in 1869. Claxton herself became a star with her appearance in the 1873 production of *Led Astray*. Following the 1876 Brooklyn Theatre Fire, discussed earlier on this tour, Claxton began her own acting company and attempted to establish herself as a theater manager. She split her time between New York and traveling shows. Her popularity continued for many years, but it is unclear if audiences came to see her talent or to see the woman from the deadly fire. She was so famous that Claxton, Georgia, the "Fruitcake Capital of the World," was named in her honor when it was incorporated in 1911.

➤ **Follow Locust Avenue to the next major intersection. Turn right and continue walking along Locust, where you**

will quickly come to Southwood Avenue. Take a little detour to your right to the monument to David Bates Douglass.

David Bates Douglass (1790–1849) was hired to transform this grazing pasture into a cemetery. Douglass had served in the War of 1812 and had been a professor of mathematics and engineering at the U.S. Military Academy. Before working on Green-Wood, he had also been the chief engineer for the Croton Aqueduct System. Among other things, he designed the High Bridge, which remains the oldest bridge still standing in New York City, to transport Croton's water across the Harlem River to Manhattan.

One of Douglass's first tasks at Green-Wood was to lay out 4.5 miles of road that followed the contours of the terrain and demonstrated the beauty of the site. This route became known as "The Tour," and it was designed and used not only to display Green-Wood's charms but also to serve as an incentive for potential lot buyers. One unexpected side effect of "The Tour" was that Green-Wood quickly became a major recreational and tourist destination for New Yorkers, who had access to almost no public parkland at all.

Under Douglass's direction, Green-Wood was carefully and artistically designed to reveal every natural feature in its most advantageous light. Trees and shrubs were planted as screens and foils in the proper locations to provide just the right feeling and mood. Roads and paths followed land contours whenever possible and wound around lakes and ponds. Douglass even had songbirds imported from Europe to assist with the ambiance.

Following his work at Green-Wood, Douglass designed garden cemeteries in Quebec, Canada, and in Albany, New York. He also served as the president of Kenyon College in Gambier, Ohio.

➤ Returning to Locust, keep walking past all the small
paths until you, once again, come to Southwood, only
this time on your left. Just past Southwood, on the right-
hand side, is William M. Tweed and family.

There are two common assumptions about William Tweed:
first, that his middle name was Marcy and, second, that
he was Irish. In truth, while his middle initial is M, it
is thought to have stood for his mother's maiden name,
Magear. And, although Tweed was born on Cherry Street
in Manhattan in 1823, he was of Scotch-Irish descent.

William Tweed was a classic Horatio Alger story, but
without a sense of morality. He left school at age 11 and
began working what turned into a series of jobs, ultimately
ending up as a partner in a brush concern. He joined state
assemblyman John J. Reilly in founding the Americus Engine Company Number 6, a volunteer fire brigade, in 1848.
Tweed served a single term in the U.S. House of Representatives in 1852 but realized that the money to be made
was in New York City politics. He quickly rose to sit on
the executive committee of Tammany Hall in 1858. He became "Boss" after being named Grand Sachem of Tammany in April 1863. Tweed was a brilliant politician and a
master at skimming large sums of money off city projects
for his personal use. By 1870 he had amassed a fortune of
more than $12 million and was the third-largest landowner
in Manhattan.

While he is best known for the vast corrupt empire,
Tweed was also responsible for building hospitals and or-
phanages and widening Broadway along the Upper West
Side. And he was also able to secure land within the new
Central Park for the Metropolitan Museum of Art. Of
course, these "good works" certainly do not negate the
$200-plus million he and the "Tweed Ring" stole from the

William M. Tweed (1823-1878), better known as "Boss Tweed," led Tammany Hall, the corrupt Democratic machine whose elected officials plundered the city treasury in the nineteenth century. Image courtesy of the Brooklyn Historical Society.

city, nor the fact that the city deficit went from $36 million in 1868 to more than $130 million by 1870.

Tweed was eventually arrested for his thefts and held for trial. While on prison leave to visit his family in December 1874, he escaped to New Jersey and just kept going. Traveling to Florida and then Spain, he had the misfortune to encounter a Spanish customs officer familiar, thanks to a Thomas Nast drawing, with Tweed's appearance. Tweed was arrested and returned to New York. He died in the Ludlow Street Jail, just a few blocks from his childhood home, on April 12, 1878.

POLITICIANS IN GREEN-WOOD

Green-Wood Cemetery has its fair share of local and national politicians buried within its gates. Most of them are not nearly as famous, or infamous, as William M. Tweed.

On the national level, Missouri senator John Henderson (1826–1913) is buried in the Foote family mausoleum. Henderson sponsored the Thirteenth Amendment, which abolished slavery. The amendment was passed, but it ended Henderson's career, as his home state did not share his sentiment. He is buried with his wife's family. Ironically, he is buried next to the Bowery B'hoy Bill "the Butcher" Poole (1823–1855). Poole, an anti-immigrant, anti-black leader of the Nativist movement, died with "Good-Bye boys. I die a true American" on his lips as his supposed last words. Poole was the model for Daniel Day Lewis's character, Bill Cutting, in Martin Scorsese's 2003 film **Gangs of New York.** A political kindred spirit of Poole's, the states' rights senator from Alabama Dixon Hall Lewis (1802–1848), is also buried here. Lewis was deeply opposed to a strong federal government and advocated Southern secession from the Union before the Civil War.

Ten-term mayor of New York City, senator, and "Father of the Erie Canal" DeWitt Clinton (1769–1828) was reinterred in Green-Wood after 16 years in Albany. During his terms as mayor, he oversaw the creation of the New-York Historical Society, the Orphan Asylum, the improvement of sanitation, the adoption of the 1811 Manhattan street-grid system, and the fortification of the New York harbor defenses in preparation of the feared British invasion during the War of 1812. Clinton ran for president in 1812, losing to James Madison by the slim margin of 30 electoral votes. Clinton also served as a three-term governor of New York State. Having Clinton's body brought down from Albany was a major coup for

Green-Wood. It helped encourage other prominent families to seek plots out here in what was seen as the wilds of Brooklyn.

Another prominent family to bring its ancestors to Green-Wood was the Livingstons. William Livingston (1723-1790) and his son, Brockholst (1757-1823), were brought here in 1844 from Manhattan. William Livingston was a two-term governor of New Jersey and signed the Declaration of Independence. Brockholst was a Supreme Court justice.

Mayor William Gaynor (1849-1913) can also be found in Green-Wood. A resident of Park Slope (see our Park Slope tour for more), Gaynor walked to Manhattan from City Hall on a daily basis during his term in office (1909-1913). Gaynor was a tremendous supporter of the 1898 Consolidation Plan. He survived an assassination attempt in 1910 and died while running for his second term. Brooklyn mayor Charles A. Schieren (1842-1915) is also buried here.

The only person to serve as mayor of both Brooklyn and New York City, Seth Low (1850-1916), is buried in Green-Wood as well. Son of the wealthy Brooklyn Heights merchant A. A. Low, Seth served as a two-term reform Republican mayor of Brooklyn from 1881 to 1885. He then served as president of Columbia College beginning in 1890 and oversaw the campus move to its current location in Morningside Heights. He helped draft the terms of consolidation for New York City and served as a one-term mayor of all five boroughs from 1901 to 1903. Seth Low was also a trustee for the Brooklyn Bridge.

Turning around 180 degrees from Tweed, take note of the massive Steinway mausoleum on top of the hill. Henry Steinway brought his family piano business to New York from Germany in the 1850s. His son, William, established the company town of Steinway, Long Island, for the mass manufacture of the instruments. Erected in the 1870s to hold up to 200 people, the mausoleum was meant to be used by many generations of Steinways. It is the largest mausoleum in Green-Wood, but it currently holds fewer than 70 people.

➤ **Continue along Locust to the next major intersection. Veer to the right-most avenue and continue for a short distance on Vista. Turn right onto Adler Avenue and then left, downhill, onto Central Avenue.**

You have essentially walked around a squat hill. At the peak is an elaborate Gothic Revival tomb designed by Richard Upjohn for none other than Henry Pierrepont.

As noted at the beginning of this walk, Pierrepont (1808–1888) was the person primarily responsible for the creation of Green-Wood Cemetery. The second son of Hezekiah B. Pierrepont, Henry Pierrepont was a city planner and businessman, in addition to managing his family's properties. He also worked to establish ferry connections across and up and down the East River. He is regarded as one of the first city planners in the United States, having been active in planning the expansion of Brooklyn following its 1834 incorporation. One year later, Pierrepont was appointed chair of a commission to lay out the streets of the new city. He donated the original fence that surrounded Green-Wood and, in 1842, purchased eight plots for himself and his family. His monument stands atop one of the few man-made hills in Green-Wood. At the time of his death, Henry Pierrepont was the last survivor of the original trustees who created the cemetery.

Henry's father, Hezekiah (1768–1838), moved to Brooklyn in 1802, after building his fortune as a merchant adventurer. Upon arrival, he bought some 60 acres in Brooklyn Heights. He was the first important suburban real-estate developer in America. As early as 1823, he was advertising and selling Brooklyn Heights lots to wealthy

Manhattanites. In that year, he advertised in the *Long Island Star*:

> Situated directly opposite the southwest part of the city [Manhattan], and being the nearest country retreat, and easiest of access from the center of business that now remains unoccupied; the distance not exceeding on an average fifteen to twenty-five minutes walk, including the passage of the river; the ground is elevated and perfectly healthy at all seasons; views of the water and landscape both extensive and beautiful; as a place of residence combining all the advantages of the country with most of the conveniences of the city.

➤ **Leaving Pierrepont, take the right turn onto Sycamore and walk up to the next intersection. Standing on the slight hillock to your right is the monument for James Stranahan.**

James S. T. Stranahan (1808–1898), like many Brooklynites, adopted the city as home in adulthood. Raised in northwestern New York State, Stranahan came to Brooklyn in 1844 to earn his fortune. Stranahan served in the state assembly and the U.S. House of Representatives. His legacy, though, comes primarily from his tenure as president of the Brooklyn Park Board, when he oversaw the creation of Prospect Park. Stranahan understood that the continued success of Brooklyn was dependent on its strong ties with Manhattan. To further those ties, he was one of Brooklyn's most vocal supporters of the Brooklyn Bridge and the 1898 consolidation of New York City.

Continue walking to your left, along Sycamore Avenue. This is one of the oldest and, in our opinion, prettiest parts of Green-Wood. Sycamore goes all the way down the hill, passing Bayside first on the right and then on the left. Sycamore Avenue then jogs right. Just past the second

Bayside and the right-leaning bend, look carefully for Gamaliel King.

Gamaliel King (1795–1875) is listed in the Brooklyn city directory as a grocer until the year 1830, and then he is listed as a carpenter. King was the architect of the 1845 Greek Revival Brooklyn City Hall, now known as Borough Hall. The building can be seen on our downtown Brooklyn tour. It is, with the exception of the cupola that was changed from wood to iron in the 1890s, the same as it was 150 years ago.

➤ **Continue along Sycamore and gaze down on the chapel.**

The firm of Warren & Wetmore—best known for designing Manhattan's Grand Central Terminal, completed in 1913—was chosen to build the chapel in 1912. It is a scaled-down version of Christopher Wren's Thomas Tower at Christ Church, Oxford. After many decades of being closed, the chapel was reopened by Green-Wood Cemetery in April 2000. It is used primarily for individual contemplation but can be reserved for services. If there is no service being held at the time of your visit, please feel free to enter.

The chapel is a wonderful place to sit and contemplate Green-Wood's extensive history, beautiful foliage, and marvelous architecture. One of the grandest and oldest garden cemeteries in America, Green-Wood is a true gem in the heart of Brooklyn.

➤ **Continue around to your right, back to the exit.**

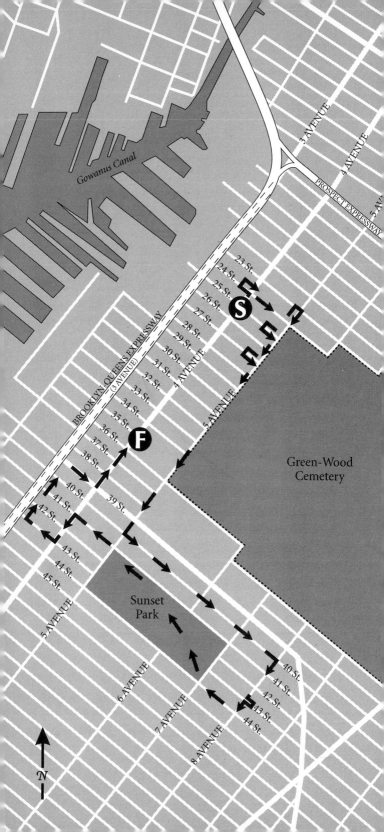

9 SUNSET PARK

"How Sweet It Is!"

➤ Start: The 25th Street M and R stop on 25th Street and 4th Avenue.

SUNSET PARK is a multiethnic residential and industrial neighborhood. From where you stand, facing east up the 25th Street hill from the subway exit, some of the neighborhood's borders are evident. To your right, you may be able to make out the red-brick apartment building that marks the southern border at 65th Street, taller than anything in the area. Behind you, the neighborhood slopes down to Upper New York Bay. To the left, it's only a few blocks to the Prospect Expressway at 17th Street. And, finally, five blocks in front of you is the eastern border at 9th Avenue. Because of its fertile farmland and the waterfront, affording easy trade with the Dutch village of New Amsterdam across the river, this land was one of the first parts of Brooklyn to be settled by Europeans, who carved out narrow farms stretching back from the river.

In 1636 William Adrianse Bennet and Jacques Bentyn made the first land purchases in Kings County (Brooklyn) when they bought 930 acres along the Sunset Park shore. Beginning in the 1640s, more Dutch settlers obtained portions of Sunset Park from the Canarsee Indian village of

Gowanus and began farming along the waterfront. The area remained rural until the mid-1800s.

The area grew rapidly in the late nineteenth century with the establishment of the Brooklyn waterfront as a major port. From the turn of the twentieth century through the 1960s, ships berthed at the piers on Sunset Park's shoreline. Indeed, the development of the neighborhood was closely linked with Bush Terminal, a complex of piers, warehouses, and factory lofts built by Irving Bush in 1890 along the Sunset Park shore, and the Brooklyn Army Terminal, built in 1919 further south in the borough. To meet the cargo-handling demands of these ships, thousands of longshoremen worked on the docks loading and unloading goods. With a steady demand for labor to work in its piers, the neighborhood became a home for many newly arrived immigrants.

Up until the mid-1960s, the northern section of the community was called "Gowanus" or "South Brooklyn." The southern section was part of Bay Ridge. In 1965 the area began to be called "Sunset Park" after the 24.5-acre park, built in the 1890s, that overlooked the neighborhood. Within the neighborhood lies the Sunset Park historic district, with over 3,200 buildings, one of the largest historic districts in New York City. Almost all the neighborhood's residential construction occurred in the late nineteenth and early twentieth centuries. The housing is a mixture of old- and new-law tenements on the avenues with frame and masonry one-, two-, and three-family homes, and limestone and brownstone houses on the side streets.

Sunset Park is a microcosm of the many immigration waves that have transformed the City of New York. After the Dutch settled the area, the first large wave of immigrants to arrive in Sunset Park came from Ireland. Fleeing Ireland's potato famine in the 1840s, many of the Irish who settled in New York City made their homes in the

A 1930s aerial view of Sunset Park, including Bush Terminal and its piers. Photo courtesy of the Brooklyn Historical Society.

northern part of Sunset Park. By 1855, one-third of the area's population was Irish. While a minority of the Irish immigrant men worked as firemen, policemen, sanitation workers, tavern owners, real-estate agents, and landlords, the majority worked as farm laborers, on the docks, and on construction crews. For women, the number-one employment opportunity in the early years was as domestic servants.

Starting in the late 1800s, following the Irish, a Scandinavian community, mostly from Finland and Norway, grew in Sunset Park, followed by Polish immigrants, who settled near 3rd Avenue and 20th Street, and Italians, who moved into the neighborhood beginning around 1900. Puerto Ricans had made their homes in New York City since the early 1900s, but it was not until after World War II, when flights began to operate between San Juan and New York City, that large numbers of Puerto Ricans arrived in Sunset Park. Since the 1980s, about half the immigrants to this neighborhood have come from China, Mexico, and the Dominican Republic. Others have arrived from countries in the Middle East, Latin America, Asia, and the Indian subcontinent.

➤ **Walk one block to 24th Street and turn left to stop at Our Lady of Czenstochowa Church.**

The area between 20th and 24th streets and 3rd and 4th avenues was the heart of Polish Sunset Park. In the 1870s and 1880s, a few Roman Catholic families from Poland began to make their home in Sunset Park near 3rd Avenue and 20th Street. By 1890 a largely Catholic Polish community, complete with a church, social clubs, and other cultural organizations, was thriving in Sunset Park.

Right Reverend Boleslaus Puchalski and other Polish immigrants established Our Lady of Czenstochowa in 1897. The church has a unique and detailed hand-carved altar brought from Poland over 100 years ago by the church's first pastor. As the congregation grew, the church built a rectory, a school, and a convent between 24th and 25th streets and 3rd and 4th avenues. In 1898 the parish of Our Lady of Czenstochowa, along with two other Polish congregations, St. Casimir's and St. Stanislaus Kostka, organized more than 300 volunteers for the Spanish-American War. If you enter the church, you can see a plaque memorializing parishioners killed during World War I; but for a single man, they all have Polish surnames.

➤ **Turn around and take 24th Street one and a half blocks to 5th Avenue, and then turn left for one block to reach White Eagle Hall.**

While Our Lady of Czenstochowa was the religious pillar of the Polish community in the early to mid-twentieth century, White Eagle Hall was its secular pillar. White Eagle was built by members of the Polish community in the early

1890s and was the center of Polish social life. Adults and children would meet here to study and play, promote the culture of the old country, and foster a Polish American identity. The building contained meeting rooms, a bar, and a dance floor where political, dancing, and singing societies like the National Polish Alliance, the American-Polish High-Hatters, and the Jurtzrenka Singing Society met and performed.

Perhaps the most influential organization that met in White Eagle Hall was the "Sokols" or Polish Falcons. The Polish Falcons was an athletic club that sponsored track and field, basketball, and baseball leagues, folk-dancing classes, and other forms of physical training. But athletics were part of a larger social project. As Ralph Foster Weld suggests in *Brooklyn Is America*, the "Falcons had other goals than the development of good physiques. In training the young in the right and wise use of their bodies they did not neglect the larger aim of good American citizenship."

➤ **Turn around and walk two blocks to 25th Street and 5th Avenue and the entrance to Green-Wood Cemetery.**

Green-Wood Cemetery is one of the largest expanses of undeveloped land in the entire borough of Brooklyn. For more information on the cemetery, please see the Green-Wood Cemetery chapter in this book and "Green-Wood Cemetery: A Garden Cemetery Revisited," in Seth Kamil and Eric Wakin's *Big Onion Guide to New York City* (New York University Press, 2002).

➤ **Turn right and go down 25th Street for less than half a block.**

On your left is Century Memorials (although the sign still reads "Brooklyn Monument Company"), which began in

1854 as two competing memorial companies founded by two Scottish-immigrant brothers, J. R. Pitbladdo and Thomas Pitbladdo. For most of the next century, the two brother created memorials for such Green-Wood notables as Peter Cooper, founder of Cooper Union University; Horace Greeley, publisher of the *New York Tribune*; and Nathaniel Currier of Currier & Ives. In 1929 Finnish-immigrant stonecutter John Hakola and his son Wayne merged the two firms into the Brooklyn Monument Company. Now called Century Memorials, the company has created memorials throughout the country, including in St. John's Church—the Church of the Generals—in Fort Hamilton, Brooklyn; a memorial for Washington Roebling, the chief engineer of the Brooklyn Bridge, on the Supreme Court Grounds at Cadman Plaza (see our Downtown Brooklyn and Brooklyn Heights chapter); and a menorah on the interior stone wall of the Community Synagogue in Port Washington, Long Island.

➤ **Turn around and walk back to 5th Avenue and turn right. Walk two blocks to 27th Street and turn right. Walk for half a block to reach St. Rocco's Church at 216 27th Street.**

As you walk along 5th Avenue with Green-Wood to your left, note the structures that make up Sunset Park. Along 5th, you'll see a mixture of warehouses and light industry, small frame houses, and some brick homes as well. As you progress further into the neighborhood later in the tour, you'll see more brownstone and limestone homes.

In 1880 fewer than 20,000 Italians lived in New York City. Twenty years later there were 220,000, and by 1930 almost 1.1 million New Yorkers were either Italian or had Italian parentage. Italians gravitated to the Lower East Side of Manhattan because their homes there were within walking distance of their jobs. In Brooklyn, Italians, especially many southern Italians and Sicilians, settled between 15th and 39th streets in Sunset Park between 1890 and 1910. The majority were single men recruited in Italy by labor bosses for construction projects in the United States, and they arrived to work as laborers, bricklayers, or masons. Between 1910 and 1915, many Italian working crews dug the tunnel for the 4th Avenue subway line, known then as the BMT and now as the M, N, R, and D lines.

Italians who settled in Sunset Park created St. Rocco's Church. Prior to 1902, most Italians attended St. Michael the Archangel Church on 42nd Street and 4th Avenue or St. John the Evangelist Church on 21st Street and 6th Avenue. In 1902 the congregation that would found St. Rocco's began worshiping in a former synagogue on 22nd Street, and a few years later Reverend Alessio de Donatis arrived in the area to organize St. Rocco's Church as a parish to serve the religious needs of the area's Italian Roman Catholic population. In 1911 the diocese purchased the Trinity Lutheran Church on 27th Street between 4th and 5th avenues and created St. Rocco's. By 1923 St. Rocco's had 15,000 members. By the 1960s, the parish could no longer claim to be predominantly Italian, as most of the older Italian and Italian American congregants had died or moved out of the neighborhood. But the religious foundation that Italian immigrants created is today continued by Spanish-speaking immigrants and Hispanic Americans. Mass is celebrated in both English and Spanish, and in 2002 the congregation of St. Rocco's celebrated its 100th anniversary.

ST. ROCCO

In November 1977, Archbishop Vittoria Ugo Righi gave Father George Ebejer of St. Rocco's Church a relic of St. Rocco, which is on view in the vestry of the church. Who was the historical Rocco?

Rocco, the son of a French governor and Italian mother was born in Montpellier, France, in 1350. In 1367, after Pope Urban V visited Montpellier, the young Rocco decided to make a pilgrimage to Rome, where he cared for those suffering from the plague, including the Pope's brother. In 1371 he traveled around Italy, only to fall ill in Piacenza, where he remained for some time. When he was alone and sick, it is said that a stray dog often took loaves of bread from a bakery and gave them to Rocco.

Returning to Montpellier in the late 1370s, Rocco was accused of spying and was subsequently arrested and imprisoned. Upon his death in prison, Rocco was identified as the son of a former governor by a cross-shaped birthmark on his chest.

Rocco's remains were taken to Venice in 1485. In 1629 he was beatified, and his followers created the Third Secular Order of St. Dominic. Rocco is held in especially high regard due to his work with plague victims, and he is known as the saint who wards off pestilence and plague. Today, worshipers invoke his name to assist them in fighting HIV-AIDS.

➤ Continue walking along 5th Avenue to the corner of 36th Street.

The Jackie Gleason Bus Depot—named after Brooklyn resident and "Honeymooner" Jackie Gleason—begins on 36th Street. In the late nineteenth century, the building on this spot was called Union Depot. From the early twentieth century until 1940, when the New York City Board of Transportation purchased the site, the depot was used as an elevated-car inspection shop. In 1944 the depot was renamed the Fifth Avenue Bus Depot and began operating as a bus garage. The current structure, which is over 260,000 square feet, was completed in 1986 and was the first depot

The Jackie Gleason Bus Depot is named after Brooklyn resident Jackie Gleason, who played Ralph Kramden, a bus driver from Bensonhurst, Brooklyn, in **The Honeymooners.** This 1955 publicity photo shows, left to right, Gleason, Audrey Meadows, Art Carney, and Joyce Randolph. Image courtesy of the Brooklyn Historical Society.

in New York City to be fully equipped to operate compressed-natural-gas buses (the same natural gas used in stoves), which produce less pollution than diesel and gas buses. As of publication, New York City Transit operates almost 100 compressed-natural-gas buses from the Jackie Gleason Bus Depot, which employs over 800 people.

JACKIE GLEASON

Jackie Gleason was born in Brooklyn, New York, in 1916 and died in 1987. He had his film debut in 1941 as Tubby, a sailor, in **Navy Blues.** In the 1960s he was acclaimed for his roles as Minnesota Fats, a pool shark, in **The Hustler** (1961), and as a mute, ragged Parisian who communicates with his neighbors in pantomime, in **Gigot** (1962). But Gleason is best known for his role as Ralph Kramden, a bus driver from Bensonhurst, Brooklyn, in **The Honeymooners,** a black-and-white television comedy that aired from 1955 to 1971 on CBS and went into syndication in 1984.

This bus depot was named after Gleason in 1988 because his character, Ralph Kramden, epitomizes the hopes, dreams, and work ethic of New York City's transportation workers. If you look closely at the sign on the southeast corner of the depot, you'll notice a striking resemblance to the New York City skyline that opened every episode of **The Honeymooners**.

> Walk alongside the Jackie Gleason Bus Depot to 40th Street and 5th Avenue.

This stretch of 5th Avenue is an excellent example of the ethnic and economic transformation of Sunset Park. The nineteenth-century economic base created by the Irish, Germans, Italians, Poles, and Scandinavians began to falter after World War II. During the war, work on the piers increased, as Brooklyn became a primary center for exporting supplies to American soldiers and our allies in Europe. After the war, however, a combination of factors led to economic decline in Sunset Park. Jobs on the piers decreased, due to the introduction of containerized shipping, which allowed goods to be taken off ships and loaded directly onto trucks. Also, families moved from Sunset Park to quieter pastures in the suburbs, and companies left the neighborhood for cheaper labor and more space outside New York City.

The economic decline of Sunset Park coincided with postwar immigration of Puerto Ricans to the city. According to 1950 census data, only 1,800 Puerto Ricans lived in Sunset Park (about 1.6 percent of the neighborhood's population), many living in deteriorating tenements under the Gowanus Expressway that other immigrants had fled because of Robert Moses's highway-building destruction. By 1970, almost 24,000 Puerto Ricans were living in Sunset

Park, making up 25 percent of the population and working along the waterfront, in restaurants, and in the garment industry.

The Puerto Ricans' arrival led real-estate agents and brokers to use "blockbusting" techniques to drive down property values. Blockbusting is the practice of encouraging a newer immigrant group, in this case Puerto Ricans, to move into a house in the hopes that current residents will flee, selling their homes below market value and driving down property values in a neighborhood. After the older residents depart, realtors and brokers inflate the home prices and sell them to unsuspecting, newer immigrants. Simultaneously, with blockbusting and economic decline, banks began "redlining" Sunset Park—refusing to give home mortgages or commercial loans to buyers. Banks were notorious for redlining nonwhite and poor neighborhoods in New York in the postwar years.

But Puerto Ricans and other Spanish-speaking groups succeeded, despite the economic decline, in revitalizing this community. Despite redlining, many opened fruit and vegetable stands, restaurants, taverns, clothing and gift shops, and other small businesses along 5th Avenue. Today, Spanish-speaking peoples from Mexico, Ecuador, the Dominican Republic, and other Latin American countries own many of the stores on 5th Avenue. The area's businessmen and political leadership have joined forces to form the Sunset Park Business Improvement District (BID). The BID is financed by a self-imposed tax on members, collected from 384 properties from 38th Street to 64th Street. The funds are used to clean graffiti from buildings, pay private sanitation companies to sweep the streets, add security during the busy holiday seasons, and support sale promotions throughout the year. As a united voice, the BID has helped restore the disintegrating shopping strip.

➤ **Turn left onto 40th Street. Walk up the hill to 740 40th Street, the location of Resurrection Church. As you walk, note the differences in the homes compared with those you saw along 5th Avenue as you walked to the Jackie Gleason Bus Depot.**

In 1991, to honor the Finnish contribution to New York City and Sunset Park, 40th Street was renamed Finlandia Street. The Finns followed the Norwegians to New York City, where they worked as skilled craftsmen, mechanics, laborers, tailors, and small-business owners. They settled in two areas: Harlem and Sunset Park. The area from 40th to 43rd streets between 5th and 9th avenues was called "Finntown" by English speakers and "Pukin Mäki" (Goat Hill) by Finns.

In 1896 the first Finns in Sunset Park established the Aid Society Imatra. Named after a waterfall in Finland, the society sought to provide aid to the growing Finnish population, and, with a labor and leftist base, it existed in pointed contrast to church activities. Imatra meetings were originally held on Court Street, then in a store on 8th Avenue, but in 1907 the Aid Society built Imatra Hall here at 740 40th Street to provide a center for meetings, dances, and summer and holiday festivities. The hall was the first building in the neighborhood to have electricity when it purchased its own electric generator rather than pay the $3,000 Edison Electric Company requested to provide power to the building.

Members of Imatra Hall organized a band and choir, a sick fund, and a reading room. As was the case with mutual-aid societies that catered to other ethnic groups, Imatra Hall became the place to which newly arrived Finns would go for housing and job information. It also housed the Ladies of Kaleva, a women's organization that provided housing assistance and employment services to recently arrived Finnish women. In 1984 Imatra Hall became Resurrection Church. Most Finns have moved out of the community to the suburbs or other parts of the city, leaving only a few descendants of the original Finnish settlers in the neighborhood who provide a critical link from the past to the present neighborhood.

➤ **Keep walking on 40th Street to 8th Avenue. Turn right onto 8th Avenue and walk to 4216 8th Avenue.**

In the early 1980s, Chinese immigrants, mainly from Hong Kong, began to converge on "Bat Dai Do," a term that translates to "Big 8th Street," the area along 8th Avenue from 45th Street to 65th Street. In the 1990s Sunset Park's Chinatown expanded to include many streets between 5th and 8th avenues, making it about half the size of Manhattan's Chinatown. Ethnic Chinese and other Asian immigrants chose Sunset Park because the 4th Avenue subway took them directly to Chinatown in Manhattan. Walking on 8th Avenue, you can see video stores with the latest films from Hong Kong, others specializing in herbal remedies, and scores of Chinese restaurants. In 2000 Bat Dai Do was home to an estimated 400 Chinese-owned businesses.

Chinese-owned businesses share the same geographic space with dozens of garment factories, or sweatshops. Sweatshop workers often toil 6 or 7 days a week for 12 to 18 hours per day, while making much less than minimum wage. In one example, in 1998 the New York State attorney general sued Hua Great Procetech—a notorious Sunset Park sweatshop that manufactured clothing for Street Beat, which sold it to Sears and others—on behalf of four garment-industry workers. Records showed that workers were paid a percentage of their wages on the books and the rest off, while working 12–14 hours per day, 6 days a week.

One thread trimmer worked 105 hours in one week, earning $1.49 per hour. The grassroots Chinese Staff Workers Association has also been fighting to improve illegal working conditions in garment factories primarily by suing owners and publicizing the practices of companies that engage in exploitative practices. Nonetheless, garment factories continue to be one of the dominant types of employers in New York for non-English-speaking immigrants from Asia and Latin America.

PURE LAND BUDDHISM

In addition to language, cuisine, and customs, Asian immigrants have brought new religious practices and beliefs to Sunset Park. At 4216 8th Avenue is one of several storefront Pure Land Buddhist temples in Bat Dai Do. Buddhism began with Shakyamuni Buddha, who lived in India more than 2,500 years ago. He, in turn, spoke of Amitabha Buddha, who existed eons before Shakyamuni's enlightenment.

Amitabha was once a king troubled by life's sufferings and vowed to become a Buddha to lead others to enlightenment. With the good karma he accumulated, he created the Western Land of Pure Bliss. In this Land, one feels no pain and all obstacles are removed, so that anyone who reaches the Pure Land can obtain enlightenment quickly and without distraction, an almost impossible achievement on earth. On reaching enlightenment, you are freed from samsara, the cycle of birth and death. According to the Pure Land tradition, in order to reach Amitabha's Buddhaland one must practice nembetsu, a Japanese term for chanting "Namo Amida Butsu" (Praise to Amitabha Buddha), and have faith in Amitabha, who transfers his good karma to eliminate adherents' bad karma.

While there are several schools of Pure Land Buddhism, each following the tenets of particular Pure Land thinkers, all schools revere Amitabha Buddha (the Buddha of Infinite Light and Life), the Amitabha Sutra (the Infinite Light Sutra), and the Contemplation Sutra. Pure Land Buddhism is the most popular type of Buddhism in East Asia and in New York City, with services held in small storefronts like this one and in adherents' homes.

➤ **Continue walking down 8th Avenue. Turn left onto 43rd Street and walk to 816 43rd Street.**

Faced with a housing shortage, a group of Finnish carpenters formed the Finnish Building Corporation, purchased land between 41st and 43rd streets and 7th and 8th avenues, and built one- and two-family homes. In 1916, 16 Finnish families jointly built in Sunset Park one of the earliest self-help cooperative apartment buildings in the United States. Each family gave $500 to the cooperative, which purchased the land at 816 43rd Street and built a four-story apartment house called "Alku I" (Beginning I), which can still be seen written on the glass above the building's entrance. When the families moved into the building, they paid a nominal monthly maintenance fee. Alku II was built in the adjacent lot—see the stone carving above the main entrance, which reads, "Alku Toinen"—to be followed by 20 more buildings in subsequent years. The cooperative effort was also found in business, where Finns pooled their capital to create a cooperative shopping center, beginning on 8th Avenue and 43rd Street, that included a sauna, a grocery store, a restaurant, and a host of other businesses. Alku I and II continue to exist as residential co-ops, and the current residents represent the multiethnic character of the community. The cooperative retail venture, though, slowly dissolved with the movement of Finns out of the neighborhood. The cooperative shopping center has been replaced with privately owned businesses that cater to the growing Asian American populations.

➤ **Walk back to 8th Avenue and turn left. Proceed to 44th Street, turn right, and walk one block. Enter Sunset Park on the northwest corner of 7th Avenue, across from PS 169. Walk to the entrance of the Sunset Park Recreation Center.**

On 24.5 acres between 5th and 7th avenues and 41st and 44th streets is Sunset Park. In 1891, 14 of these acres were set aside by the City of Brooklyn for the park. In 1905 the park was expanded to its present 24.5 acres, and the retaining walls around it were added, along with a six-hole golf course, a man-made pond, and a carousel, creating a center for community and family events. Families sat around the pond, children played on the merry-go-round, and in the winter Scandinavian immigrants often skied down the slopes.

In 1935 the park closed and underwent a large-scale Works Progress Administration (WPA) construction project that removed the pond, carousel, and golf course. In their place, the WPA erected the Sunset Park Recreation Center, which houses an Olympic-size swimming pool and a playground. Aymar Embury II created the Center in a Neoclassical/Art Deco style, with vertical columns and diamond-motif brickwork. On opening day in the summer of 1936, 7,000 people swam in the pool. Only a few years later, artillery pieces were placed in the park to protect the city from invasions during World War II.

The park remained virtually unchanged until 1984, when the pool, bathhouse, and comfort station were reconstructed and the playground was expanded in a $5 million restoration project. In 2001–2 the park received another minor makeover when volleyball courts and a new drainage system were installed. Because it is one of the highest points in Brooklyn, at 214 feet above sealevel, the park offers great views of the Statue of Liberty, the tallest structures in Brooklyn and Manhattan, and the Verrazano Bridge. Sunset Park continues to be a popular community-meeting place since it offers a serene place to exercise, have picnics, and gaze at the skyline. Its elevation and location above the bay also offers one of the best places to watch Independence Day fireworks shows.

Inside the Sunset Play Center you can see murals painted by students from PS 1, PS 94, PS 169, and JHS 136 in the neighborhood. On the wall to the right of the entrance to the play center is a long description of shell-fish in the harbor. Why? Perhaps because you can look down into the bay from the top of the hill. If you follow your way around the play center on the 41st Street side, you will come to the former carousel spot. In cement on the ground are small impressions in the shape of carousel animals, but the carousel is gone. If you come in spring and admire the flowers, thank the Sunset Park Garden Club.

Before walking out of the park, stand atop the hill and look below you. The white tower/steeple is St. Michael the Archangel Church, to the right is the red-brick Charles Dewey Middle School, and in the distance is the harbor.

➤ **Exit the park at 41st Street and 5th Avenue, diagonally opposite where you entered. Walk on 41st to 4th Avenue, turn left, and walk to the corner of 42nd Street.**

On the corner is the landmarked 1931 former Sunset Park Courthouse; notice "Municipal Court" over its entrance a few steps from the corner of 42nd Street. The Classical Revival building was designed by Mortimer Dickerson Metcalfe, who also worked on Grand Central Terminal. Today the building is used by the local Community Board 7 and the New York Police Department's Applicant Processing Division, which is also noted above the door.

➤ **Walk along 4th Avenue one more block to 43rd Street.**

On the southwest corner, the fenced-in building is the former 68th Police Precinct Station House, popularly known
as "the Castle." The building and accompanying stable—
both of which are hard to see, as obscured as they are by
weeds, fencing, and spray paint—were designed by Emile
M. Gruwe in a Romanesque architectural style and built in
1889. A corner tower dominates the station house. If you
look carefully, you'll see that the tower's first floor is decorated with a limestone band of carved dogs' faces and leaf-
shaped ornaments.

In 1898 a staff of 63 worked here: 1 captain, 4 sergeants,
3 roundsmen, 52 patrolmen, and 3 doormen. In December
1970 the 68th Precinct was moved to 333 65th Street, and
the New York City Board of Estimate declared the Castle
surplus property to be sold to the highest bidder. In 1982 it
was added to the National Register of Historic Places. The
Sunset Park School of Music was slated to move into the
building in 1998, but the school only got as far as placing
its sign on the building. The Brooklyn Chinese-American
Association purchased the property in the spring of 1999
and had made plans to convert it into residential apartments for low- and moderate-income families, but things
seem to have stalled.

Across the street is the enormous St. Michael the Archangel Church. In the late nineteenth century, Bishop John
Loughlin decided to organize a new parish, St. Michael the
Archangel, to serve the religious needs of the largely Irish
Roman Catholic population in Sunset Park and nearby. In
1870 the site for St. Michael's was purchased by the Brooklyn Archdiocese, which built a small wooden church in the
1870s and a school in 1886.

The current version was dedicated on October 1, 1905,
and cost $274,000, which won't even buy a one-bedroom

apartment in much of Manhattan these days. The tower stands 200 feet above street level, making it the tallest structure in Sunset Park.

St. Michael's Grammar School opened in 1910 on land adjacent to the church, and St. Michael's High School opened in 1926 and closed in 1960, when Xaverian High School opened on Shore Road and the students moved there. The former school building and the Xaverian Brothers Monastery on the site is now home to a Head Start program serving the community's families. The church continues to minister to the spiritual needs of Sunset Park's Spanish-speaking, Roman Catholic population with Mass celebrated in English and Spanish.

Several blocks north of the church, to your left if you are facing that way, was Little Norway. Norwegians moved to Sunset Park beginning in the late 1880s to work in maritime trades as sailors, shipbuilders, dockworkers, maritime bankers, and insurance-company officers. Initially they settled just north of Sunset Park on Hamilton Avenue. Eventually, overcrowding and poor housing led wealthier Norwegians to move into Sunset Park, which created the largest urban concentration of Norwegians in the United States, in an area stretching from 45th to 60th streets between 4th and 8th avenues.

To provide health care to the growing Norwegian community, in 1889 Norwegian immigrants founded the Lutheran Deaconesses' Home and Hospital at 4th Avenue and 46th Street. Deaconesses quickly grew to offer one of the first nurses' training programs in Brooklyn and an ambulance service by early 1893. The Deaconesses' Home and Hospital was the forerunner of the Lutheran Medical Center located on 2nd Avenue and 55th Street. The hospital moved there in 1969, after the medical center purchased the former American Machine and Foundry Company building for $1 and spent over $70 million to renovate it.

Lutheran Medical once served the large Scandinavian population, but now it serves the ethnically diverse community of today's Sunset Park and surrounding neighborhoods.

➤ **Walk west along 43rd Street one block to 3rd Avenue.**

When you reach 3rd Avenue, you will be able to feel the destruction and change wrought by the construction of the Gowanus Expressway portion of the Brooklyn-Queens Expressway, begun in 1937 (with a long pause for World War II) and finished in 1964. Although officially part of the interstate highway system, and designated I-278, the expressway has a 45 mph speed limit, absurdly sharp curves, no shoulders, and short exits. It was actually built on top of the pillars that held up the 3rd Avenue elevated train line. Stand a moment here and remember that merely two avenues behind you is a lovely park and community.

ROBERT MOSES AND THE GOWANUS EXPRESSWAY

Robert Moses—perhaps the greatest builder and destroyer of New York City—exerted considerable influence not only on the lives of the residents of Sunset Park but also on the lives of all New Yorkers past and present. He was born in New Haven, Connecticut, in 1888, graduated from Yale in 1909, and earned his Ph.D. in political science from Columbia University in 1914. Shortly after graduating, Moses started his career in city planning as a technical assistant to the New York City Civil Service Commission.

In 1924 Governor Alfred Smith appointed him the president of the State Parks Council and the Long Island State Park Commission. In this capacity he was responsible for creating almost 10,000 acres of parks on Long Island. Ten years later, in 1934, Moses was the parks commissioner of New York City, and within two years on the job he had organized the creation of 255 parks

Robert Moses's elevated Gowanus Expressway dwarfs the small buildings along 3rd Avenue and was responsible for destroying what used to be a bustling commercial street and for dividing the neighborhood of Sunset Park. Photo courtesy of the Brooklyn Historical Society.

and 11 swimming pools, the construction of the Marine Parkway Bridge, and a network of highways from the Henry Hudson Bridge to the Belt Parkway.

In 1946 Moses began to make the city even more accessible by car with the construction of the Brooklyn-Queens Expressway, numerous highway loops, parking garages, and Brooklyn's Civic Center. During his 40 years as a powerbroker in New York City, Moses also played an integral part in the construction of public-housing projects in Harlem, the Lower East Side, and Brownsville. As the head of the mayor's committee on slum clearance, he replaced what some called "slums" with 12- and 14-story public-housing apartment buildings—one housing project per month from 1947 to 1949.

In Sunset Park, Moses was responsible for creating the Gowanus Expressway, which drastically altered the neighborhood.

The huge elevated highway runs above 3rd Avenue in Sunset Park and connects the Brooklyn-Battery Tunnel, city airports, and Long Island highways and provides access to Staten Island and New Jersey via the Verrazano Bridge. Although there had been an elevated subway line on 3rd Avenue, when plans for the expressway were made public, Sunset Park residents feared the destruction that a highway would bring and began a vigilant campaign to have the expressway moved closer to the bay, one block west along 2nd Avenue. However, Moses's construction plans went ahead on 3rd Avenue, and residents' fears became a reality.

This section of 3rd Avenue was the heart of the community. The avenue had newsstands that sold foreign-language newspapers to the immigrant community, seven movie theatres, scores of small restaurants and small businesses, and more. Hundreds of businesses were removed and over 1,000 residents were displaced as construction demolished buildings to widen 3rd Avenue and build the expressway.

The 94-foot-wide Gowanus Expressway radically changed Sunset Park by creating a barrier between the industrial area west of 3rd Avenue and the residential areas to the east, blocking out the sun, making pedestrian crossing dangerous, and eventually closing off what used to be a bustling commercial street of ethnic markets.

➤ Turn right on 3rd Avenue and walk three blocks to 40th Street.

To see one happy remnant of the pre-expressway days, walk along 3rd Avenue, past light industry and pornographic video stores, listening to the roar of the expressway, to Frankel's on the northeast corner of 40th Street and 3rd Avenue. Adolph Frankel opened his store in 1890 across the avenue but was forced to move here when

An 1885 photo of the DeHart-Bergen House, built in 1671. The rural farm house used to stand on 38th Street and 3rd Avenue in Sunset Park. Photo courtesy of the Brooklyn Historical Society.

the Gowanus Expressway was constructed. Frankel sold clothes and toiletries to longshoremen, who were numerous along the docks a century ago. Frankel's has seen the ethnic and physical transformation of the neighborhood and has changed along with the community. It stopped selling toiletries when the docks closed and began to sell popular street wear and sneakers, moving through the phases in footwear from Frye boots to Timberlands to Red Wings. The store remains in the family, with Marty Frankel, the grandson of Adolph Frankel, as the sole proprietor, although, truth be told, Marty works another job as the owner of the Crossroads music club in Garwood, New Jersey. Ask him and he'll show you photos of himself with many famous musicians.

Southwest of Frankel's is the Brooklyn Army Terminal, between 58th and 65th streets along 2nd Avenue. The Military Ocean Terminal, as the ocean-supply facility was originally known, became Brooklyn Army Terminal in 1919, after the completion of a massive construction project designed by Cass Gilbert, the famous architect who designed many notable Manhattan landmarks, including the Woolworth Building, the U.S. Courthouse at Foley Square, and the New York Life Building.

At peak operation during World War II, 80 percent of the supplies and soldiers heading for Europe were shipped from the Brooklyn Army Terminal. At its largest, the terminal stretched across 97 acres and consisted of 19 structures, including two eight-story warehouses of reinforced concrete, one of which was the largest warehouse in the world. The terminal was deactivated by the federal government in the 1970s, designated a national historic landmark in 1983, and reopened in 1987 as a light-industry center.

➤ **Walk one block to 39th Street.**

Standing on 39th Street and 3rd Avenue and gazing toward the water, one has a panoramic view of the Bush Terminal. What is now Irving T. Bush Terminal was once Ambrose Park, a picnic area where in 1892 Buffalo Bill's Wild West Show played on the way to his European tour. Bush began building the terminal in about 1900 to compete with Manhattan's ports and hoped to make the complex "an industrial city within a city." Initially he had just one building and pier, a tugboat, and an old railroad engine, but by the terminal's heyday it encompassed a 200-acre complex of piers, warehouses, display rooms, and factory lofts, with fire and police departments, power plants, and over 20,000 workers. Some of the buildings in this complex are over 3 acres in size. Some claim that Bush Terminal was the model for today's "industrial parks."

In 1965 the Bush Terminal was bought by a group calling itself the Industry City Association and converted into an industrial park. Of the 18 original piers, 5 are no longer standing, but the fenced-off area where thousands of long-

An 1870s view of 3rd Avenue and 39th Street showing John O'Rourke's carpentry shop and the location of Bush Terminal. Photo courtesy of the Brooklyn Historical Society.

shoremen once worked now forms an unofficial bird sanctuary, complete with ring-necked pheasants and other local and migrating birds.

LUCKENBACH PIER EXPLOSION

On Monday, December 3, 1956, a massive explosion rocked the Luckenbach Steamship Company on the municipally owned pier on 35th Street. The explosion shot flames 500 feet in the air, shattered windows as far away as 4th Avenue, and was felt six miles away in Queens. The devastation caused by the explosion and subsequent fire was attacked by 250 policemen, 300 firefighters, scores of nurses and physicians, the Coast Guard, the Red Cross, the Civil Defense, and volunteer personnel from all five boroughs.

Two days after the fire and explosion, Kings County district attorney Edward Silver appointed a board of experts to investigate.

The board included professors of chemistry and chemical engineering, as well as the chief engineer of the New York City Department of Marine and Aviation. Initial rumors of a nuclear explosion were dispelled. Instead, fire commissioner Edward F. Cavanagh Jr. determined that torches used by ship riggers repairing a roof fell into burlap-wrapped foam rubber on the pier and caused a fire. Exposed to fire, 37,000 pounds of detonating fuses exploded, touching off a fire fueled by rubber, lacquer, and varnish.

It wasn't until several days later, when the fires were fully extinguished, that the power of the destruction became evident. The explosion sheared through the 14-inch-thick concrete floor that was reinforced with half-inch steel bars and 2 inches of asphalt. The resulting crater was 150 by 175 feet wide, covering most of the pier. There were 10 men were killed and 246 injured, and the damage was estimated at $15 million.

➤ Turn right on 39th Street and walk up the hill to 4th Avenue. Turn left and walk three blocks to the D, N, and R stop at 36th Street.

Despite Sunset Park's being one of New York's largest neighborhoods, it is not well known by many residents. As you have seen throughout the tour, the neighborhood offers the opportunity to go from garden cemetery to park to church to expressway. But more importantly this community allows the contemporary observer the opportunity to witness, if only peripherally, how a polyglot community composed of individuals from all parts of the globe sustains itself and negotiates what it means to be American.

To be sure, the community is in transition. With rising rents and home prices in Manhattan and nearby Brooklyn communities, Sunset Park residents are negotiating gentrification—the restoration and rebuilding of seemingly deteriorating properties for purchase by middle- and upper-class buyers. Such a process has positive and negative effects. On the one hand, it provides a larger economic base for the community. On the other hand, it forces some working-class immigrant and migrant groups out of the community. Another major transition in the neighborhood is being planned by Community Board 7, the local governing body, along with real-estate developers. The two groups are working to create a waterfront park west of the Gowanus Expressway, and some are advocating to replace the Gowanus with an underground expressway. Just as the construction of Gowanus Expressway transformed Sunset Park in the mid-twentieth century, perhaps burying it in the early twenty-first century will do so again.

OCEAN PARKWAY

NEPTUNE AVENUE

W. 5 STREET

SURF AVENUE

BOARDWALK

W. 8 STREET

W. 8 ST.

W. 10 ST.

W. 12 STREET

S

HENDERSON WALK

STILLWELL AVENUE

STILLWELL AVE.

SCHWEICKERTS WALK

W. 15 ST.

KENSINGTON WALK

W. 16 ST.

W. 17 ST.

Keyspan Park

W. 19 ST.

W. 19 ST.

W. 20 ST.

NEPTUNE AVENUE

W. 21 ST.

SURF AVENUE

W. 22 ST.

F

W. 23 ST.

W. 24 ST.

W. 25 ST.

W. 27 ST.

W. 27 ST.

W. 28 ST.

BOARDWALK

W. 29 ST.

W. 30 ST.

Atlantic Ocean

N.

10 CONEY ISLAND

The "Nickel Empire"

➤ **Start: Stillwell Avenue subway station, last stop on the F, D, and Q lines.**

CONEY ISLAND is the stuff of legends. Even its name is fabled, though most accept that it's a corruption of the Dutch word *konijn*, meaning "rabbit." Over the course of this walking tour, you will be offered vivid reminders that once upon a time Coney was, for many, the living, breathing embodiment of recreation and amusement, a pleasure palace par excellence. Never before, and for many not since, has one small stretch of island been the repository of such a wide agglomeration of bizarre fantasy, fantastical excess, and cultural edification. If Paris is France, Steeplechase-amusement-park impresario George Tilyou once proclaimed, then Coney Island between June and September is the world.

The small island or peninsula off the coast of the Atlantic Ocean is some six miles long and comprises the neighborhoods of Coney Island proper and Brighton Beach, as well as Manhattan Beach on the island's east side. Rem Koolhaas in his classic *Delirious New York*, referring not only to Coney's physical geography but also its vibrant sensuality, described the island as a "clitoral appendage at the entrance to New York harbor." The focus of this tour will be a concentrated stretch of that clitoral appendage ranging approximately between 8th and 21st streets. While we will refer to places beyond these limits, most of the major historical and contemporary sites fall within these boundaries.

For many, of course, the notion of Coney Island evokes both the memory of and nostalgia for an amusement-park culture that make today's Disneyland or Great Adventure seem timid by comparison. With names connoting other-worldliness and outer-consciousness like Dreamland and Luna Park, Coney Island, once dubbed "Sodom by the Sea," was the place for both the working and middle classes to participate in escapist and often fantasy-laden activities.

While the Golden Age of Coney is often considered to be the first part of the twentieth century during the heyday of the great amusement parks—Dreamland and Luna Park—Coney's Silver Age was certainly the Depression through World War II, when the island became home to the so-called Nickel Empire. During this period, Coney became the choice destination for millions of immigrants and working families seeking a respite (by means of a nickel ride on the subway) from the cramped quarters of New York's tenements. Although Steeplechase Park continued in operation until 1964 and Astroland opened in 1962, post–World War II Coney was a lackluster site. The construction of Robert Moses–like housing projects and the possibility of other destinations, like Jones Beach, through the extension of the parkway system (again Moses) led to the accelerated demise of Coney Island as a recreational hotspot. But in recent years a renaissance has taken hold, with a new museum and ballpark and city monies designated for the revitalization of the neighborhood. Coney Island is indeed in the throes of rebirth.

Construction is underway to the tune of $200 million to revamp the gargantuan 1921 terminus subway station. By 2005, if plans remain on schedule, there will be a lovely canopy of steel and glass over a new building, platforms, and tracks. Why the generosity? Former mayor Giuliani was inspired by the projected revitalization of Coney as catalyzed by a gleaming new minor-league baseball stadium (more on that below). Can future mayors sustain the former mayor's promises?

➤ **Walk across Surf Avenue to the corner of Surf and Stillwell Avenue.**

Standing here in front of Nathan's Famous, you may think nothing's changed since the last century. Even though the franks are now $1.75, the 1920s signage and décor hark back to a bygone era. Relish (pun intended) the classic crinkle-cut fries, fried clams, and fresh-squeezed lemonade.

Formed in 1916, a year before America's entrance into World War I, Nathan and Ida Handwerker revolutionized frankfurter consumption with the advent of the nickel hot dog. While the origins of that great American food item are contested, many agree that the frankfurter—just the beef part—derives eponymously from Frankfurt, Germany. Only with the introduction of the bun did the hot dog as we know it emerge.

The German immigrant Charles Feltman, whose hot dog stand on Coney Island advertised "frankfurter sandwiches," is most often credited with the hot dog's invention. Nathan Handwerker had previously been in the employ of Charles Feltman when the latter's business expanded to include restaurants, beer gardens, and a hotel. In the fateful year 1916, Nathan Handwerker broke away from Feltman and formed his own business, ingeniously reducing the frank in price from 10 cents to 5 and becoming as a consequence the greatest ever hot dog entrepreneur. The rest, as they say, is history. Feltman himself, whose once-packed restaurant (the site of today's Astroland Park; see below) is remembered fondly by Coney devotees, is for most people today the equivalent of an Antonio Salieri or Pete Best—a forgotten progenitor to those who came after.

And for those who think Nathan's represents small-scale mom-and-pop business at its finest, think again. The last eight decades have transformed Nathan's into a bona fide multinational corporation. Not only can one now find a Nathan's outlet at a local Home Depot store, but one can also consume their footlongs in Israel and Egypt.

Relax with your frank and fries in the sitting area on Schweikert's Walk. And for the bravely gluttonous, the Fourth of July brings in frankfurter fireworks with the annual Nathan's hot dog eating contest. At press time, the reigning champion is rail-thin Takeru Kobayashi of Japan, who in 2002 downed a stomach-numbing 50½ Nathan's franks in just 12 minutes, besting the 50 he ingested in 2001. Kobayasahi's weight over the course of the event ballooned from 113 to 129 pounds (to put Kobayashi's feat into perspective, the portly hot dog lover Babe Ruth once scarfed down a measly 12 franks between doubleheader games and was promptly rushed to the hospital for indigestion). Despite 20 billion hot dogs consumed in the United States annually, only one American has won the Nathan's competition since 1996. The hot dog is no longer the unique preserve of Americans.

And what's for dessert? Well it should be noted that Coney Island was also once a center for the candy industry, boasting a dozen candy stores on Surf Avenue. The invention of saltwater taffy and the Eskimo Pie are part of Coney's history. Later in the tour, at the old Child's

Nathan's Famous, circa 1962, on Surf and Stillwell avenues in Coney Island. The great Brooklyn icon has seen little change. Photo courtesy of the Brooklyn Historical Society.

Restaurant, you will get a view of all that remains of this history.

> **Walk east along Surf Avenue to West 12th Street.**

As you leave Nathan's, look across the street on the west side of Stillwell Avenue at the large 1920s building with the Shore sign. This was the old Coney Island Theatre Building (1925), last employed as the Shore Theatre.

Note Faber's Fascination. Now a rather grim video arcade, (Nat) Faber's Fascination once housed the famed Fascination game, a game similar to Bingo. In another guise, Fascination was also a popular electronic maze game from the early 1960s.

Then pass Herman Popper and Bro., currently art gallery space. In 1904 Herman Popper and his frère had a distillery, and then a saloon, here. Though defaced in other ways, the lovely Roman-brick façade and signage remain. Next is the Eldorado Auto Skooter, your chance to go (disco) bumper car-ing on Coney, the other place being several hundred feet away in Astroland. It runs $3.50, but you gotta be 42 inches tall to get behind the wheel.

The Coney Island Museum (1208 Surf Avenue) is open only on weekends (12 p.m. till sundown). This small (one flight up) museum is a treasure-trove of Coney Island lore and memorabilia. Not only functioning as an artifactual center for Coney's cultural history, the museum is also a research center for scholars and students and a cultural center with lectures and other happenings. And for some first-rate souvenirs, which one can savor as legitimately purchased at Coney itself (rather than, say, on eBay), the gift shop is one of a kind (there's always the website, of course: www.coneyislandusa.com).

➤ **Turn right on West 12th and walk toward the Bowery.**

As you venture toward Astroland, the amusement park in Coney these days, here lies another wonderful vestige of the past: the sideshow (this one dates from 1987). Sideshows by the Seashore, located in a 1917 building where the singing waiters of Child's Restaurant once crooned, offers you Bambi the Mermaid; Ula, the Painproof Rubber Girl; and Eak, the Illustrated Man. They claim that it is the last place in the United States where one can enjoy the thrills and mysteries of a genuine ten-in-one circus sideshow. Indeed, this professional nonprofit theater is the only of its kind committed to preserving the sideshow's legacy. For only 5 bucks ($3 for kids under 12) one gets a rousing 45-minute show. Remember, this is the stuff of legends: once upon a time, a young Erich Weiss, better

Dreamland amusement park featured Lilliputia, a city of 300 residents, including, at various times (left to right) Baron Magri, Count Magri, and Mrs. General Tom Thumb (formerly Countess Magri). Image courtesy of the Brooklyn Historical Society.

known as Harry Houdini, worked as an escape artist (where else?) at a Coney sideshow.

SIDESHOW

Although historically P. T. Barnum should be credited with raising sideshow-freak events to an art form, it was Missouri showman Samuel Gumpertz who transported the freak-show experience to Coney Island. Dreamland, that fantastical short-lived amusement park stroke of brilliance, was host during its opening season in 1904 to Gumpertz's Midget City, Lilliputia. By inviting 300 "midgets" (today the preferred term is Little People)—who had been scattered across North America at assorted fairs—to

Dreamland, Gumpertz overnight radically transformed the experiential possibilities for millions of persons seeking to be transported from their quotidian lives.

The most famous Lilliputians were the Count and Countess Magri (the countess's marriage to the beloved Tom Thumb popularized her). The Little People had their own parliament, a fire department that responded to hourly false alarms, and a mini-city designed to resemble fifteenth-century Nuremberg, Germany! It was the radical success of this enterprise that led Gumpertz to even more daring imported extravaganzas. Gumpertz traveled the world, bringing back with him scores of what were then considered "exotic persons."

In 1905, for example, Gumpertz helped transport to Coney 212 Bantocs — Spanish-speaking Filipinos from America's latest colonial prize — experts in blowing poison darts through reed guns, as well as in wire and brass crafts making. He brought from Burma women who could extend their necks 14 inches through the addition of brass rings. And from Borneo (partially out of competition with Barnum, as the latter had been there first) Gumpertz leased from a tribal chieftain, for 200 bags of salt, 19 "Wild Men." All told, Gumpertz brought during his tenure with Dreamland 3,800 persons from around the globe to Coney. Gumpertz's prize for these efforts: he was made Dreamland's general manager in 1908.

Even amid the overall atmosphere of adventure and lunacy at other amusement parks like Luna Park and Steeplechase (of which more below), Dreamland was still in a class by itself. In terms of its design and architecture, it paid homage to the great 1893 Columbian World Exposition in Chicago, with its white classical buildings and statuary. At its very center, based on the Giralda Tower in Seville, Spain, and adorned at the top by a large falcon, was a monumental 375-foot-high central tower, which at the time was the largest structure in Brooklyn proper (and which was over 100 feet taller than the real Giralda).

Every night 1 million lights were lit to flood Dreamland (compared with the 250,000 that lit Luna Park). Its spectacular en-

The magnificent entrance to Dreamland amusement park. Image courtesy of the Brooklyn Historical Society.

trance portal along Surf Avenue was 150 feet deep and 75 feet high with gigantic columns outfitted in gold on either side. Once inside, along with the aforementioned (orientalist) sideshows, there were innovative rides like the great Shoot the Chutes, the largest water slide ever constructed, and lifelike reproductions such as the Canals of Venice Ride, with a mammoth night-time model of Venice set inside a smaller-scaled Ducal Palace with authentic gondolas carrying passengers along a simulated Grand Canal.

And then there were radical medical offerings such as the Baby Incubator Building where Dr. Martin Couney, at his nurse-staffed hospital, displayed prematurely born babies. To cover expenses he charged 10 cents to view these children, this during a time when America's medical establishment didn't approve of his methods and when most hospitals lacked incubators. As it turned out, Couney had a phenomenal record over his tenure saving babies' lives (6,500 of the 8,000 babies placed in his care survived!). To encourage visitors, Couney hired the young English immigrant Archibald Leach (later known as Cary Grant) as a barker.

For those wishing to pay their respects to the area that Dreamland once occupied, simply walk down Surf Avenue to West 8th Street, where the Aquarium now stands. The price of admission back then? 10 cents – the equivalent of two hot dogs at Nathan's. Tragically, on the evening of May 27, 1911, Dreamland became engulfed in fire, starting, ironically enough, at Hellgate, a boat ride through the caverns of hell. It was never rebuilt.

➤ **Walk toward the Bowery into Astroland Park.**

Steeplechase's amusement-park impresario George Tilyou laid this street to guide people to his newly opened (1898) Steeplechase Park. Nicknamed "the Bowery" (originally Ocean Avenue), it resembled Manhattan's own Bowery, rife as it once was with vaudeville theaters, cabarets, and restaurants.

Astroland Park, which dates from 1962, though lacking the various exotic and edificational trappings of Coney's amusement parks of yore, still has a number of rather significant elements to appreciate and enjoy.

Perhaps most legendary among Astroland's rides is the justly famed Cyclone, considered by aficionados to be the greatest roller coaster in the world. Once part of Coney's Steeplechase Park, which closed in 1964, the Cyclone dates from 1927, the year of the Yankees' Murderers' Row team. Giving a 1-minute-and-50-second ride at 60 mph, it is the last working roller coaster on Coney today. The great aviator and Nazi sympathizer Charles Lindbergh once told *Time* magazine that "a ride on the Cyclone is greater than flying an airplane at top speed." And Emilio Franco, a coal miner from West Virginia who was from birth unable to speak, is said to have regained his voice on the Cyclone, uttering his first words ever: "I feel sick"! The Cyclone has been a New York City landmark since 1988 and a national

The 1927 Cyclone is the last working roller coaster in Coney Island and one of the few wooden roller coasters in the nation. The Cyclone is both a New York and national historic landmark. Photo courtesy of the Brooklyn Historical Society.

historic landmark since 1991. For the faint of heart, here are some statistics that may keep you on the sidelines: 6 180-degree turns; 12 drops, including an initial one of 85 feet at a 60-degree angle; 16 changes of direction; and 27 elevation changes.

But if you're really concerned whether this 75-year-old heart-palpitation-inducing contraption holds up, have a word with Walter Williams, who is (at press time) the caretaker of the Cyclone. For three hours every morning, Williams taps each inch of steel track with a hammer to check for loose nuts and screws and looks painstakingly for any rotting wood. Who wouldn't trust a guy that intones, "I take care of her, I see after her. I fix her, and I make sure she's okay. I love the Cyclone, like you would love your wife"?

Dating from Astroland's inception in 1962, the Astrotower is a 272-foot-tall space tower offering a 360-degree rotation as it ascends. Feltman's 1903 Carousel was removed to make way for this "tower to the stars." Willy Buhler of Bern, Switzerland, constructed this "space needle" at a cost of $1.6 million.

While not commercially part of Astroland, Deno's 1920 Wonder Wheel is situated on the West 12th Street side near the Boardwalk within the Astroland Park environs (it is actually owned and operated by Deno's Amusement and Kiddie Park). Standing 150 feet tall, it was until recently the largest ferris wheel in the world (that honor now goes to the Millennium Wheel on London's South Bank). The Wonder Wheel was constructed with Bethlehem steel and built on site; it maintains 16 swinging and 8 stationary cars. The only stoppage in the history of the Wonder Wheel was on July 13, 1977, during the New York City blackout, when the owners hand cranked the wheel to bring the riders down safely. The Wonder Wheel became an official New York City landmark in 1989. The origin of the ferris wheel? It was created by Pittsburgh, Pennsylvania, bridge builder George W. Ferris and was the engineering highlight of the 1893 Chicago Exposition.

A 1988 report by the Landmarks Preservation Commission referring to rides like the Cyclone and the Wonder Wheel noted that "most of these rides succeeded because they combined socially acceptable thrills with undertones of sexual intimacy."

Within Deno's Amusement Park you will find the age-old amusement-park game Skeeball, invented by J. D. Estes of Philadelphia in 1909. Skeeball is a game of (slight) skill, wherein players roll nine balls down a 10-foot alley, with the object of landing them in scoring rings with differing values. As players accrue points, they earn tickets that can be exchanged for prizes of varying value.

➢ Walk over to the Boardwalk and head west.

Coney Island in the summer, as seen from the sea in a photograph by Harry Kalmus in 1950. Photo courtesy of the Brooklyn Historical Society.

(Although the tour will head west on the Boardwalk, we suggest a detour briefly the other way, especially when with kids, to check out the New York Aquarium, which was once the number-one tourist attraction in New York City at its previous site in Manhattan at Castle Clinton. It was moved here after World War II by Robert Moses, in what many consider a fit of pique after he didn't get his way in the form of a bridge from Battery Park to Brooklyn and had to settle for a tunnel instead.)

The Boardwalk (properly the Riegelmann Boardwalk). You've seen it in movies, experienced it as a child, heard about it through family, but nevertheless here it is, the real McCoy: Coney Island's Boardwalk. First laid in 1923 and originally two miles long (lengthened to three in 1941, stretching eastward to Brighton Beach), the Boardwalk literally changed the landscape of Coney Island while democratizing the larger area. Created over the original surf line, most waterfront property in Coney was until that time privately held by bathhouse proprietors. But by 1920 the subway had been extended so that the traffic on a summer Sunday skyrocketed from 100,000 to 1 million. Coney needed to find some way to manage such numbers; the creation of a Boardwalk with access to the Atlantic was the ticket. And with the subway fare 5 cents (same as a Nathan's hot dog) the age of the "Nickel Empire" was born.

The Boardwalk's namesake is Edward Riegelmann, the borough president of Brooklyn who oversaw its development. The Boardwalk was a turning point in Coney's demographic, as immigrants from all over the city began to venture out in droves. And with the beach becoming open to everybody in 1923, Coney Island was transformed from a middle-class destination to one open to all segments of society.

Heading east, the Boardwalk trails into Brighton Beach, or "Little Odessa," as it's called for the thousands of former Soviet immigrants who have settled here since the 1980s. For a truly ethnic experience, take in one of the restaurants or nightclubs lining Brighton Beach Avenue.

➢ **Walk west down the Boardwalk to the ruins of the Thunderbolt (between West 15th and 16th).**

The open space before you was once home to a great rival roller coaster to the Cyclone: the Thunderbolt. Built in 1925 (beating the Cyclone by two years) and revolutionizing the use of steel rather than wood, the roller coaster had a great run until 1983, when it fell into disuse, standing fallow until sadly uprooted and carted off (without warning) in November 2000. Some say that the roller coaster ruin had become simply too unstable; others contend that then-mayor Giuliani paid heed to developers' concerns that the gargantuan ruin would be an eyesore to the neighboring baseball stadium being constructed (see below). When it stood next to the former Steeplechase Park, the Thunderbolt was made economically viable through the spillover of visitors.

Secondary to the roller coaster but part of the Thunderbolt's illustrious history was the curious 1895 house, originally the Kensington Hotel, that lay directly underneath the belly of the coaster. It was for decades—until 1988, actually, when Fred Moran's widow, Mae, moved out —the home of the Moran family, which ran the roller coaster. The Moran story was popularly depicted by Brooklyn-raised Woody Allen in his classic film *Annie Hall*. A partial explanation for Alvie Singer's (Woody Allen) complicated neuroses was that he grew up in the house underneath the Thunderbolt.

Look at the tall metal structure that is the Parachute Jump. Built originally for the 1939–40 World's Fair in Queens and designed for training troops, the Parachute Jump's function was transformed in 1941 after its purchase by Steeplechase-amusement-park impresario Edward Tilyou (son of George) for $150,000. As an amusement ride, it allowed riders to free-fall from its 262-foot perch before deploying a parachute, offering in the process a spectacular panoramic view of Coney Island. The Parachute Jump maintained 12 chutes, each with a seat intended for two passengers. The ride was extremely popular during the war years, but in the 1950s and 1960s interest waned and the Jump became too labor intensive since it required three operators for each chute.

Unlike the Thunderbolt, the Parachute Jump—sometimes known as Brooklyn's "Eiffel Tower"—was landmarked on July 1977. As a result of landmarking, it has achieved several notable facelifts including the replacement of steel members and a paint job that returned its original red sheen. It is the lone remnant from Tilyou's Steeplechase Park and lasted even three years longer than

The landmarked Parachute Jump allowed the willing to drop from its 262-foot perch by parachute, offering in the process a spectacular panoramic view of Coney Island. No one has jumped from it since 1967. Photo courtesy of the Brooklyn Historical Society.

the great amusement park itself, offering its last jump in 1967.

Ask most Americans what comes to mind when they think of Brooklyn, and if they don't say Coney Island, the next choice will likely be the Dodgers, despite the Dodgers having run away to Los Angeles after the 1957 season. After 44 years, baseball in Brooklyn is back. Since the opening of Keyspan Park, home to the Single A franchise of the New York Mets, a Brooklyn stadium is drawing sold-out crowds to witness the national pastime.

Keyspan Park, following in the recent tradition of corporate stadium namings, takes its name from the company that supplies gas and electricity to Brooklyn and that was formerly known as Brooklyn Union Gas. But even with corporate sponsorship, the park still cost the taxpayers $39 million for its construction. The old Dodgers' Ebbets Field, by the way, was named for Charles Ebbets, who acquired the Flatbush stadium land for around $100,000. Keyspan Park was opened for the 2001 season with a seating capacity of 6,500 and a reasonable ticket price of $6–10, if you can get them. The Cyclones bright red color is taken from—where else?—the roller coaster's sign itself. Dead centerfield, by the way, is a cool 412 feet away.

Keyspan Park stands exactly on the site of the great 15-acre Steeplechase Park. Of the big three amusement parks —Steeplechase, Luna Park, and Dreamland—Steeplechase was the oldest, being established in 1897, and lasted the longest, closing only after the 1964 season (the ballpark is the first building on the site since Steeplechase's demolition; Donald Trump's father, Fred Trump, was to have built some condos here, but the project never got off the ground). Its name derives from the great Steeplechase Race, one of the park's greatest attractions, a simulated horserace on iron rails along a 1,100-foot track. In the ride, six double-saddled mechanical horses took parkgoers around the outside of the park, over hurdles and a stream bed. Body weight paid off here: since the ride was gravity driven, heavier riders had a distinct advantage.

Steeplechase was the brainchild of George Tilyou, a man whom Ric Burns and Richard Snow in their documentary *Coney Island* called "the first impresario of controlled chaos." Tilyou's enchantment with the celebrated ferris wheel while on his honeymoon at the 1893 Columbian Exposition gave rise to his amusement-park fascination.

A devilish joker grin—the Funny Face, as it was dubbed—welcomed visitors from Steeplechase's entrance

The entrance to Steeplechase Park in 1907, featuring the devilishly grinning "Funny Face." Postcard illustration courtesy of the Brooklyn Historical Society.

on the Boardwalk (see that famous grin recycled back at Sideshows by the Seashore today). Tilyou also laid out the Bowery, as noted above, to guide visitors to his park. Distinct from Luna Park and Dreamland, with their emphases on exotic and orientalist trappings, Steeplechase paid more attention to "mainstream" rides and attractions, especially those that helped engender greater physical closeness between the sexes. Notable here are the Whichaway, a swing that gyrated its passengers in all directions; the Barrel of Love, where persons were strapped in a revolving drum that literally barreled down numerous inclines; and the Dew Drop, in which one climbed up a 50-foot tower, sat down, and then was repeatedly twirled around on a billowing platform.

Steeplechase burned down in 1907. But unlike Dreamland, which called it quits following its 1911 conflagration, Steeplechase was destined to rebuild. Credit here must be given to Tilyou's entrepreneurial savvy: masterminding the reconstruction and taking a cue from P. T. Barnum's playbook, Tilyou ingeniously recognized the willingness of American suckers to pay for anything and thus charged people admission to watch the smoldering ruins. And pay they did. Within nine months Steeplechase was rebuilt.

In its second incarnation, Tilyou put a number of the rides indoors to make them impervious to inclement weather, thus creating the glass-housed Beaux-Arts Pavilion of Fun. The Pavilion included such amusements as the Earthquake Stairway, which had a flight of steps split down the center, and the Human Roulette Wheel, which spun until passengers sitting on it were flung to the perimeter. Indeed, whereas Luna Park and Dreamland offered an otherworldly character, Steeplechase was where parkgoers went to have fun. Pure, unadulterated fun. The largest ballroom in New York State, by the way, was located here as well.

➤ **Keep walking west down the Boardwalk to West 21st Street.**

Built in 1924 and outfitted with extraordinary terra-cotta nautical designs—for example, the Neptune holding a trident that adorns the arches and assorted fish roof carvings—Child's Restaurant was designed for working-class families. Retrospectively, though, it is perhaps best remembered for functioning as a firebreak during a terrible July 1932 fire that swept Coney's oceanfront, leaving around 1,000 persons homeless and causing $5 million in damages. In the 1950s the Ricci family purchased the property, and they have operated the Tell Chocolate Company from the building ever since. Not long ago, in the 1980s, there were 150 employees making sweets and $2 million in profits. In 2001, alas, they were down to one staff person and $200,000.

Looking for something a little more substantial after a

long day noshing at Nathan's and on the Boardwalk? Walk over to 1524 Neptune Avenue, three blocks north from the Boardwalk, and have top-of-the-line pizza at Totonno's. None other than Lou Reed has hailed it as the best around. And the native New Yorker and Coney Island aficionado would know: he wrote a song on his 1996 record *Set the Twilight Reeling*, called "Eggcream," in which he waxes poetic about the pizza joint. And let's not forget his 1970s record *Coney Island Baby*.

➤ From 21st Street, you can walk back to the D, F, or Q train at Stillwell Avenue or relax on the Boardwalk for a while.

SOURCES

Alleman, Richard. *The Movie Lover's Guide to New York*. New York: Harper and Row, 1988.

Baker, Paul. *Stanny: The Gilded Life of Stanford White*. New York: Free Press, 1989.

Burns, Ric. *Coney Island* (video). Santa Monica: Direct Cinema, 1991.

Burrows, Edwin G., and Mike Wallace. *Gotham: A History of New York City to 1898*. New York: Oxford University Press, 1999.

Callender, James. *Yesterdays on Brooklyn Heights*. New York: Dorland Press, 1927.

Caro, Robert A. *The Power Broker: Robert Moses and the Fall of New York*. New York: Knopf, 1974.

Carter, Robin V. *Park Slope: Its People, Its Past, an Oral History Anthology*. Brooklyn: Park Slope Senior Citizens Center, 1969.

Cleaveland, N. *Green-Wood Illustrated*. New York: R. Martin, 1846.

Culbertson, Judi, and Tom Randall. *Permanent New Yorkers: A Biographical Guide to the Cemeteries of New York*. Chelsea, VT: Chelsea Green, 1987.

deMause, Neil. *The Complete Illustrated Guidebook to Prospect Park and the Brooklyn Botanic Garden*. New York: Silver Lining Books, 2001.

Denson, Charles. *Coney Island Walking Tour Map and Guide*. Berkeley, CA: Dreamland Press, 1998.

Edmiston, Susan, and Linda Cirino. *Literary New York: A History and Guide*. Boston: Houghton Mifflin, 1976.

Glueck, Grace, and Paul Gardner. *Brooklyn: People and Places, Past and Present*. New York: Harry Abrams, 1991.

Halporn, Roberta. *New York Is a Rubber's Paradise: A Guide to New York City's Cemeteries in the Five Boroughs*. Brooklyn: Center for Thanatology Research, 1998.

Homberger, Eric. *The Historical Atlas of New York City*. New York: Henry Holt, 1999.

Israelowitz, Oscar. *New York City Subway Guide*. New York: Israelowitz Publishing, 1989.

Jackson, Kenneth T., ed. *The Encyclopedia of New York City*. New Haven: Yale University Press, 1995.

Jackson, Kenneth T., and John B. Manbeck, eds. *The Neighborhoods of Brooklyn*. New Haven: Yale University Press, 1998.

Jerardi, Eric J. *Gravesend, Brooklyn: Coney Island and Sheepshead Bay*. Dover, NH: Arcadia Publishing, 1996.

Kasson, John F. *Amusing the Million: Coney Island at the Turn of the Century*. New York: Hill and Wang, 1978.

Lancaster, Clay. *Old Brooklyn Heights: New York's First Suburb*. New York: Dover, 1979. Originally published 1961.

———. *Prospect Park Handbook*. New York: Long Island University Press, 1972.

Manoni, Mary. *Bedford-Stuyvesant: The Anatomy of a Central City Community*. New York: Quadrangle/New York Times, 1973.

McCullough, David W. *Brooklyn and How It Got That Way*. New York: Dial Press, 1983.

McCullough, Edo. *Good Old Coney Island: A Sentimental Journey into the Past*. New York: Fordham University Press, 2001. Originally published 1957.

McInnis, Bryant Johnson. *Glory in a Snapshot: A Photographic Look at Bedford-Stuyvesant — Then and Now!* Vol. 1. New York: Word for Word Publishing, 1999.

Ment, David, and Mary S. Donovan. *The People of Brooklyn: A History of Two Neighborhoods*. Brooklyn: Brooklyn Educational and Cultural Alliance, 1980.

Meyer, Richard, ed. *Cemeteries and Gravemarkers: Voices of American Culture*. Logan: Utah State University Press, 1992.

Morris, Edmund. *Theodore Rex*. New York: Modern Library, 2002.

Morrone, Francis. *An Architectural Guidebook to Brooklyn*. Layton, UT: Gibbs Smith, 2001.

New York Department of Planning. *Sunset Park*. New York: Department of Planning, 1977.

O'Connell, Shaun. *Remarkable, Unspeakable New York*. Boston: Beacon Press, 1995.

Olmsted, Frederick Law, Jr., and Theodora Kimball, eds. *Forty Years of Landscape Architecture: Central Park*. Cambridge, MA: MIT Press, 1973.

Osborne, Ben. *The Brooklyn Cyclones: Hardball Dreams and the New Coney Island*. New York: NYU Press, 2004.

Powers, John. *A Concise Encyclopedia of Buddhism*. Oxford: Oneworld Publications, 2000.

Register, Woody. *The Kid of Coney Island: Fred Thompson and the Rise of American Amusements*. Oxford: Oxford University Press, 1991.

Reynolds, Donald Martin. *Monuments and Masterpieces: Histories and Views of Public Sculpture in New York City*. New York: Macmillan, 1988.

Richman, Jeffrey. *Brooklyn's Green-Wood Cemetery: New York's Buried Treasure*. Brooklyn: Green-Wood Cemetery, 1998.

Robbins, Michael W., and Wendy Palitz, eds. *Brooklyn: A State of Mind*. New York: Workman, 2001.

Rybczynski, Witold. *A Clearing in the Distance: Frederick Law Olmsted and America in the Nineteenth Century*. New York: Scribner, 1999.

Sanchez, Toby. *The Sunset Park Neighborhood Profile*. Brooklyn: Brooklyn in Touch Information Center, 1989.

Sexton, Andrea Wyatt, and Alice Leccese Powers, eds. *The Brooklyn Reader: Thirty Writers Celebrate America's Favorite Borough*. New York: Crown, 1994.

Sharp, John Kean. *History of the Diocese of Brooklyn, 1853–1953*. New York: Fordham University Press, 1954.

Snow, Richard. *Coney Island: A Postcard Journey to the City of Fire*. New York: Brightwaters Press, 1984.

Snyder-Grenier, Ellen M. *Brooklyn: An Illustrated History*. Philadelphia: Temple University Press, 1996.

Solomon, Professor. *Coney Island*. Baltimore: Top Hat Press, 1999.

Stern, Robert A. M., Thomas Mellins, and David Fishman. *New York 1880: Architecture and Urbanism in the Gilded Age*. New York: Monacelli Press, 1999.

———. *New York 1960: Architecture and Urbanism between the Second World War and the Bicentennial*. New York: Monacelli Press, 1995.

Sunset Park Restoration Committee. *Sunset Park: A Time Remembered*. Brooklyn: Sunset Park Restoration Committee, 1979.

Walker, Altina. *Reverend Beecher and Mrs. Tilton: Sex and Class in Victorian America*. Amherst: University of Massachusetts Press, 1982.

Weld, Ralph Foster. *Brooklyn Is America*. New York: Columbia University Press, 1950.

———. *Brooklyn Village, 1816–1834*. New York: Columbia University Press, 1938.

Willensky, Elliot, and Norval White. *AIA Guide to New York City*, 4th ed. New York: Three Rivers Press, 2000.

Wilson, Jeff. *The Buddhist Guide to New York*. New York: St. Martin's/Griffin, 2000.

Wolfe, Gerard R. *New York: A Guide to the Metropolis*, 2nd ed. New York: McGraw-Hill, 1988.

Wyatt Sexton, Andrea, and Alice Leccese Powers. *The Brooklyn Reader: Thirty Writers Celebrate America's Favorite Borough*. New York: Crown, 1994.

Younger, William Lee. *Old Brooklyn in Early Photographs*. New York: Dover, 1978.

ABOUT THE CONTRIBUTORS

LEONARD BENARDO has advanced degrees in political science from Columbia University and a degree in history from the University of Michigan. He presently works for a large private foundation in New York City but would prefer to spend more time at home in Park Slope with his wife and young son. Leonard has been a tour guide with Big Onion since 1997.

JENNIFER FRONC has an M.A. in historical studies from the New School for Social Research and is a Ph.D. candidate in U.S. history at Columbia University. Her work focuses on vice and social reform in twentieth-century New York City. She lives in Williamsburg and has been a guide with Big Onion since 2000.

SETH KAMIL holds advanced degrees in American history from Columbia University. He is founder and president of Big Onion Walking Tours and Big Onion Historical Consulting. Kamil's Ph.D. dissertation is titled "The Management of Misery: Homelessness in New York City, 1857–1940." He is the coauthor of *The Big Onion Guide to New York City* (New York University Press, 2002); the author of "Tripping down Memory Lane:

Walking Tours on the Jewish Lower East Side," an essay in *Remembering the Lower East Side* (Indiana University Press, 2000); and a contributor to the *Encyclopedia of New York City*. Seth lives in Park Slope.

ANNIE POLLAND received her Ph.D. from Columbia University. Her dissertation was titled "New York's Immigrant Jews and Their Religion, 1890–1930." She is the Deputy Director of Education for the Eldridge Street Project and has been a Big Onion guide since 1998. Annie currently lives in Brooklyn.

THORIN TRITTER received his Ph.D. in American history from Columbia University in 2000 and has been teaching in the History Department at Princeton University for the past three years. He began leading walking tours with Big Onion in 1994 and has contributed to several city guidebooks. His articles have been published in a number of academic journals, including the *Journal of Urban History*, the *New-York Journal of American History*, Harvard University's *Business History Review*, and *Afro-Americans in New York Life and History*. He is currently finishing work on a book about the newspaper industry in New York City.

ERIC WAKIN has an M.Phil. in U.S. history from Columbia University and an M.A. in Southeast Asian studies and an M.A. in political science from the University of Michigan, Ann Arbor. Eric is a native New Yorker who was born in Manhattan, raised in Queens, and lives in Brooklyn. He is the author of *Anthropology Goes to War: Professional Ethics and Counterinsurgency in Thailand* (University of Wisconsin/Center for Southeast Asian Studies, 1992) and *Asian Independence Leaders* (Facts on File, 1997) and the coauthor of *The Big Onion Guide to New York City*

(New York University Press, 2002) and two travel guides for Lonely Planet. He has been a Big Onion guide since 1995.

JAMIE WILSON is a doctoral candidate in American history at New York University. His research focuses on the twentieth-century history of Harlem. Jamie was a Big Onion tour guide from 2001 to 2002.

INDEX

In the text, buildings are often identified by street number. In the index, **bold text** identifies the building's address and distinguishes it from the page numbers that follow. *Italicized page numbers* signify an illustration and its caption.

ABOUT BIG ONION WALKING TOURS

Since 1991 Big Onion Walking Tours has led innovative and exciting tours through New York's ethnic neighborhoods and historic districts. Big Onion leads student and adult group tours as well as lectures on numerous aspects of New York City history. Big Onion Walking tours are wonderful for fundraisers, schools, alumni associations, corporate events, orientation for newcomers, visiting clients, relatives, and families.

Big Onion Walking Tours is directed by Seth Kamil. All guides hold advanced degrees in American history or a related field, have at least two years teaching experience, and are licensed by the City of New York. Big Onion Walking Tours is a member of NYC & Company: The Convention & Visitors Bureau.

Big Onion Walking Tours
476 13th Street
Brooklyn, NY 11215
tel: (212) 439-1090
fax: (718) 499-0023
www.bigonion.com